HARPER'S NEW TESTAMENT COMMENTARIES

GENERAL EDITOR: HENRY CHADWICK, D.D.

THE EPISTLE OF JAMES

A COMMENTARY ON
THE EPISTLE OF JAMES

SOPHIE LAWS

LECTURER IN NEW TESTAMENT STUDIES
KING'S COLLEGE, LONDON

1817

HARPER & ROW, PUBLISHERS, SAN FRANCISCO
Cambridge, Hagerstown, Philadelphia, New York,
London, Mexico City, São Paulo, Sydney

Library of Congress Cataloging in Publication Data

Laws, Sophie.
    A commentary on the Epistle of James

    (Harper's New Testament commentaries)
    Bibliography.
    Includes indexes.
    1. Bible. N.T. James—Commentaries.   I. Bible. N.T. James. English.
Laws. 1980.   II. Title.
BS2785.3.L38   227′.91077   80-8349
ISBN 0-06-064918-6

80 81 82 83 84 10 9 8 7 6 5 4 3 2 1

CONTENTS

67989

PREFACE

ON completing this commentary on the Epistle of James, my thanks are due above all to Dr Henry Chadwick, for entrusting the task to an untried postgraduate student, for waiting the unconscionable time she took to accomplish it, and for helpful advice in the final stages. I am also grateful to Dr Hedley Sparks, who supervised my research work, and to friends and fellow-teachers at King's College London, who encouraged, or goaded, me on to write. My parents have always followed the progress of the book with interest, as has my husband, who even assisted with its typing. For that, if for nothing else, its dedication must be to him:

James for John: the man of law

London, Michaelmas, 1979   SOPHIE LAWS

ABBREVIATIONS

1. GENERAL

AG *A Greek-English Lexicon of the New Testament,* by W. F. Arndt and F. W. Gingrich (a translation and adaptation of W. Bauer's *Griechisch-Deutsches Wörterbuch*), Chicago 1957.

ANET *Ancient Near Eastern Texts Relating to the Old Testament,* ed. J. B. Pritchard, 3rd edn, Princeton 1969.

Charles *The Apocrypha and Pseudepigrapha of the Old Testament,* ed. R. H. Charles, 2 Vols, Oxford 1913.

ExT *The Expository Times.*

HTR *Harvard Theological Review.*

Hennecke- *New Testament Apocrypha* by E. Hennecke, ed. W.
Schneemelcher Schneemelcher, ET ed. R.McL. Wilson, 2 Vols, London 1963, 1965.

JBL *Journal of Biblical Literature.*

JSS *Journal of Semitic Studies.*

JTS *Journal of Theological Studies.*

LS *Greek-English Lexicon,* ed. H. G. Liddell and R. Scott; new edn 1940.

LXX The Septuagint.

MT The Massoretic Text.

MM *The Vocabulary of the Greek New Testament illustrated from the Papyri and other Non-Literary Sources,* By J. H. Moulton and G. Milligan, London 1915–1929.

OCD *The Oxford Classical Dictionary,* ed. N. G. L. Hammond and H. H. Scullard, 2nd edn, Oxford 1970.

NTS *New Testament Studies.*

SB *Kommentar zum Neuen Testament aus Talmud und Midrasch,* by H. L. Strack and P. Billerbeck, 5 Vols, München 1922–1956.

TDNT *Theological Dictionary of the New Testament,* ed G. W. Bromiley (translation of G. Kittel's *Theologisches Wörterbuch*), Grand Rapids, Michigan 1964–1976

ZNW *Zeitschrift für die Neutestamentliche Wissenschaft.*

2. ENGLISH TRANSLATIONS OF THE BIBLE

AV The Authorised (King James) Version.

GNB Good News Bible.

JB Jerusalem Bible.

NEB	New English Bible.
RSV	Revised Standard Version.
RV	Revised Version.

3. EDITIONS OF THE GREEK NEW TESTAMENT

Kilpatrick	Η ΚΑΙΝΗ ΔΙΑΘΗΚΗ, ed. G. D. Kilpatrick for the British and Foreign Bible Society, 2nd edn, London, 1958.
UBS	*The Greek New Testament*, ed. K. Aland, M. Black, C.M. Martini, B. M. Metzger and A. Wikgren for the United Bible Societies, 3rd edn, Münster 1975
WH	*The New Testament in the Original Greek*, ed. B. F. Westcott and F. J. A. Hort, Cambridge and London 1881.

INTRODUCTION

CONSIDERED as a part of the Christian canon of holy scripture, the epistle of James is an oddity. It lacks almost all of what might be thought to be the distinctive marks of Christian faith and practice. Some have suggested that it was originally not a Christian document at all, but a Jewish text interpolated to bring it into Christian use; yet if this were so, it would still be remarkable that the added veneer should be so thin. The best known comments on the epistle are those of Martin Luther. In his 1522 Preface to the New Testament, he judges that 'St John's Gospel and his first epistle, St Paul's epistles, especially Romans, Galatians, and Ephesians, and St Peter's first epistle are the books that show you Christ and teach you all that is necessary and salvatory for you to know, even if you were never to see or hear any other book or doctrine. Therefore St James' epistle is really an epistle of straw,[1] compared to these others, for it has nothing of the nature of the gospel about it.' Luther placed James, with Hebrews, Jude and the Revelation of John, at the end of his translation of the New Testament, out of their usual canonical order. In his Preface to the Epistles of St James and St Jude, he denies that James is the work of an apostle, because of what he sees to be its opposition to Paul in its interpretation of justification, and because 'it is the office of a true apostle to preach of the Passion and resurrection and office of Christ, and to lay the foundation of faith in him. . . . All the genuine sacred books agree in this, that all of them preach and inculcate [treiben] Christ'. Luther's misgivings about the presence of the epistle in the canon are hardly unprecedented; as he himself comments, the history of its slow acceptance into the canon may indicate that they were felt from an early stage.

In historical terms, the chief interest of the epistle of James is in its evidence of the way the nature of Christianity was un-

[1] An allusion to 1 Cor. iii. 12.

1

derstood by this author, his readers, and, maybe, by those who accepted his work as a part of their scripture. Yet also, as even Luther admitted about the work of this 'good, pious man', 'there are many good sayings in him'.[1] In his re-interpretation of traditional ideas in new situations, in his insistence on the right practice of prayer and of charity, and in his appeal to the nature of man and the nature of God in establishing rules for conduct, the author of the epistle deserves a continued hearing.

The introduction to a commentary is essentially a conclusion, presenting to the reader the views that the commentator has formed about the character and intention of his text in the course of his study of its contents and his attempt to elucidate the author's argument. This introduction will, then, assume an interpretation of various verses of the epistle for which detailed exegesis will be found in the commentary.

THE ENVIRONMENT OF JAMES

The epistle of James affords notoriously scanty material for answering the traditional questions of an introduction, as to the date of the document, the identity of the author and the situation and geographical location of both himself and those whom he addresses. It is best to begin by sketching in broad general terms the world of thought and experience to which this author belongs.

In the first place, he belongs firmly in *the world of early Christianity*. There is no textual warrant for eliminating the two references to Jesus Christ in i. 1 and ii. 1,[2] and even apart from these there are other clear indications of the author's

---

[1] Quotations from Luther's Prefaces are from *Luther's Works* Vol. 35, Word and Sacrament I, ed. E. Theodore Bachmann, Philadelphia 1960, pp. 362, 396 and 397.

[2] As did L. Massebreau, 'L'épitre de Jacques—est-elle l'œuvre d'un Crétien?', *Revue de l'Histoire des Religions*, 32, 1895, pp. 249–283; and F. Spitta, 'Der Brief des Jakobus', in his *Zur Geschichte und Litteratur des Urchristentums*, 2, Göttingen 1896, pp. 1–239; both arguing for the exclusively Jewish character of the epistle.

INTRODUCTION

Christian character. The teaching of Jesus as found in the synoptic tradition is reflected in i. 5, i. 17, ii. 5, ii. 8, ii. 19, iv. 3, v. 12 and perhaps also v. 20. The discussion about faith and works in ii. 14–26 is conducted in terms which presuppose some acquaintance with the Pauline argument about justification; it cannot be read as a Jewish reaction to Paul, because of the author's failure to realise that Paul's attack is directed to notions of works of the Law, but must represent a debate conducted within Christian circles. James uses the language of Christian eschatology in v. 7 f.; and the language of Christian initiation (whether specifically of baptism or more generally of conversion) is drawn on in i. 18, 21 and ii. 7. Close similarities to the teaching of other New Testament authors, especially the author of 1 Peter, may reflect common use of developing patterns of Christian ethical instruction (i. 2–4, i. 21, iv. 6–8). In designating Jesus as 'the glory' in ii. 1, James shows an acquaintance with one line of development of Christological thought; and he follows the initiative of earliest Christianity in entitling him 'the Lord', in i. 1, ii. 1, v. 7 f., v. 14 f. It is under the authority, and in the power, of Jesus that the elders of the community anoint the sick, and that community is termed *ekklēsia*, the Church (v. 14). Yet the omission of what might be thought to be central and indispensable Christian themes is glaring. There is no reference to Christ's death and its effects or to his resurrection; none to the gift and activity of the Holy Spirit; none to the sacrament of the eucharist. Example of endurance is found in the prophets and in Job, v. 10 f., rather than, as by the author of 1 Peter, ii. 21–23, in Christ; and in contrast to the practice of every other New Testament author (except the author of the Apocalypse), the title 'Lord' is still more frequently a title of God (i. 7, iii. 9, iv. 10, iv. 15, v. 4, v. 10, v. 11). By contrast with thinkers such as Paul, John or the author of Hebrews, the Christianity of James will inevitably be judged as superficial and undeveloped.

Secondly, James shows a clear acquaintance with *the world of Judaism*. In affirming the proposition that 'God is one', ii. 19, he affirms the central tenet of Jewish faith, perhaps even in terms of its central prayer. His characteristic condemnation

3

of the 'double-minded' man, i. 8, iv. 8, reflects the Jewish
theme of doubleness as a cause of sin, and in particular, as for
James, of deficiency in prayer. Parallels may be drawn from
many areas of Judaism to James's extolling of the Law as
'perfect' and as 'the law of freedom' (i. 25, ii. 12) and to his insistence that it be kept in full (ii. 10). James frequently quotes
the Jewish scriptures and appeals to examples drawn from
them (ii. 8, ii. 11, ii. 21–25, iv. 6, v. 11, v. 17 f.); retains the
title 'Lord of Sabaoth' for God, v. 4; and uses the Jewish term
for the place of punishment, Gehenna, iii. 6. His piety, the
theme of the righteous poor (i. 9, ii. 5, v. 6) and the importance of charity (i. 27, ii. 15 f.), can be seen to have its
roots in Jewish tradition. Yet it may be doubted that Judaism
is really the framework of the author's life. He is one of the
few New Testament authors to mention neither the Jews nor
Israel by name, and his address to his readers as 'the twelve
tribes of the Dispersion', i. 1, is most readily understood as
directed to Christians in their character as the true Israel
(though that would not of course preclude their being also in
fact Jews by race). He makes no mention of Judaism's
characteristic institutions: circumcision; the keeping of the
Sabbath and the food laws; rules of ritual purity and separation (see on i. 27); the worship of the Temple (and his
sunagōgē in ii. 2 is not necessarily the Jewish place of
meeting). It might be argued that he had no occasion to mention such matters, or that he took them for granted, but it is
striking that he does not appreciate that the Pauline argument
on faith and works involved a dispute about the Torah. His
own appeal to the Law, when made explicitly, is to a very
limited area: Leviticus xix. 18 (ii. 8) and the Decalogue (ii.
11), and the context and manner of his appeal to the latter
calls in question the extent of his 'whole' law. His appeal to
scripture, too, is generally simple and straightforward. The
elements of 'Jewishness' in James are thrown into relief by the
lack of pronounced Christian colouring, but their extent
should not be exaggerated.

James's scriptural quotations are drawn from the Septuagint, and he knows the Greek Old Testament so intimately
as to make telling use of allusions to it as well as formally

4

citing quotations (thus in i. 10, iii. 9, iii. 18, iv. 5, v. 4). The third 'world' to which he belongs is *the Hellenistic world*: the shared culture of the eastern Mediterranean area within the Roman Empire that resulted from the conquests of Alexander the Great and the subsequent founding of Greek cities with their characteristic features of agora, stadium, theatres, temples and gymnasia (an account of the attempt thus to Hellenise the city of Jerusalem may be found in 2 Macc. iv. 7–15). The citizen of this world would be expected to have a general education in rhetoric, grammar and elementary philosophy. James's language is Greek, and he uses it with a certain feeling for cadence and an especial fondness for alliteration (e.g. i. 2, i. 6, i. 14, i. 25, iii. 5, 17, iv. 9); the imperfect hexameter of i. 17 is probably of his own devising.[1] He opens with the conventional form of greeting of a Hellenistic letter, i. 1, and makes use of some of the devices of the diatribe, a form of moral address, both written and oral, developed in the Cynic and Stoic schools but widely adopted by popular preachers of many persuasions, including Paul (e.g. ii. 18, iii. 10, iv. 13; see Ropes, pp. 10–16). Some of his striking metaphors have little biblical background, but are commonplace in Greek and Latin literature (the horse and the ship in iii. 3 f., cf. the images of man's control of the animal kingdom in iii. 7, and of the mist in iv. 14). The pious proviso he commends in iv. 15 has no biblical precedent, but is a familiar Hellenistic idiom. James shows some acquaintance, too, with the language of philosophy, though very much at the level of the catch-phrase with little appreciation of its original content (i. 21, iii. 6); and he makes clumsy play with the technical vocabulary of astronomy (i. 17). Also in catch-phrase terms, he shows a familiarity with the language of magic, as it is found in the rich store of magical papyri (ii. 19, iv. 7); the practice of magic was, of course, an area of religious

---

[1] An examination of James's Greek style would be out of place in this commentary, but may be found in the commentaries of Mayor, pp. ccxlix–cclix, and Dibelius, pp. 34–38. W. L. Knox draws attention to what he sees as peculiarities of the epistle's Greek, in constructing his theory of it as composed of original text plus Hellenistic commentary, 'The Epistle of St James', *JTS* XLVI, 1945, pp. 10–17.

syncretism, where Jewish, Greek, Oriental and ultimately Christian elements intermingled. In general, then, James's environment would seem to be the meeting of Christian, Jewish and Hellenistic thought, at a popular and unsophisticated level.

THE SETTING OF JAMES

The attempt to establish more precisely the situation of James within this general environment will focus on three areas: first, the social situation of James and his readers in the life of the Hellenistic world; secondly, their location among the various groups of early Christianity; and thirdly their geographical location. The attempt to define these three areas will also be conducted in three ways: through assessment of internal indications, of literary affinities, and of the external attestation of the epistle.

The appeal to *internal evidence* from the epistle as to its situation is problematical on the grounds of its genre and the character of its content. The epistle of James is a literary letter. Its opening address is not to a specific community in a particular place to which it is to be despatched, like Paul's to the Corinthians, Philippians or Thessalonians. James addresses Christian readers in general, as the people of God in its dispersion, and any of them might be supposed to profit from what he writes. His letter form is a common convention employed alike by Roman authors such as Seneca and Pliny (though some of Pliny's are genuine letters), Jews like the authors of the epistles of Aristeas and Jeremiah, and Christians like the author of the epistle of Barnabas (see Ropes, pp. 6–10; A. Deissmann, *Light from The Ancient East*, revised edn. ET London 1927, pp. 227–233; and art. 'Letters, Latin' in *OCD*). Congruously, his material is of general applicability, rather than a response to a specific situation. Uncertain prayer, abuses of speech, quarrelsomeness and envy, are not the particular problem of any one community. James draws his material from a variety of sources, and the structure of his writing is loose. Sometimes there is a passage of sustained argument, as in ii. 1–9, ii. 14–26, iii. 1–12; more often the author moves from one subject to another with only a loose train of thought discernible (as in i. 2–8, iv. 1–10, v. 1–11). These characteristics of eclecticism and lack of continuity in the content of James's teaching lead Dibelius to classify the document as *paraenesis* and strongly to discourage any attempt to deduce its situation from the author's choice of subject matter and examples (see his Introduction, sections 1 and 7, pp. 1–11 and 45–47). It may, however, reasonably be supposed that although the author thought of his work as having a general interest, he probably also had some idea of its initial readership; that his selection from the vast stock of ethical material, Jewish, Hellenistic and Christian, probably reflects something of his own interests or of the character of the Christian community with which he is most immediately familiar; and that the illustrations used to reinforce his general admonitions would only serve to do so if they bore some relation to the actual experience of those who read them. Thus, for instance, when James expounds his warning against discrimination in terms of a picture of the community's meeting (ii. 2 ff.), it may be supposed that some such situation as he sketches would be recognisable. The conventional scriptural terms in which to illustrate such a warning would be those of the law-court; James reflects a knowledge of this in v. 4, but he does not simply take it over. Similarly, the behaviour of merchants is not necessarily the obvious example from which to draw warnings about the transitoriness of human life and the folly of human boasting (iv. 13–16). One may presume that the author chose it because he thought his readers would appreciate it.

The problem of detecting internal pointers to a real situation is most acute in assessing James's remarks about rich and poor. James's language on this subject is at its most stylised, with the balanced antitheses of i. 9 f., the apocalyptic thrust of v. 1–3 and the Old Testament imagery of v. 4. Moreover, an equation of rich as wicked and poor as pious had long been a convention in some areas of Jewish thought (it is seen notably in psalms such as x, xlix and cxl, and in the Psalms of Solomon), passing thence into Christian tradition (for a full survey of the relevant material, see the article by E. Bammel,

7

THE EPISTLE OF JAMES

πτωχός in *TDNT* vol. VI pp. 888–915, also Dibelius pp. 39–45). James may, then, be seen as simply including in his collection of ethical material a familiar idea; and no further deductions should be drawn. However, it is arguable that the tradition of the poor as the righteous was most fervently maintained by those who were in fact actually poor: the Qumran community called themselves 'the poor', and in their self-chosen isolation may well have literally been so; the Jerusalem Church, called 'the poor' in Gal. ii. 10; Rom. xv. 26, needed real support (cf. Acts xi. 28–30); the designation of Jewish Christians in Palestine as Ebionites, from the Hebrew *'ebyon*, poor, later satirised by Origen,[1] may have its origin in part in their experiences during and after the two Jewish revolts. Where such conditions did not obtain, the advantages of wealth might be appreciated, and the tradition modified.[2] James himself modifies it: the poor are chosen to be 'rich in faith' and thus inherit the kingdom (ii. 5; cf. the variation in the parallel passages of Lk. vi. 20; Matt. v. 3). Nor is his language on this subject merely conventional, but is distinctively adapted. Twice he employs his characteristic method of Old Testament allusion to add force to his argument (i. 10, v. 4). His precise delineation of the rich man of ii. 2 is in terms probably evocative of a particular type in his and his readers' experience. His rhetorical question about the activity of the rich as oppressors draws on the language of baptism (ii. 6 f.), and he may be seen there as recalling actual experiences of his Christian readers, however difficult these are to reconstruct. Choosing as his example of discrimination the relative treatment of rich and poor at a community meeting, he very deliberately links this to the central Christian commandment of Lev. xix. 18 (ii. 8); and he demonstrates

[1] Origen explained the name variously as deriving from their poverty of understanding (*De Princ.* iv. 3.8), their poor opinion about Christ (*Comm. in Matt.* xvi. 12), or the poverty of their interpretation of the Law (*Cont. Cels.* ii. 1).
[2] This position is argued by D. L. Mealand in 'The disparagement of wealth in New Testament times', an unpublished M. Litt. thesis for the University of Bristol, 1971; also in M. Hengel, *Property and Riches in the Early Church*, ET London 1974, especially chapters 2 and 4.

the futility of 'workless' faith not only by scriptural example but also in a pointed parody of the piety that neglects charity to a 'brother or sister' (ii. 15 f.).

It seems reasonable, then, to suppose that the inclusion of teaching on rich and poor, thus creatively presented, reflects a real concern of the author himself. He does not idealise poverty *per se*, but his antipathy to the rich as a class is explicit. From the force of his language it would seem that this attitude is not shared by the Christian group he knows most intimately. Although there may have been needy members whose situation should call forth charity, this does not mean that the whole community was poor. If ii. 2 ff. represents, however exaggeratedly, a possible situation, it would seem that they would not readily identify with someone in real poverty. They may well have perceived the advantages of attracting a wealthy patron or wealthy converts (ii. 2 f., perhaps such might be drawn from the prosperous merchants of iv. 13); as Hermas confidently saw the mutual benefit of rich and poor believers: the rich supplying the poor's needs, the poor making intercession for the rich (*Sim.* ii). James, however, writes to punctuate such confidence by exposing, as he sees it, the character of the rich at present (ii. 6, iv. 13–16) and their future fate (i. 10 f., v. 1–3, 5).

James's language may, then, give some indication of the social situation or social attitudes of himself and his readers. It is doubtful if it supplies any evidence of their geographical situation. D. Y. Hadidian has argued that the imagery of the epistle is at times drawn from the Palestinian scene:[1] thus i. 6, i. 11, iii. 11 and v. 7, but the wording of the first three is too imprecise to support his conclusions, while the fourth may readily have been derived from the LXX, especially as James is in context presenting a consciously 'biblical' situation. He chooses to couch his attack on the rich in terms which are pointedly evocative of a whole tradition of divine judgment on injustice; the picture cannot be taken to indicate that his

---

[1] D. Y. Hadidian, 'Palestinian Pictures in the Epistle of James', *ExT* LXIII, 1951–52, pp. 227–228. L. E. Elliott-Binns, *Galilean Christianity*, London 1956, pp. 45–52, argues for the epistle's origin in Galilee.

THE EPISTLE OF JAMES

readers were an agricultural community, far less a Palestinian agricultural community. His reference to traders (iv. 13), and his image of the ship (iii. 4), have been taken to indicate a seaport setting, but there is nothing to show the former as necessarily travelling overseas, while the latter is again a familiar image, though not this time of biblical origin.

A further attempt to place the epistle in its setting may be made through observing *affinities with other documents*, and their setting; but again precise links are difficult to establish convincingly. Strack-Billerbeck cite numerous parallels between James and Rabbinic literature (SB IV, pp. 751–761), but the resemblances are of a very general kind. Similar ethical questions are treated, and the same doctrinal principles employed: consideration of the nature of man; the sanction of the law of the one God. The closest similarities are to the simple maxims of the Mishnah tractate *Aboth* (see parallels cited on, e.g., i. 6, i. 19), where the Rabbinic tradition itself is seen at a primitive stage and as still broadly in the wisdom tradition. James's use of scripture shows no acquaintance with the subtlety of learned Rabbinic exegesis to establish *halakah* or to provide midrashic expansion of biblical narrative. Paul shows his education in the use of scripture in such passages as Rom. iv. 2–8; 1 Cor. x. 1–4; Matthew and John have a knowledge which they use polemically (e.g. Matt. xxiii. 16–22; Jn vii. 22–23), but there is no comparable evidence for such knowledge on the part of James.[1] Similarly, there have inevitably been attempts to link James, like other NT documents, with the Qumran manuscripts.[2] James's phrase 'Father of lights' (i. 17) is compared with the 'Prince of lights' of the Manual of Discipline (1 QS iii. 20; cf. CD v. 18);

[1] See on ii. 25, v. 10 f., v. 17. The suggestion of M. Gertner that James can be seen as a systematic exposition of Ps. xii. 1–5 ('Midrashim in the New Testament', *JSS* 7, 1962, pp. 283–291), founders on the absence of quotation of that text; there seems no reason why the author should edit out his main text when he elsewhere relies on explicit quotation.
[2] A. R. C. Leaney, *A guide to the Scrolls*, London 1958, pp. 91 ff.; T. H. Gaster, *The Scriptures of the Dead Sea Sect*, London 1957, pp. 24–27; G. R, Driver, *The Judaean Scrolls*, Oxford 1965, pp. 543 f.; W. I. Wolverton, 'The Double-Minded Man in the Light of Essene Psychology', *Anglican Theological Review* 32, 1956, pp. 166–175.

his murdered 'righteous one' (v. 6) with Qumran's martyred 'teacher of righteousness'. These specific links are unconvincing, and the parallels which exist (e.g. on i. 6 ff., i. 25, ii. 10) are again in areas of general interest in Judaism. The differences between James and Qumran are more striking than any resemblances: James does not employ the sect's characteristic method of *pesher* exegesis; has none of its interest in rituals of purification or grades of initiation; no echo of its nationalist hopes; no evidence of its hierarchical community structure; nor does his community seem to have been a closed society, but rather one acquainted with mercantile life (iv. 13) and law courts outside its own discipline (ii. 6), and which admitted visitors to its meeting (ii. 2). The Jewish character of James cannot plausibly be seen to derive from links with either of these two distinctive areas of Judaism.

Striking similarities of language may be found between James and 'testamental' literature, especially the Testaments of the Twelve Patriarchs.[1] The Testaments show, like James, a great interest in the doubleness of man's character, and its evil effects (see parallels cited on i. 8, especially from the Testaments of Asher and Benjamin; Test. Benj. vi. 5 condemns there being 'two tongues, of blessing and of cursing', cf. Jas iii. 10). However, the Testaments do not employ James's distinctive term *dipsuchos*, using instead the idiom of 'two inclinations' or of being 'double-faced', while on the other hand James shows no knowledge of their association of doubleness with the work of Beliar. The probability is that each is independently developing a common and familiar theme. Similarly, James and the Testaments urge the putting to flight of the devil (parallels on iv. 7), but here they are likely

---

[1] These parallels may have provoked the theory of Meyer that the epistle is in origin the 'testament' of *Jakōbos*, Jacob, to his twelve sons (A. Meyer, *Das Rätzel des Jakobusbriefes*, Giessen 1930; substantially adopted by B. S. Easton, *The Epistle of James*, Interpreter's Bible Vol. 12, New York 1957). This theory founders like that of Gertner on the absence of the essential structural features supposed, in this case the names of the twelve sons, and on the extraordinary versatility of the author, who is seen to make reference to them through a knowledge not only of the LXX but also of the Hebrew text of the OT, and through playing on the meanings of Hebrew names (onomastic).

both to be drawing on the language of popular magic and exorcism. The resemblances are not sufficient to link James with the setting of the Testaments; nor would such a link clearly establish the origin of the epistle, since the date of the Testaments themselves is disputed, as is their original character, whether Jewish or Christian.[1]

Within certainly Christian literature, the striking parallel between Jas v. 12 and Matt. v. 33–37, a passage peculiar to Matthew in the gospel tradition, immediately suggests a close relationship between the epistle and that gospel, and that the setting of the former should be found in relation to that of the latter. Further parallels might seem to substantiate this. Some of the vocabulary characteristic of Matthew's edition of his material is found also in James: *dikaiosunē* (Jas i. 20, iii. 18; Matt. iii. 15, v. 6, 10, 20, vi. 1, 33, xxi. 32); *teleios* (Jas i. 4; Matt. v. 48, xix. 21); *ekklēsia* (Jas v. 14; Matt. xvi. 18, xviii. 17); *parousia* (Jas v. 7; Matt. xxiv. 3, 27, 37 and 39). In content, too, James might seem to draw upon Matthew, reflecting the Matthean beatitudes on the merciful and peacemakers (Matt. v. 7, 9) in ii. 13 and iii. 18. Both warn against care for the morrow: Matt. vi. 34; Jas iv. 13 f., and about seeking the status of teacher: Matt. xxiii. 8; Jas iii. 1. Initially impressive, these parallels need to be weighed carefully. With

---

[1] See the discussion by M. de Jonge, 'The interpretation of the Testaments of the Twelve Patriarchs in recent years', in his edition of *Studies on the Testaments of the Twelve Patriarchs*, Leiden 1975, pp. 183–192.

M. R. James notes a number of parallels between James and another 'testamental' document, *The Testament of Job*, in his edition (*Texts and Studies*, V. 1, Cambridge 1899), but it is unlikely that any of these would have received notice had it not been that James and the author of the *Testament* both characterise Job as a man of *hupomonē*. This is to some extent an interpretation of the biblical picture, but not such an extraordinary one as to demand a link between the two writers. M. R. James judged the *Testament* to be a second century Jewish Christian work; S. P. Brock, the most recent editor of the work, *Pseudepigrapha Veteris Testamenti Graece II*, Leiden 1967, considers (in a private letter) that it could be of the first century BC or AD. Its date and character are thus uncertain, so that it too would contribute little to the dating and placing of James even if some relationship were argued.

the parallels of vocabulary, *dikaiosunē* and *teleios* are ethical terms with a considerable biblical (LXX) background; *ekklēsia* one might expect to find in any early Christian document; *parousia* becomes a technical term in Christian eschatology, found frequently elsewhere in the NT,[1] and James lacks Matthew's other and more distinctive eschatological terms, *palingennesia* (xix. 28) and *sunteleia tou aiōnos* (xxiv. 3, xxviii. 20). It may be that the two beatitudes underly James's statements about mercy and peacemaking, but these are in a form so different from the Matthean that it cannot be certain, and with the second an alternative source in OT allusion may be suggested. In dealing with care for the morrow, the two authors' targets differ, Matthew's being over-anxiety and James's over-confidence; while in the warning to teachers James shows no consciousness of Matthew's specific attack on those who covet the Jewish title 'Rabbi'. Similarly, when the two draw on teaching of Jesus in the Q tradition, they develop it differently: Jesus' call to ask in order to receive is by Matthew referred to receiving 'good gifts' in general; by James related specifically to the gift of wisdom (Matt. vii. 7, 11; Jas i. 5; cf. Lk. xi. 9, 13; James later returns to this theme, in iv. 3, to consider the problem of asking which is not followed by receiving, a development not found in Matthew). The beatitude on the poor is in Matthew spiritualised as an address to the 'poor in spirit', and in James becomes a double promise to the poor to be 'rich in faith' and to inherit the kingdom (Matt. v. 3; Jas ii. 5; cf. Lk. vi. 20). Even with the prohibition of oaths which is the most striking parallel between the two, their wording of the positive ruling is sufficiently dissimilar as to give a different meaning to the whole, and James also lacks both Matthew's direction of this

---

[1] A. Feuillet argues that Matthew and James both use it specifically of the historical judgment of Israel, 'Le sens du mot Parousie dans l'Evangile de Matthieu. Comparaison entre Matth. xxiv et Jac. v. 1–11.', in W. D. Davies and D. Daube, ed., *Studies in the Background of the New Testament and its Eschatology*, Cambridge 1956, pp. 261–280. His argument rests on an identification of 'the righteous one' of Jas v. 6 with Jesus, and on a strict application of chronological order in Matt. xxiv, distinguishing the events of vv. 27 and 30, and is unconvincing in both respects.

teaching to an attack on Jewish casuistry with oath formulae (Matt. v. 34–36, cf. xxiii. 16–22) and his theological rationalé for the prohibition, namely that man's oaths constitute an arrogant appeal to God's sphere where man has no control. M. H. Shepherd, arguing for a relationship between Matthew and James, concludes that 'the Gospel of Matthew provides the author of the Epistle with support for the presentation of his themes, and it gives him in his treatment of these themes such theological depth as he has',[1] but Matthew's theological dimension is absent in this case.

The parallels which exist between Matthew and James are in sayings which could readily be absorbed into the general stock of Christian ethical teaching. The majority of them are found in the sermon on the mount which Matthew himself characterises as Jesus' teaching to the crowds (Matt. vii. 28 f.); Matthew, of course, in presenting this teaching calls attention to the authority of Jesus the teacher, while James makes no such appeal. For the setting of James to be established in relation to that of Matthew, the two authors must be shown to share each other's more characteristic interests and concerns. James's affirmation of the 'whole law', ii. 10, is superficially similar to that in Matt. vi. 17 ff., but whereas it is clear that for Matthew this involves the whole Torah (*loc. cit.* and Matt. xxii. 40; James's inter-relation of Lev. xix. 18 and xix. 15, argued on ii. 4, is not comparable to Matthew's implication of 'all the law and the prophets' in the great commandment), including the maintenance of its ritual prescriptions (Matt. xxiii. 23, and the omission of Mk vii. 19b in the parallel passage Matt. xv. 17), and maybe even extending to its oral interpretation (xxiii. 2), James's explicit appeal to the Law is, as has already been noted, much more limited: only to Lev. xix. 18 and the Decalogue, which might have been seen as the law sanctioned by Jesus (cf. Mk xii. 29 ff. and x. 17 ff.).

---

[1] Massey H. Shepherd, 'The Epistle of James and the Gospel of Matthew', *JBL* 75, 1956, p. 47. Shepherd accounts for the imprecise wording of the parallels by suggesting that James derived his knowledge of Matthew from hearing the gospel read in Church, rather than from reading it himself; it is unclear if he thinks that this reading is taking place in the original Matthean community, to which James would therefore belong.

Alongside his maintenance of the Law, Matthew takes up a polemical attitude to its Jewish, chiefly Pharisaic, interpreters, most notably in chapters v. 20–vi. 18 and xxiii (his warnings about oaths and the desire to be teachers have already been seen to be thus slanted), and indeed towards the Jewish people (Matt. xxi. 43, xxiii. 35 f., xxvii. 25). James contains no such explicit attack, nor can it be seen to be implicit in his writing at any point; again as already noted, he shows no apparent interest in the Jewish people. His own most specific attack is on the Pauline interpretation of justification, as he understands it, and this in turn is unlikely to be a concern of the author of Matthew. Even were Matthew's defence of the Law to be seen as a reaction to Paul's treatment of it, that would be precisely the element in Paul's argument of which James seems to be ignorant. His dispute with 'Paul' is not a dispute about the Law. Finally, James's suspicion of the rich has already been discussed; Matthew, by contrast, may be seen to tone down the antipathy to riches found in his source material (compare Matt. v. 3 with Lk. vi. 20 and 24; possibly the inclusion of the conditional clause in Matt. xix. 21, cf. Mk x. 21, is intended to moderate the instruction to the rich young man; certainly there is not that hostility to the rich *per se* found in the Lukan material, e.g. Lk. i. 53, xii. 16–21, xvi. 19–25).[1] The conclusion must surely be that although Matthew and James both draw on a similar tradition of the teaching of Jesus, not only do they use and interpret it differently, but they are engaged in different debates. Their characteristic concerns are so dissimilar that they must be seen as employing their common material in different situations.

The relation of James's argument about justification by faith or by works, in ii. 21–25, to Paul's exposition of justification in Gal. iii and Rom. iii–iv is fully discussed in the commentary on that passage, and will not be rehearsed here in advance. James's argument must presuppose Paul's, but it is in the highest degree unlikely that it presupposes Paul's as the apostle himself presents it in his letters. Rather, James has

[1] For the suggestion that Matthew envisages a community of some affluence, see G. D. Kilpatrick, *The Origins of the Gospel according to Saint Matthew*, Oxford 1946, p. 125 f.

15

heard Paul's affirmation of justification by faith used as a slogan to justify not libertinism, as Paul himself experienced it being used (Rom. iii. 8, vi. 1), but a pious quietism that saw expressions of trust in God as doing away with the need for active charity. The probability is, however, that those who so used it did so as having the authority of Paul, and that James knew this.

The question here is of the relevance of this relationship for defining the setting of James; of where such a misuse of Paul's teaching would be likely to have arisen and been encountered. The original context of his argument, the rejection of Judaising tendencies in the Churches and so of the Law as the means of justification, has been left behind, and 'works' are clearly not understood as works of obedience to the Law but as 'good works' in terms of general charitable activity. This translation can be seen to be made by writers who sought to be faithful to Paul. The pseudonymous 'Paul' of Tit. iii. 5 writes that God saved us 'not by works done in righteousness (*ouk ex ergōn tōn en dikaiosunē*) which we did ourselves, but according to his mercy'. More strikingly, Clement of Rome, who knows and quotes Paul's epistle to the Romans, performs the same translation: 'we ... are not justified through ... works which we wrought in holiness of heart, but through faith, whereby the Almighty God justified all men' (1 Clem. xxxii. 4). Clement goes on to raise the rhetorical question, 'What then must we do, brethren? Must we idly abstain from doing good, and forsake love?' (xxxiii. 1); precisely the argument that James has encountered. It is suggested by J. B. Lightfoot (*The Apostolic Fathers*, Part I, *S. Clement of Rome*, Vol. 2, London, 1890, n. *ad loc.*) that Clement knows James as well as Paul, and writes to reconcile their two positions. This is unlikely. There is no reflection of James's language in Clement independent of the way that James himself reflects Paul, and although Clement elsewhere like James couples the examples of Abraham and Rahab (see on ii. 25) he does not appeal to them in this context as examples of those who 'work righteousness' but rather appeals to the example of God himself, who 'adorned himself with works' in creation (1 Clem. xxxiii. 2–7). When Clement raises the question of abstaining from good works, it is a hypothetical argument; he lacks James's polemical tone and it is unlikely that he has encountered any who actually put the argument forward. He would rather seem to be following, in his own terms, the style of Paul's argument in Rom. vi. 1 f. What Clement and Titus show is how Paul's language could be used outside the context of his original controversy, and be given new content accordingly. While their intention is no doubt to be faithful to the apostle, his language is thus opened to new possibilities of misinterpretation.

That such misinterpretation occurred in communities which had connections with Paul in their past, communities which he had founded or to which he had written, cannot be ruled out; they were not guaranteed to keep his teaching sacrosanct. E. Trocmé, in fact, sees the epistle of James (or the central section of it) as giving a depressing picture of the latter history of Pauline Churches.[1] He links James's criticism of this misuse of the Pauline formula with criticisms of behaviour in the context of worship (Jas ii. 2 f., ii. 15 f., iii. 9 f.), and stresses the connection in context between the unbridled tongue and the rôle of teachers (iii. 1 f.). This he thinks reflects the unrestrained conduct of Christian meetings in the Churches founded by Paul (cf. 1 Cor. xi. 3 ff., xiv), which is foreign to the cultic tradition to which the author of James belongs. James's violent reaction to the notion of favouring a rich visitor (ii. 5 ff.) is similarly seen to be aimed at what Trocmé regards as the 'conservatisme social' of Paul and his Churches (exemplified in Rom. xiii. 1–7; 1 Cor. vii. 17–24; Eph. vi. 5–9; Col. iii. 22–iv. 1; Philem.). These are tenuous links. The benefits of patronage are likely to have been perceived by Christian communities other than just those of Pauline origin; and there is no indication that James's teachers were impelled by the charismatic gifts of Corinth. The evidence supports only a more general conclusion. The situation of James is one in which Paul is seen to have considerable authority, so that his characteristic language continues to be appealed to outside its original context, and to

[1] E. Trocmé, 'Les Eglises pauliniennes vue du dehors: Jacques 2,1 à 3,13', *Studia Evangelica* II, 1964, pp. 660–669.

provoke controversy. Neither the appeal nor the controversy appears, however, to focus on Paul's writings. In this respect James may be interestingly compared with the author of 2 Peter. For the latter, Paul's prestige must be acknowledged: he is 'our brother Paul';[1] and the appeal to him by 'the ignorant and unlearned' causes controversy; though the subject of the controversy is not here stated. This controversy, however, is conducted in the knowledge of some collection of Paul's epistles (2 Pet. iii. 15 f.). James and those with whom he engages are at one remove from Paul, in that the original thrust of his argument is absent, but the contact with Paul is still, as it were, with Paul in 'oral tradition'.

Finally, within Christian literature, parallels exist between James and the first epistle of Peter. On three occasions James seems to follow a line of argument and to use vocabulary close to Peter's: i. 2–4, cf. 1 Pet. i. 6–7; i. 18, 21, cf. 1 Pet. i. 23–ii. 2; iv. 6–8, cf. 1 Pet. v. 5–9 (iv. 1, cf. 1 Pet. ii. 11 may be seen to provide a fourth parallel, but the idea of inner warfare is not uncommon, and James and Peter differ in their identification of the antagonists involved). Again, the passages are discussed individually in the commentary, and their evidence as to the setting of James may be briefly assessed. As with James and Matthew, the contrasts between the distinctive concerns of James and Peter are too strong for it to be probable that they derived their common material in the same situation. Both, certainly, describe the communities they address as the *diaspora*, but for both this is an ideal rather than an empirical description (see on i. 1), and it is not an idea peculiar to them. One of the striking characteristics of James is his lack of interest in the figure of Jesus; Peter by contrast focuses on Jesus as redeemer and as example (e.g. 1 Pet. i. 19–21, ii. 21–25, iii.

---

[1] James, unlike 'Peter', does not name Paul in his dispute. This can be variously interpreted. It might be argued that Paul's prestige is now such that James cannot seem to criticise him directly; or conversely that the position of 'the apostle' is not yet such that it must always be acknowledged: there can be an immediate engagement with his teaching. The omission could thus be seen as a sign of either a late or an early setting for the epistle, but in either event the argument must be from silence and evaluated accordingly.

18 f. and 22). Peter writes out of the experience of hostile pressure on the Christian community, and in the expectation that this will be intensified (e.g. 1 Pet. ii. 12, iii. 13 ff., iv. 22 ff., v. 9; the epistle is here taken to be a unity, addressed to a single and specific situation, as also argued by J. N. D. Kelly, *The Epistles of Peter and of Jude*, London, 1969, pp. 5–10). Peter relates this anticipation to an expectation of imminent eschatological crisis (1 Pet. iv. 7, 17); James also affirms the eschatological expectation (v. 5, 7), but he reinterprets the traditional language of tribulation so that it refers to the trials of everyday life (see on i. 2, i. 12 f., i. 27, v. 7, 10 f. and below, p. 28 f.).

The content of the parallel passages is ethical exhortation, and for the first two other NT parallels exist. With Jas i. 2–4 can also be compared Rom. v. 3–4, and with Jas i. 18, 21 also Col. iii. 8–10 and Eph. iv. 22–26. Even in the third case, the individual elements of James's threefold pattern can be shown to be drawn from familiarly used sources, or to express ideas found variously elsewhere. The probability is that James and Peter alike make use of developing patterns of Christian ethical instruction, though the context of these patterns is uncertain. It has been suggested that such patterns evolved in the context of the practice of baptism, either as catechesis or as liturgical forms. P. Carrington and E. G. Selwyn have suggested reconstructions of catechetical forms,[1] but James does not fit wholly satisfactorily into their schemes. M.-E. Boismard has argued for baptismal hymns in James and Peter;[2] but this is an unconvincing hypothesis in view of the considerable difference in expression by the two authors of their common ideas, since the poetic rhythm of a hymn might be expected to preserve its language intact. James would not, anyway, provide evidence for the use of such forms in the baptismal context; although he echoes baptismal themes (i. 18, 21, ii. 7), his concern is clearly with the continuing in-

---

[1] P. Carrington, *The Primitive Christian Catechism*, Cambridge 1940, pp. 22–65; and E. G. Selwyn, *The First Epistle of St Peter*, 2nd edn, London 1947, Essay II pp. 384–400.

[2] M.-E. Boismard, *Quatres hymnes baptismales dans la première épître de Pierre*, Paris 1961, especially pp. 105 f. and 133 ff.

struction of the believing community (if baptismal forms were detected in the epistle, this would then provide a warning against too rigid an association of form with situation).

James and Peter may thus be seen to draw alike on the common stock of Christian ethical teaching. However, within the range of parallels, the language of these two in their common passages is sometimes particularly close: as in the phrase *poikilois peirasmois* (i. 2; 1 Pet. i. 6), the noun *dokimion* (i. 3; 1 Pet. i. 7), the idea of the *logos* (i. 18; 1 Pet. i. 23, perhaps also in i. 21 cf. 1 Pet. ii. 2), and their common quotation of Prov. iii. 34 (iv. 6; 1 Pet. v. 5). Neither author can plausibly be argued to be using the other's work, but a somewhat looser relationship may be suggested; that is, that they draw on this common Christian material not in the same specific situation but as it was presented in the same area or region of the Church.

The third possible means of identifying the situation of James is by examining its *external attestation* and so discovering where it was first current. The first author to quote James, explicitly and with citation, is, however, Origen (c. A.D. 185–255). Recent study of the history of the canon of the New Testament is increasingly cautious about detecting knowledge of a document in default of specific reference to it or exact quotation of it, and this caution is especially necessary in respect of James. The epistle contains so much familiar, traditional material that another document may readily show parallels with it but yet be completely independent. For example, there are resemblances between James and the 'Two Ways' sections of the *Didache* and epistle of Barnabas (see on i. 5 f., 8, ii. 1), but this is ethical material of well-known pattern and content, and no parallels exist with distinctive material outside that section to link James specifically with either document. Conversely, the detection of an author's knowledge of a document depends on the contingency of its being useful for his purpose to quote it. Absence of reference need not argue ignorance. Again, this consideration is especially relevant to James, which may have been known, but, because of its general ideas and lack of distinctive Christian interpretation, not have lent itself to quotation. However, if there is a consistent lack of reference by authors in a particular area, this can be taken to argue that the document was not current there. This appears to have been the case for the epistle of James in the Church of Syria. No writer from the Syrian Church, from Ignatius of Antioch onwards, can be seen to use the epistle. It first appears in Syriac translation in the Peshitta, c. 412, but even then its general use was not assured, and Theodore of Mopsuestia and Theodoret, notably, make no reference to it.

There is a similar neglect of the epistle in the Western Church from the late second to the mid fourth century. The description of Abraham as a 'friend of God' by Irenaeus and Tertullian can be seen as the common use of a familiar phrase (see on ii. 23), as also can Irenaeus's reference to a 'law of freedom' (cf. on i. 25). James is absent alike from the Muratorian canon list, usually taken to represent the scriptures of the Roman Church c. 200, and from the Mommsen Catalogue (or Cheltenham List) thought to represent the Church in Africa in 359.[1] In the latter part of the fourth century it begins to be quoted by authors such as Ambrosiaster, Hilary and Priscillian, and its use is securely established by Augustine and Jerome. Augustine complains of the unusual badness of the Latin text of the epistle (*Retract.* ii. 32), and its Latin textual history and characteristics seem different from those of the other catholic epistles, suggesting that it was translated at a later stage (thus B. F. Westcott, *A general survey of the history of the Canon of the New Testament*, 7th edn London 1896, p. 270 f.; see also the discussion by Ropes, pp. 80–84). That the epistle of James was not current in the Western Church at a comparatively late stage in the history of the canon there seems clear; what is debatable is whether it had been known at an early stage. Clement of Rome does not appear to have known it. His treatment of faith and works has been discussed above (p. 16 f.); it has some similarity to James's, but is surely independent. His appeal to Rahab as well as to Abraham is to a popular exemplar (see on ii. 25),

---

[1] For a brief account of these canon lists, see the entries in *The Oxford Dictionary of the Christian Church*, 2nd edn, F. L. Cross and E. A. Livingstone, London 1974.

and his description of the latter as 'friend of God' may be explained like that of Irenaeus and Tertullian (cf. again on ii. 23). Dispute centres rather on the relationship between James and the other Roman document among the 'Apostolic Fathers', the *Shepherd* of Hermas. Older commentators like Mayor and Hort were sure that Hermas knew and used James, but the majority of subsequent commentators have thought otherwise (so Ropes, Dibelius, Mitton; Chaine thinks it is less probable that Hermas used James than that Clement did; Cantinat cautiously suggests 'une utilisation plus ou moins directe', p. 32). J. Drummond, in the valuable study by the Oxford Society for Historical Theology,[1] examines suggested parallels and concludes that 'the passages which point to actual dependence on James fail to reach, when taken one by one, a high degree of probability, yet collectively they present a fairly strong case, but we should be hardly justified in placing the Epistle higher than class C', i.e. where dependence is not very probable.

This conclusion should be challenged. Mayor (pp. lxxiv–lxxviii) gives a formidably long list of parallels in thought and expression, but what is impressive is not this number (Hermas is after all a long work) but the concentration of parallels in some particular contexts. Thus in *Mandate* ix Hermas attacks double-mindedness, *dipsuchia*, and in particular its effect on prayer. Prayer should be made in faith, without wavering, or the petitioner will receive nothing (*Mand.* ix. 1–6, cf. Jas i. 6–8; ix. 6 uses the phrase *dipsuchos anēr* as in Jas i. 8). The object of prayer is to know the great compassion of God, *polueusplanchnia*, ix. 2, a compound noun not found in the LXX or other earlier literature, but related to the compound adjective *polusplanchnos* in Jas v. 11. The *Mandate* concludes by personifying *dipsuchia* as the 'daughter of the devil' and contrasting it as an 'earthly spirit' with faith which is 'from above' (ix. 9–11, cf. James's contrast of 'earthly ... devilish' wisdom, and the wisdom which is 'from above', iii. 15, 17, with which may also be compared the contrast of spirits 'from above' and 'earthly' in *Mand.* xi.

---

[1] *The New Testament in the Apostolic Fathers*, Oxford 1905, pp. 108–113.

5–8). In *Mandate* v Hermas discusses irascibility, *oxucholia*, a word peculiar to him. One of its effects is that it leads men astray from righteousness (*Mand.* v. 2. 1), as James says of *orgē*, anger, that it cannot effect righteousness (i. 20). Especially Hermas claims that it leads astray the *dipsuchoi*; and its issue is that a man becomes dominated by evil spirits and 'unstable in all his actions' (v. 2. 7, cf. Jas i. 8). It sets up a conflict with, and may finally expel, 'the holy spirit which dwells in you' (v. 1. 2, v. 2. 5 f., cf. Jas iv. 5, with which also compare *Mand.* iii. 1). Again, in *Mandate* xii, Hermas urges resistance to 'the evil desire'. It must be 'bridled' (the rare verb *chalinagōgeō* is used), since it is tamed only with difficulty (*Mand.* xii. 1. 1 f., cf. James on the tongue, i. 26, iii. 2, 8). If resisted, it will 'flee far from you' (xii. 2. 4), as also will the devil (xii. 5. 2, cf. Jas iv. 7). In rather serving the good desire, man must master the commandments, as he exercises mastery over God's creation (xii. 4. 2 f., cf. Jas iii. 7); and he must fear God 'who is able to do all things, to save and to destroy' (xii. 6. 3, cf. Jas iv. 12). Hermas has no exact quotation of James, but, as is consistent with its presentation as new revelation, the work contains no explicit quotation of any document, save the apocryphal *Eldad and Modad* in *Vis.* ii. 3. 4. Nor does he derive distinctive ideas from the epistle; the *Mandates* like James draw on the common stock of ethical teaching, and though both make much use of the Jewish theme of doubleness as a cause of sin, Hermas's exploration of this in terms of two spirits or two desires, though it has Jewish parallels (see on i. 8), is foreign to James. The strong impression is, however, that Hermas is familiar with James, that the language of the epistle colours his exposition of his ideas, and that where he once takes up an expression, other reminiscences tend to follow. That being so, whatever its later history, the epistle was known at an early stage within the Western Church.

How early it was known in the Church of Alexandria is also debatable. It is a natural assumption that Origen knew it from its currency in that Church. Eusebius says of Clement that '... in the *Hypotyposeis* ... he has given concise explanations of all the canonical scriptures, not passing over ... the epistle of Jude and the remaining catholic epistles' (*HE* vi. 14. 1). Cassiodorus, Clement's translator, in the later part of the sixth century, specifies that Clement 'made some comments on the canonical epistles, that is to say, on the first epistle of St Peter, the first and second of St John, and the epistle of St James, in pure and elegant language' (*Inst.* viii), but there is no trace of a knowledge of James in the extant writings of that omnivorous reader, and it is probable that Cassiodorus's 'James' is a slip for 'Jude' which Clement certainly did comment on (see on i. 1). Origen also, however, had close connections with the Palestinian Churches of Caesarea and Jerusalem (Aelia), and he came to reside permanently in Caesarea from A.D. 232. Origen's references to the epistle come in works written after this move to Caesarea. For example, explicit reference to the epistle is found in his *Commentary on John*, which was substantially completed during the Caesarean period,[1] whereas in *De Principiis*, a work of the Alexandrian period, no such quotation is found (see on iv. 17). It would seem quite possible, then, that Origen accepted the epistle on the authority of the Church in Palestine, and that his description of it as 'the epistle of James which is current' (*en tē pheromenē Iakōbou epistolē; Comm. in Jn* xix. 6), may reflect his appreciation that it was not everywhere known and accepted. The suggestion that he adopted it from its currency in the Church in Palestine may receive tentative corroboration from the fact that the epistle is also quoted, though without attribution, in the Pseudo-Clementine *Epistles to Virgins*, which are thought to be of third-century Palestinian provenance.[2] After Origen, the epistle is accepted by authors in the Alexandrian tradition, though his disciple Eusebius classes it among his 'disputed' documents (*HE* iii. 25. 3, cf. ii. 23. 24 f.), most probably in recognition of its still limited currency; and two third-century Alexandrian papyri, 𝔭 20 and 𝔭 23, contain fragments of it.

It would seem, then, that James was known in Rome at the

---

[1] *Comm. on Jn* xix. 6 alludes to Jas ii. 20, 26; fragments 6 and 38 to Jas i. 17; fragment 126 to Jas iii. 15.
[2] Thus J. Quasten, *Patrology* Vol. I, Utrecht 1950, p. 58 f. *Ep.* i. 11 quotes Jas iii. 1 f. as 'scripture', and alludes to iii. 15 and i. 5, and i. 12 probably alludes to Jas i. 27.

time of Hermas, but that there is then no certain evidence of it until the time of Origen, who may well have met the epistle first in the Church of Palestine.[1] This century of silence between the two witnesses need not seem extraordinary. James may well have had a measure of circulation after it was first written, and then, because of the general character of its contents, have fallen into disuse unless a particular Church had a special interest in retaining it. The Church of Jerusalem had such an interest. After A.D. 135, the Church of Jerusalem was the gentile Church of Aelia, but was concerned to affirm its origins in the earliest community led by James, the brother of Jesus. It exhibited his chair (Euseb. *HE* vii. 19. 1), and its liturgy was attributed to him; it is therefore likely to have preserved an epistle bearing his name, even if it was one not remarkable as a presentation of Christian faith. However, the earliest evidence of a knowledge of the epistle comes from Rome. If James was not a letter intended for despatch to a particular destination, but a literary letter, then it is likely that it would be earliest read in its place of origin. A Roman origin for James would be consistent with features of the epistle already noted. In its presentation of patterns of ethical teaching, it is strikingly similar to 1 Peter, a document usually considered to be of Roman origin. James is aware of a lively currency of the Pauline language of justification, and the Roman Clement also shows this language in use, albeit to different effect. James's distinctive and unusual adjective *dipsuchos* is part of a word-group used with most obvious familiarity by the Roman authors Clement and Hermas. The chief objection to the idea of Roman origin is that the epistle makes no reference to the best-known event in the early life of the Church in Rome, its persecution by Nero in A.D. 64

---

[1] Hermas is notoriously difficult to date. In the second *Vision*, ii. 4. 3, the author is presented as a contemporary of Clement, *c.* A.D. 96, who will send a 'little book' to foreign cities for him. In the Muratorian Canon he is identified as a recent writer, the brother of Pius, bishop of Rome from A.D. 139–154. Neither is very reliable evidence. The former may only reflect an image of Clement as Church correspondent; the latter is a tendentious statement made in argument against reading the *Shepherd* as 'scripture'. The book cannot be more firmly dated than in the early decades of the second century.

(contrast 1 Clem. v–vi); but this could be answered by seeing the epistle as written either before or very considerably after that date, or as coming from a community which was not involved in the event. It is highly unlikely that even at its first beginnings in that great city Christianity in Rome constituted a single Church; there were probably several communities of different character (as the different characters of Clement and Hermas themselves suggest) and with different experience.[1] That the epistle of James had its origin in some part of the Roman Christian community is a plausible, if not provable, hypothesis.

THE CHARACTERISTIC IDEAS AND INTERESTS OF JAMES

Thus far the emphasis has been on what James has in common with other writers, and on his debt to various forms of tradition. Yet, as has already been remarked, his selection of material, even if that material be traditional, may be taken to reflect his own interests, and in presenting it he may be seen to put his own stamp upon it. His concern with rich and poor has already been discussed. Another concern indicated by the frequent appearance of the subject is with speech, its use and abuse. The subject is treated in a variety of forms. In i. 19 there is a simple three-fold admonition to be swift to hear and slow to speech and anger; in i. 26 a warning to the would-be 'religious man' to 'bridle his tongue', similar in form to the definition of the 'perfect man' as the one who makes no error in speech; i. 22–24 argues the need for consistency in word and action, an argument echoed in ii. 12; in iii. 3–8 there is a highly rhetorical attack on 'the tongue', drawing on a variety

---

[1] Cf. Graydon F. Snyder, *The Apostolic Fathers*, Vol. 6, *The Shepherd of Hermas*, Camden N.J. and Toronto 1968, pp. 19 f.

B. H. Streeter also thought that Hermas knew and used James, and argued for the epistle's Roman origin, but for reasons that are now unconvincing: e.g. that Rahab (ii. 25) was peculiarly a model of faith in Rome; that it was in Rome that a Christian meeting place was called a 'synagogue' (ii. 2); and that in Rome in particular the Church was attracting wealthy converts (ii. 2 f.); *The Primitive Church*, London 1929, pp. 189–200.

of metaphors of different origin; and in v. 12 a prohibition of one particular mode of speech, the use of oaths. In iii. 9 f. James exposes another form of inconsistency, that between speech to God and speech to man, 'from the same mouth comes blessing and curse'.

Speech to God, prayer, is another of his interests. In i. 5 he counsels prayer for wisdom; but prayer must be of the right quality, that is, wholehearted, i. 6 f. James there recognises the possibility of unanswered prayer, as also in iv. 2c–4, where the explanation is that prayer is for ends inimical to God. In v. 13–18 he counsels prayer in different circumstances, and gives instruction for the resort to prayer in the particular situation of sickness. This advice is reinforced with the assurance that 'the active prayer of a righteous man is very powerful' (v. 16), as the prayer of Elijah demonstrates. Prayer forms may be echoed in the language of ii. 19 and iii. 9, and, from a different background, in the prophylactic formula of iv. 15; while ii. 16 cites a prayer, though in this case an ineffective one. The idea of prayer is linked to the idea of faith: v. 15 describes the saving prayer as 'the prayer of faith'; i.6 warns that it is only prayer made in faith and without doubt to which God responds; and the prayer of ii. 16 is presented as an expression of that faith which, being unaccompanied by works, is worthless. This characteristic association of faith and prayer shows that faith is not for James simply formal assent to propositions about God, as is sometimes deduced from ii. 19. (It is anyway wrongly deduced, since the statement about God is presented as one that evokes response rather than formal assent, even from the demons.) Faith is that attitude to God which is expressed in prayer, but is also necessarily issuing in action.

The epistle of James is the most consistently ethical document in the New Testament, but its various warnings, precepts and words of encouragement are not based on a theological principle in any way remotely comparable to, for instance, Paul's drawing of ethical conclusions from his proclamation of the death and resurrection of Christ in Rom. vi. Only in the sequence of Jas i. 21–22 is it indicated that the saving word of the gospel carries with it an imperative. J. L.

27

Houlden judges that, 'the ethics of the Epistle of James are, from the point of view of conceptual pattern, the simplest in the New Testament: no theological impulse overtly provides them with backing and the writer embraces a simple belief in practical charity, humble endurance and control of the tongue as the keys to moral life' (*Ethics and the New Testament*, Harmondsworth 1973, p. 66). Houlden acknowledges James's vision of the 'law of liberty' in i. 25 and ii. 12, which he sees as centring on the command to love of one's neighbour, as in ii. 8; but even the command of *agapē*, variously interpreted as the basic principle of Christian behaviour in Matt. xxii. 37–40; Jn xiii. 34 f. and 1 Jn iv. 7–21; Rom. xiii. 8–10, does not appear to unify James's collection. Lev. xix. 18 is cited in ii. 8 (and alluded to in iv. 11), and the particular issue of discrimination brought into relation to it, but as the 'royal law' it is not a governing principle, but rather one commandment which has, however, a certain primacy of importance.

Another notion which appears in some of James's ethical teaching is of the sanction of eschatological reward and punishment. There is a promise of future reward for the one who endures trial (i. 12), for the poor (i. 9, ii. 5), and for the repentant (iv. 10); and the coming of the Lord is an encouragement to patient endurance (v. 7 f.). An expectation of judgment underlies the various warnings of ii. 12 f., iii. 1, iv. 11 f., v. 9 and v. 12; and the future menaces the rich (i. 10 f., v. 1–7). In linking his encouragement to endure with eschatological hope, James uses familiar language but with a somewhat different content. In other documents it is clear that what is to be endured is extreme suffering, attack on the people of God, the so-called 'messianic woes' (see on i. 12). James gives no indication in i. 2 of the nature of the 'various kinds of trials' to be encountered, but his examples of endurance in v. 7, the farmer, and v. 11, Job, suggest that he thinks of the everyday difficulties facing the individual rather than of a particular crisis; and in i. 27 he uses the almost technical term *thlipsis* of the perennial plight of widows and orphans. In i. 13 ff. he follows the promise to the one who endures (i. 12) with a discussion of the experience of temptation. If the sequence is more than a simple verbal link, it may be that the trial he thinks of is the personal battle against temptation to sin. It is also notable that he presents the end of the chain of probation in i. 2–4 as the achieving of personal integrity. It seems possible that for James's community the traditional marks of eschatological hope were not apparent (cf. 2 Peter iii. 3 f.); they did not seem to be called upon to face the onslaught that would usher in the kingdom. James therefore seeks to keep the hope alive with a re-interpretation of its traditional signs.[1]

Much more pervasive, however, than an appeal to law or to eschatological reward and punishment, is James's indictment of disunity and inconsistency in human behaviour. Man is torn apart by conflicting desires (iv. 1), rendering his prayer ineffective (iv. 3); and prayer is also rendered ineffective by doubt (i. 6 ff.). The man who separates hearing and action deceives himself (i. 22–24); and to divorce faith and works is to make faith worthless (ii. 14–17). Disunity mars human relationships, with 'discrimination between persons', especially between rich and poor (ii. 1–9). It may also be demonstrated in the difference between a man's attitude to God and to his fellow man, with the tongue an especial instrument of this disunity, since 'with it we bless the Lord and Father, and with it also we curse men, who are made in the likeness of God' (iii. 9). Those who would combine their prayer to God with the 'friendship of the world' are associating two incompatible things and are stigmatised accordingly as 'adulteresses' (iv. 3 f.). James's characteristic pejorative adjective is *dipsuchos*, 'double-minded' (i. 8, iv. 8); in iv. 8 he addresses the call to repentance alike to *dipsuchoi* and to *hamartōloi*, 'sinners', and from the parallelism it would seem that for him these terms are virtually synonymous: doubleness is of the essence of sin. The corollary of this must be that the ideal state for man to achieve is one of singleness or integrity, and this positive point is also made. The aim of enduring trial is that 'you may be whole and complete' (i. 4);

[1] With this interpretation, contrast Reicke's association of the epistle with the troubled period of the later years of Domitian, *The Epistles of James, Peter and Jude*, 2nd edn, New York 1964, especially pp. 5 f. Reicke finds reference to actual persecution in i. 2 f., i. 12, ii. 6, iv. 1 f., iv. 6 and v. 10 f.

29

and the man who can bridle the tongue, the instrument of duplicity in iii. 9, is 'the perfect man, able also to bridle the whole body' (iii. 2). He will also, presumably, be the wise man, since disunity is foreign to wisdom (iii. 17). The theme of doubleness as evil, and singleness or unity as the state to be desired, has parallels in Jewish, Greek, and even gnostic, thought (see on i. 8); James gives it a strongly practical, ethical content.

Both congruous and contrasting with this emphasis on the doubleness of man is an emphasis on the singleness of God. The affirmation of faith 'that God is one' is to be commended (ii. 19); granted that it has appropriate consequences. It is a statement of the integrity and consistency of that one God, and this point is variously made elsewhere in the epistle. In i. 5, God is said to give *haplōs*, an adverb which conveys the idea both of generous and of wholehearted giving; hence it may be asserted that 'every gift that is good ... is from above', from the unchanging God (i. 17). The singleness of God is also the sanction for obedience to the whole law, since 'he who said "Thou shalt not commit adultery", said also "Thou shalt not murder" '; and as there is one lawgiver, so also there is one judge (iv. 2). It is tempting to associate these two similar themes, of the singleness and consistency of God, and the doubleness and inconsistency of man, and to suggest that underlying James's condemnation of the latter and his exhortation to singleness is the idea of ethics as the imitation of God. This is an ethical principle familiar in his world. It is debated whether it is already present in the OT, in Lev. xi. 44, 45, xix. 2,[1] but it was clearly employed by the Rabbis (G. F. Moore, *Judaism*, vol. II, Cambridge Mass. 1927, pp. 109–111, gives a number of examples, including *Sotah* 14a which explores the idea in considerable detail; cf. also I. Abrahams, *Studies in Pharisaism and the Gospels*, First

[1] Contrast E. J. Tinsley, *The Imitation of God in Christ*, London 1960, pp. 50 ff., and T. W. Manson, *Ethics and the Gospel*, London 1960, p. 18 f., with W. Michaelis, art, μιμέομαι, *TDNT* vol. V pp. 359 ff. and B. Lindars SSF, 'Imitation of God and Imitation of Christ' in *Theology* LXXVI, 1973, pp. 394–402, and *Duty and Discernment*, ed. G. R. Dunstan, London 1975, pp. 100–110.

Series, Cambridge, 1917, p. 16 f.). The attributes of God most frequently held up for imitation are his gracious and merciful qualities, which can be put into practice by men in acts of charity. Within the Greek world, the idea is given classic expression in Plato's *Theaetetus*, in the advice that '... we ought to try to escape from earth to the dwelling of the gods as quickly as we can; and to escape is to become like God, so far as this is possible; and to become like God is to become righteous and holy and wise' (176a; cf. *Republic*, 501b, 613a; *Laws*, 716b–c).[1] Epictetus quotes Zeno, the founder of Stoicism, as saying that 'To follow the gods is man's end' (*Discourses*, ii. 14. 11–13), as does his fellow-Stoic Seneca (*De Providentia*, i. 5). Philo, debtor to Jew and Greek, alludes to the *Theaetetus* passage in *De Fuga* 82, and makes frequent use of this ethical principle of imitation: man's true end is a likeness to God who begat him (*De Opif.* 144); beginners, and children, should imitate their Father and Teacher (*De Sacrif.* 64–68); it is a salutary thought that the virtue of man is only an imitation and copy of the divine (*Quod det.* 160–61). Philo provides the closest parallel to the suggested development of the theme of imitation in James, that man should be one as God is one, in a work in which the Platonic elements of his thought are most overt, *De Gigantibus*. There Philo argues that God is perfect, so that he who turns to God turns from the imperfect; the wise man is one 'averse to change and mutability', and the experience of true stability and immutable tranquillity is to be found beside the immutable God (45–49). With this tranquillity Philo contrasts the 'war in peace' of human societies, and in the individual (51; cf. Jas iv. 1); he associates twofoldness and speech; it is contemplation of the One by the soul that alone brings stability (52; cf. James on the tongue as the instrument of doubleness in iii. 8ff.).[2]

---

[1] A full discussion of the theme in Plato's writings is given by G. G. Rutenber, *The Doctrine of the Imitation of God in Plato*, Philadelphia 1946.

[2] The parallel with *De Gigantibus* was suggested in private correspondence by the Revd D. L. Mealand of Edinburgh University, and is here gratefully acknowledged. Cf. also *De Mut. Nom.* 27–34; *Quod Deus Immut.* 82–85; *Quaest. Exod.* ii. 29.
 Log. 61 of the Gospel of Thomas could provide another close parallel,

The connection between the two ideas, of the doubleness of man that should be singleness, and the singleness of God, is never made explicit by James; the two are simply juxtaposed in the epistle (as, indeed, God's oneness and man's singleness are juxtaposed in Deut. vi. 4 f.). When he appeals to the character of man as made 'in the likeness of God' (iii. 9), it is with an interest in the object rather than the subject of action: to insist on consistency in treatment of God and of his image rather than that man should live in accordance with that character, imitating God in whose likeness he is. The argument that this theme of imitation underlies James's ethical instruction rests on the familiarity of the theme, and on the obvious congruity of the two ideas juxtaposed. If God is one, and man should be one, it is obvious that man's aim is the imitation of God. If this is admitted, then it can be said of James as of other NT authors that his ethical teaching has a theological basis. He would be employing an ethical principle used by other NT authors, for the imitation of God is urged in Eph. v. 1; cf. Matt. v. 48, Lk. vi. 36; 1 Pet. i. 15 f.; but for Christian authors the theme of imitation is more characteristically that of the imitation of Christ (thus, explicitly, Jn xiii. 15; 1 Cor. xi. 1; 1 Thess i. 6; 1 Pet. ii. 21). If James is using this theme, he is, typically, not doing so in its distinctively Christian form.[1]

THE EPISTLE OF JAMES AND EARLY CHRISTIANITY

In the second section of this Introduction, it was argued that James cannot be associated with any specific area of early Christianity as reflected in other documents of the NT. The

---

for in the translation of Thomas O. Lambdin God is spoken of as 'the Undivided'; man is filled with light if undivided, but with darkness if divided (*The Nag Hammadi Library in English*, ed. James M. Robinson, Leiden 1977, p. 125); but the logion is obscure and translations accordingly vary (two variations may be found in Hennecke-Schneemelcher I, on p. 298 and, in an Appendix by R. McL. Wilson, p. 517).

[1] The argument for the theme of imitation as underlying James's ethical teaching is presented in more detail in an article 'The Doctrinal Basis for the Ethics of James', Sophie Laws, *Studia Evangelica* (forthcoming).

epistle must be considered by and in itself as providing a picture of one form of Christian community and thus contributing to an appreciation of the variety of early Christianity; and it is, as always, easier to define what it is not than what it is. The Christianity of James is not an 'enthusiastic' or 'charismatic' Christianity. Unless in iv. 5 (which is unlikely), there is no reference to the presence and activity of the Holy Spirit. Prophets are figures of the past, serving as moral examples (v. 10), not part of contemporary experience. Rather the community values teachers; and in his warning against an over-readiness to assume that rôle (iii. 1) the author makes no reference to a need for charismatic endowment for it (contrast Rom. xii. 6 f. and 1 Cor. xii. 28 f.). He castigates abuse of the tongue, in speech to man and to God, but knows nothing of the abuse of 'tongues' that troubled Paul (1 Cor. xiv). In v. 14 f. he advises on seeking healing within the Church, by means of anointing and prayer, and it is certainly inadequate to see the anointing as simply a common therapeutic measure. However, those who anoint and pray over the sick man are 'the elders of the Church', and it is not said that they act as a result of a spiritual gift either to heal (again contrast 1 Cor. xii. 9) or to leadership. James certainly assumes that within the Christian community people will experience physical healing, but this assumption is not part of a general atmosphere of enthusiasm. There is even less to associate James with 'gnostic' tendencies in early Christianity. He has no apparent interest in Jesus as a redeemer-figure; and his definition of wisdom is in ethical and not esoteric terms (iii. 17), as also his opposition to 'the world' is ethically and practically expressed (i. 27, iii. 6, iv. 4). Only in his use of *psuchikos* as a pejorative adjective (iii. 15) is there an echo of what came to be the technical language of gnosticism; but its force here is no more than that of a catchword.

Christianity for James and his community is not then a matter of participation in a charismatic movement, of initiation into esoteric knowledge, or of sacramental participation in the mystery of salvation. Primarily, it is a way of life before God, a moral code (cf. the definition of 'true religion' in i. 27).

Precepts for behaviour are backed by a notion of salvation associated with conversion and baptism (i. 18, 21), and with reclamation from sin (v. 19 f.), and also by an expectation of judgment (ii. 12 f., iv. 12, v. 9, 12). The time of judgment is the time of the coming of Christ the Lord (v. 7 f.), though how Christ is involved in the exercise of judgment is not indicated. Christ is also a factor in the present in the regulation of conduct, which must be assessed in relation to faith in him (ii. 1). In the determining of this way of life the teaching of Jesus plays a part, adapted to the author's interests as it is in the synoptic tradition; and in his understanding of Christianity the author comes into conflict with a tradition of the teaching of Paul. There is some measure of organisation in the community, for meetings (ii. 2 ff.); and there are forms of leadership, the teachers of iii. 1 and elders of v. 14; though there is no definition of criteria for office, like those given in the Pastoral epistles (cf. 1 Tim. iii. 1–13; Tit. i. 5–9), nor is it clear whether teacher and elder are distinct offices, or if teaching might be one function of an elder (cf. 1 Tim. v. 17). Interestingly, although there are women members of the community (ii. 15), there is no reference to a specific rôle for women within the Church, and no guidance for their behaviour within the community or in marriage (iv. 4 is of course metaphorical); a fact perhaps obscured by the insistence in the ET of Dibelius on rendering James's *adelphoi* as 'brothers and sisters'.

Some of these features might be variously taken as indications of the epistle's representing an early or a late stage in the development of Christianity. Contact with the teaching of Jesus independent of gospel fixity might seem to indicate an early date; but there is no reason to think that the writing of the gospels brought the oral tradition to an end, and indeed the enthusiasm of Papias, however misplaced, for the living rather than the written word (Eusebius, *HE* iii. 39. 3 f.), indicates that it did not. The adoption of the gospel form has the effect of identifying teaching as Jesus'; James provides evidence of another way of retaining and preserving it, absorbed without differentiation into the general stock of ethical material (cf. the incorporation of what may be recognised as

34

gospel material into the 'Two Ways' of *Did.* i–ii; and contrast Paul's careful identification of the teaching of the Lord in 1 Cor. vii. 10–12 with his use of it in Rom. xiii. 7). It is not important to James to indicate where his precepts derive from Jesus, and it must be uncertain if he is in fact conscious of this distinct origin of some parts of his material (though in ii. 8 he singles out the 'royal law' as having an especial status). It is also of interest that James draws on material that would be regarded as belonging to different sources for the gospels: ii. 8, 19 reflecting Markan material; i. 5, 17, ii. 5 and iv. 3 that common to Matthew and Luke and usually designated 'Q'; and v. 12 being peculiar to Matthew. This may serve to indicate that while the three may be regarded as distinct strata in the creation of the gospels, they did not necessarily exist in isolation from each other in oral tradition.

As contact with the oral tradition of the teaching of Jesus might be thought to indicate an early date for James, so the absence of charismatic elements and presence of institutional features, together with the lack of prominence of the kerygma of Christianity and an emphasis instead on Christian behaviour, might be taken to indicate a later period. In two respects James has affinities with 2 Peter, which is generally taken to be among the latest, if not the latest, of the NT documents: both seek to re-interpret traditional eschatological hopes (cf. above, p. 29; and 2 Pet. iii. 1–13), and both tackle problems arising from the Pauline tradition (above, p. 18; 2 Pet. iii. 15 f.). However, while 2 Pet. admits and interprets delay in the fulfilment of eschatological hope (iii. 8 f.), James affirms its imminence (v. 8 f.); and while 2 Pet. writes in the knowledge of some collection of Paul's letters, James's contact with Paul is in 'oral tradition'. These contrasts are not, conversely, arguments for an earlier situation for James as against 2 Peter: the parousia hope may well have been held more persistently in some areas of the Church than in others; and a tradition of the teaching of Paul have continued in some circles alongside or even independent of an increasing knowledge of his letters (as may be indicated by the authors of Acts and the Pastoral epistles, both in their ways Pauline disciples, yet whose knowledge of his writings is debatable). It is highly implausible to think of simple lines of development in the history of early Christianity: of a fading of the imminent parousia hope; of a move from the charismatic to the institutional; or from a kerygmatic to a moralistic Christianity; and to attempt to date James by plotting his position along such lines. Rather we should think of a diversity of forms of early Christianity co-existing; and the interesting question is not the probably insoluble one of the date of James, but by whom the form of Christianity represented by the epistle might be appropriated.

James is commonly spoken of as 'Jewish Christian',[1] and this in itself poses a problem of definition.[2] At the very least, such a description of James must take account of the Hellenistic elements in the epistle;[3] though it is increasingly demonstrated, notably by M. Hengel,[4] that absolute lines of demarcation between 'Judaism' and 'Hellenism' do not exist, and that even Judaism in Palestine was part of the Hellenistic world. James Dunn describes Jewish Christianity as itself a spectrum within the total spectrum of early Christianity, embracing both the earliest Jerusalem community and the sects accounted heretical from the second century onwards. He isolates three traits as characteristic of this heretical Jewish Christianity, which may be traced back into the New Testament writings: adherence to the Law; exaltation of James and denigration of Paul; and adoptionism.[5] These traits might seem discernible in James, thus locating him within the total spectrum: the epistle upholds 'the law'; written in the name of James it attacks a notion recognisably Pauline in origin; and

[1] C. F. D. Moule comments that James would be important evidence of the Jewish Christian element in the NT period, 'if only we knew anything about its provenance and purpose'. *The Birth of the New Testament*, 2nd edn, London 1966, p. 158.
[2] For discussion of the problem, see R. Murray S.J., 'Defining Judaeo-Christianity', *Heythrop Journal* xv, 1974, pp. 303–310, and A. J. F. Klijn, 'The Study of Jewish Christianity', *NTS* 20, 1973–74, pp. 419–431.
[3] See above, p. 5.
[4] M. Hengel, *Judaism and Hellensim*, ET London 1974.
[5] James D. G. Dunn, *Unity and Diversity in the New Testament*, London 1977, pp. 239–266; cf. H. J. Schoeps, 'Ebionite Christianity', *JTS* IV, 1953, pp. 219–224.

its references to Christ are distinctly limited. Yet the correspondence is superficial. The references to Christ are too brief to argue the nature of the author's understanding of his person, though the description of him as 'the glory' (ii. 1) might indicate a tendency in the 'orthodox' rather than the 'adoptionist' direction; James's attack on the notion of justification by faith alone contains no explicit or implicit attack on Paul himself, although James is probably conscious that the idea is thought to carry Paul's authority; and it has been argued above that James's 'law' is unlikely to be the Jewish Torah in its entirety.[1]

It is this last factor that stands in the way of regarding James as Jewish Christian in the sense that his is a Christianity professed by one who would also call himself a Jew and retain the practice of Judaism as the framework of his life. His 'Judaism' consists, broadly, in the affirmation of belief in the One God; the notion of obedience to a law which, when its content is referred to, appears in terms of the great moral commands; and in a close if not particularly scholarly knowledge of the LXX. It is probable that these were precisely the elements of Judaism absorbed by those gentiles who stood on the fringe of the Hellenistic synagogues, and were known as 'god-fearers' (*sebomenoi* or *phoboumenoi tou theou*).[2] Not becoming full proselytes, these people were attracted to Judaism as one among the philosophies of the Graeco-Roman world. Acts indicates that early Christian preachers drew adherents from precisely this group: Cornelius (x. 2, 22), Lydia (xvi. 14), Titus Justus (xviii. 7), and others in Pisidian Antioch (xiii. 16, 26, cf. 43?), Thessalonica (xvii. 4), and Athens (xvii. 17). To them Christianity offered the same attractions as Judaism, the acknowledgement of the One God, the high moral standard, and the appeal to the ancient holy book; but without the civic and social disadvantages of full membership of the national Jewish religion. They stood on the fringe of Judaism; but as Christians they could be full members of a community which

[1] See p. 4.
[2] The classic study of the god-fearers remains that by K. Lake in F. J. Foakes Jackson and K. Lake, *The Beginnings of Christianity*, Vol. V, London 1933, pp. 74–96.

had in baptism its own rite of initiation. The appropriation of the person of Jesus might no doubt vary from regarding him as a saviour figure, as a teacher, as the present Lord whose authority is to be acknowledged in daily life, or as the future judge.

The epistle of James would make good sense as a document from this area of early Christianity, and its echoes of other popular philosophies would also fall into place. It represents a form of the gentile mission independent of Paul's, and not, as for him, involving a radical disjunction from Judaism. (It may well be that the origins of Christianity in Rome, already established before Paul's contact with it, Rom. i. 8, may be in part sought in this area.) James is 'Jewish Christian' in the sense that Judaism has provided for non-Jews a bridge to Christianity, and the elements attractive to them in it are retained in their Christianity, together, it would seem, with the use of forms of organisation that would have been familiar from the synagogue. Beside the ways in which an understanding of Christ has, for Paul and the authors of Hebrews and the Revelation, transformed inherited ideas and language, the appropriation of Christianity by James may seem superficial. Yet the epistle is important in showing one form in which Christianity made its initial appeal in the Roman world, and one example of what 'conversion' to Christianity might mean. Most certainly the future development of Christianity does not lie with James's interpretation of it, but this interpretation may have been more widespread and influential in the early period than the epistle's now isolated position in the New Testament canon would suggest.

THE AUTHOR

The traditional questions of an Introduction, of the date and place of origin of a document, its purpose and its probable recipients, would be easily answered if the identity of its author were known. The 'James' of the opening greeting of this epistle is traditionally identified as James the leader of the Christian community in Jerusalem from a time quite soon after its first beginnings, called by Paul 'the Lord's brother'

INTRODUCTION

(Gal. i. 19; cf. Mk vi. 3), and later known as 'James the Just'.[1]
Evidence about this James comes from gospel references to
the unbelieving brothers of Jesus (Jn vii. 3 ff.; cf. Mk iii. 21,
31 ff.), from Acts, and from Paul's references in Galatians and
1 Corinthians. Outside the NT, varying accounts of his martyrdom are given by Josephus (*Ant.* xx. 200, a passage
generally considered to be authentic, and quoted by Eusebius,
HE ii. 23. 21–24), Hegesippus (preserved by Eusebius, *HE* ii.
23. 3–18), and Epiphanius (*Haer.* lxxviii. 13 f., which
draws on and elaborates Hegesippus); of which the latter two
contain a good deal of clearly legendary embellishment. With
such fragmentary and uncertain information available about
him, it is difficult to make judgments about what James of
Jerusalem might or might not have written.[2] Little weight can
be put on similarities between the epistle and the speech and
letter of James in Acts xv, since the historical accuracy of

[1] In the works of Origen extant in Greek, the epistle is cited as by 'James'
(cf. p. 24; *Comm. in Jn* frag. 126, 'James the apostle'). This James is identified as 'the brother of the Lord' only in Rufinus's translation of Origen's
Commentary on Romans, iv. 8. (The *Comm. in Rom.* was written at
Caesarea and contains explicit references to the epistle, but is extant only
in Latin; references are given by Mayor, pp. lxxxif.) In his *Commentary on
Matthew* x. 17, on Matt. xiii. 55 f., Origen comments that Jude the brother
of Jesus is the author of the epistle under that name, but makes no similar
comment on James the brother. This is surprising, especially as the
Comm. in Matt. is a document of the Caesarean period, but the explanation may simply be that Origen had plenty else to say about James, but
only that about Jude. There is no reason to suppose that he identified the
James of the epistle with any other James, and his disciple Eusebius is certainly quite clear as to the author's identity.
It is not necessary here to discuss the relationship of James to Jesus,
which so exercised Jerome. Discussions may be found in the older commentaries, e.g. Mayor, pp. v–lv, and Ropes, pp. 54–62, and in J. B. Lightfoot's essay, 'The Brethren of the Lord', in his Commentary on *Galatians*,
10th edn, London 1890, pp. 252–291.
[2] A notable debate relating to the date of James and thus to the authentici-
ty of the traditional authorship is conducted by G. Kittel and K. Aland in
a series of articles: G. Kittel, 'Der geschichtliche Ort des Jakobusbriefes',
ZNW 41, 1942, pp. 71–105; K. Aland, 'Der Herrenbruder Jakobus und der
Jakobusbrief', *Theologische Literaturzeitung* 69, 1944, pp. 97–104; G.
Kittel, 'Der Jakobusbrief und die Apostolischen Väter', *ZNW* 43,
1950–51, pp. 54–112.

THE EPISTLE OF JAMES

Luke's report is debatable, and many of the suggested parallels are anyway familiar expressions. (Those usually cited are Jas i. 1 cf. Acts xv. 34; i. 16, 19, 25, cf. xv. 25; i. 27 cf. xv. 14, 29; ii. 5 cf. xv. 13; ii. 7 cf. xv. 17; v. 9 f. cf. xv. 19. Even J. A. T. Robinson, who argues for the traditional authorship and a date *c.* A.D. 48 for the epistle, assesses these as not very significant evidence, *Redating the New Testament*, London 1976, p. 130 f.) It is certainly no longer possible to assert with complete confidence that James of Jerusalem could not have written the good Greek of the epistle, since the wide currency of that language in Palestine is increasingly appreciated. J. N. Sevenster in his monograph on that subject[1] uses the epistle of James as a test-case for his investigation, and concludes that it 'must not be deemed impossible'[2] that James the brother of Jesus could have acquired the facility to compose a letter in reasonable literary Greek. Yet other familiar objections still seem to hold good. It must seem extraordinary that a Christian with such an especial knowledge of, indeed relationship with, Jesus, should give him so small a place in his writing, more especially as this Christian was not only a witness, although apparently an unsympathetic one, of Jesus' earthly career, but also a witness of his resurrection (1 Cor. xv. 7; this tradition was, according to Jerome, elaborated in the *Gospel to the Hebrews, De Viris Illustribus* 2), an experience which may be supposed to have brought him to faith. Again, the tradition about James of Jerusalem is unanimous in presenting him as a Christian who continued to attach great importance to the observance of the Jewish Law, especially in cultic matters. Thus Luke shows him as presiding over the council held to decide what observance should be required of gentile converts (Acts xv. 13–21), and as suggesting to Paul a demonstration of piety in relation to the ritual discharge of vows (xxi. 18–24). Paul himself

[1] J. N. Sevenster, *Do you know Greek?*, subtitled 'How much Greek could the first Jewish Christians have known?', Leiden 1968, especially pp. 3–21 and 189–191; cf. M. Hengel, *Judaism and Hellenism* Vol. I pp. 58–61 and 103–106.
[2] Sevenster, *op. cit.* p. 191.

recalls the intervention of 'certain people from James', whatever may have been their precise rôle or their authority, as provoking the crisis in Antioch over table-fellowship between Jewish and gentile Christians (Gal. ii. 12). Josephus lists James among those arraigned for law-breaking by Ananus the High Priest, but also records the intervention of the Pharisees, in protest against Ananus's own illegal action: an intervention unlikely if they had thought that law-breakers were being justly punished (*Ant.* xx. 200). The accounts of Hegesippus and Epiphanius present James as revered among the Jews themselves for his piety, in particular his devotion to the Temple (Euseb. *HE* ii. 23. 6; Epiph. *Haer.* lxxviii. 14). The traditions vary, and are of doubtful reliability, but they show that James of Jerusalem was remembered as a Christian loyal to the Torah; and this memory is not consistent with what has been argued above as to the attitude of the author of the epistle to 'law'. James of Jerusalem, of all people, might be expected to appreciate the impact of the Pauline slogan of 'justification by faith and not by works'.

The author of the epistle, then, has adopted the convention of pseudonymity familiar in both Jewish and Graeco-Roman literature. No more than genuine authorship, however, is the adoption of precisely this pseudonym a key to his situation. Certainly James of Jerusalem was the hero of heterodox Jewish Christianity, as he is in the pseudo-Clementine *Homilies* and *Recognitions* (in contrast to their villain, Simon Magus, a thinly-disguised Paul). There he is appointed by Christ to be 'bishop of bishops, who rules Jerusalem, the holy Church of the Hebrews, and the Churches everywhere' (*Rec.* i. 44). The *Protevangelium Jacobi*, an infancy gospel popular among the Ebionites (though not necessarily originating from them, see O. Cullmann in Hennecke-Schneemelcher I, p. 372 f.), is attributed to him (*PJ* xxv. 1); and Epiphanius records that the Ebionites also used a document called *The Ascents of James* (*Haer.* xxx. 16). Yet this respect for James is by no means confined to Jewish Christianity. The gnostic Gospel of Thomas describes James as the one 'for whose sake heaven and earth came into being' (log. 12). Also in the Nag Hammadi library are the *Apocryphon of James* (I. 2), a tractate

THE EPISTLE OF JAMES

couched in the form of a letter from James;[1] and the *First* and
Second Apocalypse of James (V. 3, 4),[2] the former a dialogue
between Jesus and James, the latter a discourse of James
before his martyrdom. All three documents are clearly gnostic
in character. No doubt James appealed to the gnostics as one
for whom, as for Paul, Thomas and Matthias, belief or
knowledge came in an encounter with the exalted rather than
the earthly Jesus. Within the mainstream of Christian
development, Eusebius records Clement of Alexandria as
explaining the reason for the early leadership of James:
Peter, James and John 'did not lay claim to glory, as men who
had been preferred in honour by Him, but selected James the
Just as Bishop of Jerusalem' (*HE* ii. 1.3, cf. 23.1);
while Epiphanius shows Jesus himself entrusting James with
his throne over the world (*Haer.* lxxviii. 7). James of
Jerusalem was a very considerable figure in the tradition of
early Christianity; it is not surprising that an author of the
background and situation which has been suggested here
should have chosen the name of this early leader of the earliest
centre of the Church in which to write a letter that, while envisaging the problems of a particular community, is yet
applicable to the whole Israel of God, dispersed throughout
the world.[3]

---

[1] ET in James M. Robinson, ed., *The Nag Hammadi Library*, pp. 29–36.
Despite the letter form and opening address, 'James writes to . . .', there is
no sign of knowledge of the canonical epistle.

[2] Ibid, pp. 242–248 and 249–255.

[3] To regard the epistle as pseudonymous is, of course, to provide another
fixed point for its dating. It can hardly be supposed that the pseudonym of
James would be adopted during James's own lifetime; rather this reflects
his having become a revered figure of the past. The martyrdom of James of
Jerusalem is placed by Josephus in the interregnum between Festus and
Albinus, A.D. 62, and by Hegesippus immediately before Vespasian's
invasion of Palestine, probably therefore A.D. 67. The former is generally
considered reliable, the latter being a telescoping of events to show the
siege and ultimate fall of Jerusalem as retribution for James's fate. For the
writing of the epistle, then, A.D. 62 serves as the *terminus a quo*, and the
writing of the *Shepherd* of Hermas as the *terminus ad quem*.

SELECT BIBLIOGRAPHY

James is well served by older commentaries in English, which include

F. J. A. Hort, *The Epistle of St James* (commentary to iv. 7), London, 1909

R. J. Knowling, *The Epistle of St James* (Westminster Commentary), London, 1904

J. B. Mayor, *The Epistle of St James*, 3rd edn revised, London, 1913

J. H. Ropes, *A Critical and Exegetical Commentary on the Epistle of St James* (International Critical Commentary), Edinburgh, 1916

Among modern commentaries are

E. C. Blackman, *The Epistle of James* (Torch Bible Commentary), London and Naperville, Ill., 1957

B. S. Easton, *The Epistle of James* (Interpreter's Bible, vol. 12), New York, 1957

C. L. Mitton, *The Epistle of James*, London and Grand Rapids, Mich., 1966

B. Reicke, *The Epistles of James, Peter and Jude* (Anchor Bible), 2nd edn, New York, 1964

E. M. Sidebottom, *James, Jude and 2 Peter* (The Century Bible), London, 1967

R. V. G. Tasker, *The General Epistle of James* (Tyndale New Testament Commentary), London, 1956

German commentaries include

M. Dibelius, *Der Brief des Jakobus* (Meyers Kommentar), 11th edn by H. Greeven, Göttingen, 1964. English translation, *James*, by M. A. Williams (Hermeneia), Philadelphia, 1976

F. Mussner, *Der Jakobusbrief* (Herders Theologischer Kommentar zum Neuen Testament), Freiburg, 1964

H. Windisch, *Die Katholischen Briefe*, (Handbuch zum Neuen Testament) 3rd edn, Tübingen, 1951

French commentaries include

J. Cantinat, C.M., *Les Épîtres de Saint Jacques et de Saint Jude* (Sources Bibliques), Paris, 1973

J. Chaine, *L'Épître de Saint Jacques* (Études Bibliques), 2nd edn, Paris, 1927

J. Marty, *L'Épître de Jacques: Étude critique*, Paris, 1935

Articles, and other studies of specific issues in the epistle, are referred to in the Introduction. An exhaustive bibliography, brought up-to-date by the translator, may be found in the ET of Dibelius.

THE EPISTLE OF JAMES

1. ADDRESS AND GREETING
i. 1

(1) James, servant of God and of the Lord Jesus Christ, to the Twelve Tribes in the Dispersion: Greetings.

The epistle opens in conventional letter form, with identification of writer and recipients, and salutation. The writer identifies himself as **James**, *Iakōbos*, the Greek form of the Jewish name 'Jacob'; he writes in the character of James the brother of Jesus, leader of the Christian community in Jerusalem before the fall of that city (see Introduction, pp. 38–42).

He further describes himself as **servant** *of God and of the Lord Jesus Christ*. The description of a worshipper as the *servant, doulos*, lit. 'slave', of his god is common in Hellenistic religion, especially the mystery religions, and may be seen as the natural corollary of calling the god 'Lord', *kurios*, a title with connotations of ownership and absolute mastery (though cf. the rejection of that logic in Jn xv. 15). The term has precedents in the LXX, where all Israel may be referred to as God's *douloi* (e.g. Deut. xxxii. 36), but where also it may denote particular important individuals such as Moses (1 Kgs viii. 53, 56; Mal. iii. 24), or David (1 Kgs viii. 66), and prophets (Jere. vii. 25; Amos iii. 7; cf. *pais* in Dan. ix. 10). Correspondingly, in early Christian documents *servant of God* denotes both believers in general (e.g. 1 Pet. ii. 16; Hermas, *Vis.* i. 2. 4), and particular individuals such as prophets (Rev. x. 7, xi. 18) and apostles (Acts iv. 29; Tit. i. 1; Paul describes himself and Timothy as 'servants of Christ' in Phil. i. 1, cf. Gal. i. 10; and the self-designation *servant* is joined to that of 'apostle' in the addresses of Rom. and 2 Pet.). James may so describe himself, then,

45

either to identify himself with his readers, as a worshipper writing to fellow worshippers whom he will later call 'brothers' (so Ropes, who comments that Paul uses this form of description only in Romans and Philippians, 'epistles in which he is consciously striving to avoid the assumption of personal authority'); or, as a pseudonymous writer, to assert his place of authority in the Church and in the line of God's great servants of the past (so Dibelius). He certainly writes with an implicit authority, and in iii. 1 classes himself with the properly restricted group of teachers, but the single word of self-designation cannot really be seen as strongly emphasising either claim or disclaimer. The author presents himself to his readers as a Christian worshipper, and as one whose right to address them requires no further explanation or justification.[1]

His service is directed both to **God** and to **the Lord Jesus Christ**. The phrase *theou kai kuriou Iēsou Christou* could in fact be translated as referring solely to Jesus Christ, described as 'God and Lord', but that Jesus should be called 'God' unequivocally would be very unusual in the light of NT practice (Jn xx. 28 is an outstanding exception), and is hardly to be expected of this author with his distinctly limited christological interest. Some MSS seek to clarify the distinction between the two objects of service by identifying God as Father, *theou patros*, and Jesus as *Lord* (so 69, 206, 429), while some versions, in the absence of a definite article in Greek, add the qualification 'our Lord'. This recognition by scribes of an awkwardness in the text, together with the fact that the acknowledgement of two-fold service is unparalleled in the addresses of other NT epistles, might seem to lend support to those who, like Spitta, see the reference to Jesus as a

[1] The author of Jude, by contrast, further identifies himself as 'brother of James' (Jude 1). Clement of Alexandria, according to Cassiodorus's Latin translation of his *Hypotyposeis* (cited by Lightfoot, *Galatians*, p. 279), saw this as a mark of humility, since a greater kinship might have been claimed, but more probably there is an appeal to the better-known authority to support the author's own. Dibelius (Introduction, p. 39) thinks that the address of Jude presupposes a knowledge of the epistle of James, but there is no other indication in Jude of such knowledge, and the form of description can be readily accounted for by the general, early prestige of the figure of James.

Christianising interpolation into the original designation of the author as servant of 'God the Lord', Yahweh. There is no textual evidence for this shorter reading, and it is anyway unlikely in view of other evidence of the Christian character of the document. In calling Jesus **Lord**, James follows general Christian practice, apparently from a very early initiative, since the title appears in its Aramaic form in the prayer of 1 Cor. xvi. 22 (cf. Rev. xxii. 20), and is also found in what appears to be a confessional formula in Rom. x. 9 (cf. 1 Cor. xii. 3). It was an initiative of potentially great christological significance, since *kurios* is used in the LXX both to translate the Hebrew *adōnai*, used of God, and to render the divine name. James does not explore the implications of the title, and indeed more frequently applies it to God than to Jesus (e.g. i. 7, iii. 9, iv. 10, v. 10). **Christ**, by contrast, seems to have lost the titular sense; it goes with **Jesus** as effectively part of the proper name of the Lord.

The recipients of the letter are identified as **the Twelve Tribes in the Dispersion**. *Twelve Tribes* is an obvious way of referring to the Jewish nation (cf. Acts xxvi. 7; 1 Clem. lv. 6); and *Dispersion, diaspora*, is a familiar term for the phenomenon of Jews resident among gentiles outside Palestine, variously denoting the fact of that residence (e.g. Deut. xxviii. 25; Jere. xli. 17), the Jews so resident (e.g. Jn vii. 35; 2 Macc. i. 27), and the place in which they reside (e.g. Judith v. 19; Test. Asher vii. 2). The address could seem, then, to define the readers in racial and geographical terms, though the geographical definition would be more than somewhat open (cf. the address of 1 Peter to the 'chosen sojourners of the Dispersion' in the provinces of Asia Minor, 1 Pet. i. 1). The epistle would then be understood as addressed to Jews or Jewish Christians in the world outside Palestine (so, e.g., Mayor, Hort and Chaine). However, the address cannot be satisfactorily explained as simply an empirical definition. Although its *Dispersion* was an actual fact for the Jewish nation, its being *Twelve Tribes* was rather a description of its ideal composition as, since the fall of the Northern Kingdom of Israel to Assyria in 721 B.C., ten of those tribes were thought to be effectively 'lost' (cf. Ass. Mos. iv. 8 f.; 2 Bar. i. 2; in *Ant.* xi. 133 Josephus explains that there are two tribes in Europe and Asia subject to the Romans, and ten tribes beyond the Euphrates, 'countless myriads', whose number cannot be ascertained), and their reconstitution had become a hope for the future, the new age (so Is. xi. 11–16; Jere. xxxi. 8; Ezek. xxxvii. 15–22; Zech. x. 6–12; 2 Esd. xiii. 39–47; and also the letter of Baruch to the nine and a half tribes, in the hope of their return in the last times, 2 Bar. lxxviii ff., esp. lxxviii. 5–7). For James to address his readers in terms of this ideal would be comparable with other evidence that the Christian community thought of itself as the true Israel of God's time of salvation (e.g. Rom. ix. 24–26; Gal. v. 16; Heb. iii. 6, iv. 9; 1 Pet. ii. 9 f.). The idea of the twelve tribes is variously retained by Christian authors: the Q tradition includes Jesus' promise that his disciples will judge the twelve tribes of Israel (Matt. xix. 28; Lk. xxii. 30); Revelation envisages a sealing of the twelve tribes, or their representatives, for deliverance (Rev. vii. 4–8); while Hermas uses the term to denote the universal number of believers, 'these twelve tribes which inhabit the whole world are twelve nations', as they are now, in need of judgment and purification (*Sim.* ix. 17. 1 f.).[1]

Since the Christian community also thought of itself as one whose present character was temporary (Phil. iii. 20 f.; Heb. xiii. 14), it was natural that it should appropriate to itself the language of Israel as the sojourning people of God. Addresses to Churches in this 'dispersion' character are found in 1 Pet. i. 1 (cf. ii. 11) and the introductions to 1 Clement, the Epistle of Polycarp and the *Martyrdom of Polycarp*, cf. also Hermas, *Sim.* i. 1; Diognet. v. 5. If the main intention of the address is to define the community theologically in its Christian character (so also, e.g., Ropes and Dibelius), the question whether its members are of Jewish origin remains undecided; the 'dispersion' community of 1 Peter indeed seems to have had a predominantly gentile background (1 Pet. iv. 3, cf. i. 14, 18). To describe a Christian community as fulfilling or in-

[1] The Qumran community, which also saw itself as the 'true Israel', in the wilderness, appears to have employed a division of the community symbolically into twelve tribes, represented by the twelve laymen who formed (with three priests) their supreme council (1 QS viii. 1; cf. G. Vermes, *The Dead Sea Scrolls in English*, 2nd edn Harmondsworth 1975, p. 17 f.).

heriting the rôle of Israel need not, of course, imply that there
had been an absolute break with the empirical Jewish people;
however, other evidence will be necessary in order to argue
that the membership of the Christian 'Israel' here addressed is
in fact Jewish in origin. (To see the readers as defined here in
their theological character is also, of course, to leave undecided the question whether the author intends his work to
be of general reference, or whether he writes with a specific
community in mind.)

To these readers the author addresses **Greetings**, using the
infinitive *chairein*, the regular form of salutation in Hellenistic
letters, found frequently in the papyri, in the LXX in the
letters of Alexander, Demetrius and Jonathan (1 Macc. x. 18,
25, xii. 6, cf. 2 Macc. i. 11), and in the NT in the letter of
Lysias to Felix (Acts xxiii. 26) and the Jerusalem encyclical
(Acts xv. 23). The Jewish salutation would commonly be
'Peace' (as in the records of royal letters in Dan. iv. 1, vi. 26;
Ezra iv. 17; cf. 2 Macc. i. 1). James's opening address contrasts markedly with other early Christian epistles, none of
which use the letter style with such formality, but mostly
open with a wish or prayer for 'grace and peace' for their
readers (so all the Pauline, Pastoral and Petrine epistles; Rev.
i. 4 f., the address to the seven Churches; 1 Clem. and Ep.
Poly.; Ignatius's 'abundant greeting', *pleista chairein*, in
Magn., Trall., Smyrn., and *Poly.* is comparable, though his
designation of writer and addressees is more elaborate than
James's).

2. TRIAL AND INTEGRITY

i. 2–8

**(2) My brothers, regard it as wholly a matter for joy
whenever you fall into various kinds of trials, (3)
knowing that the testing of your faith brings about endurance; (4) and let endurance do its whole work, so
that you may be whole and complete, lacking in
nothing. (5) If any of you lacks wisdom, let him ask of**

God who gives to all freely and without grudging, and it will be given him. (6) But let him ask in faith, nothing doubting, for the man who doubts is like a wave of the sea, blown about and tossed by the wind. (7) Let not that man expect that he will receive anything from the Lord; (8) he is a double-minded man, unstable in everything he does.

The formality of the opening address is modified in the verse immediately following it, in two ways. First, it is linked into the opening passages of instruction by a verbal echo: those whom the author has given greetings, *chairein*, he now urges to regard their trials as a ground for joy, *charan*. Secondly, he addresses them in direct, personal terms as **my brothers**, a recurrent phrase throughout the epistle (e.g. i. 16, 19, ii. 1, 5, iii. 1, 10, v. 12, 19). This address to his readers as brothers is also characteristic of Paul (e.g. Rom. vii. 4; 1 Cor. i. 10 f.; Gal. i. 11; Phil. iii. 1), while Matthew refers to the disciples of Jesus as 'brethren' (Matt. xxiii. 8, cf. xviii. 15) and Luke to the earliest Jerusalem community as 'the brethren' (Acts i. 15 f.). However, although the term is characteristically Christian it is not peculiarly so, being used of fellow-Jews in Acts ii. 29, xiii. 26 (cf. Rom. ix. 3), in Jewish religious communities such as the Essenes (Josephus, *BJ* ii. 122), and generally for close associates (e.g. Jud. xix. 23; 1 Sam. xxx. 23); as also for members of Hellenistic religious associations (MM cites, e.g., associates at the Serapeum at Memphis).

The section, vv. 2–8, is given a structural unity by verbal links such as that between vv. 1 and 2; thus vv. 4 and 5 are linked by the verb *leipō*, and vv. 5 and 6 by *aiteō*. It may be argued whether these links are purely structural, or whether they reflect a discernible sequence of thought. In vv. 2–4, however, the chain of words and phrases expresses an idea of progressive experience. The readers should **regard it as wholly a matter for joy** (lit. as 'all joy'; not that suffering is the occasion for all the joy there is, but that it should occasion only joy, unmixed with other reactions) when they come under trial, for in trial is the testing of faith which produces endurance, which, when carried through, leads to the achieve-

ment of a complete character. A similar chain is found in 1
Pet. i. 6–7: the readers should rejoice when grieved by *various
kinds of trials* (the same phrase, *peirasmois poikilois*, is used
by Peter as by James, who carries on the alliteration with his
verb *peripesēte*; Dibelius comments that the adjective *poikilos*
is a favourite one for portraying a variety of torments and
persecutions, citing *inter alia* 3 Macc. ii. 6; 4 Macc. xvii. 7;
Hermas, *Sim*. vi. 3. 3, 4); for their faith, proven in trial, will
receive praise and glory at the revelation of Christ. A simpler
chain, on the same theme, is found in Rom. v. 3–4, where
rejoicing in suffering is in the knowledge that suffering
produces endurance; endurance, approved character; and approved character, hope, which will not be disappointed. The
correspondences are not so close as to argue literary interdependence between the three Christian writers, but rather
suggest that all three are making use of an established pattern
of ethical instruction, on the theme of the value of endurance
under trial. Their differences are due to each writer's
developing this pattern in relation to his own interests and
situation.

Neither James nor Peter defines the nature of the **various 2
kinds of trial** which they envisage, but Peter speaks of his
readers being 'grieved' by them, and compares their proving
action with that of fire (i. 7, cf. iv. 12, where the coming fiery
trial is to be seen as sharing in the suffering of Christ). He is
probably therefore thinking of external pressure, hostility or
persecution producing actual suffering; of a particular crisis,
perhaps already in progress. Paul's use of *thlipsis*, suffering,
with its connotations of eschatological tribulation (see on Jas
i. 27) indicates that he envisages the situation in which endurance is demanded in similar terms, whether or not he sees
a crisis as imminent for the Roman Christians. They both
therefore stand in the tradition of Jewish martyrology, where
endurance is demanded in the crisis of persecution (cf., e.g., 4
Macc. iv. 11, ix. 30; Judith viii. 25 ff.; and further on i. 12). It
is consistent with this that both Peter and Paul also see the
final link in the chain in eschatological terms. For Peter,
his readers' proven faith will receive praise at the revelation of
Christ, as yet unseen, but coming (i. 7 f., cf. i. 13); for Paul the

final term is hope, described in v. 2 as hope of the glory of God. James gives no indication that he sees the *trials* in such particular terms. His use of *hotan*, **whenever**, could indicate that he is thinking of a recurrent experience, and he may be consciously generalising the language to relate it to the trials of everyday life (cf. on i. 12, 27, v. 7 f.). He thus rather follows in the tradition of Ben Sira, who sees testing and endurance as the perennial experience of life in God's service (Ecclus ii. 1–6; cf. Test. Jos. ii. 7). There is no eschatological term to James's series, either: the process of probation leads to an achieving of personal integrity, apparently an end in itself.

3   The expression of both the first and the third elements in James's sequence is difficult. The noun *dokimion* usually means 'test' in the sense of 'the means of testing' (so Prov. xxvii. 21, LXX), which would be awkward in this context. The various trials are no doubt the means by which faith is tested, but it is rather in the experience of which they are the means that endurance will be worked out. In 1 Pet. i. 7 the noun appears to carry the sense of that which is established by testing, tried character or genuineness (so Ps. xi. 7, LXX): it is not the means of testing faith, nor the test itself, which will receive praise, but the proven genuineness of faith. For this sense, the normal expression would be the neuter adjective *dokimon* (cf. Jas i. 12), found as a variant reading for *dokimion* in both Peter and James (in p 74 for both, and some individual MSS for each). This sense, however, will suit James no better, for *to dokimion* is in his context clearly something that yields a result rather than itself a resultant fact. The most satisfactory meaning for it to carry in James is that of 'test' as **testing**, a sense which Dibelius denies that it can carry, but which is cited by AG and LS. Incidentally, the use by Peter and James of the same word in a similar context but with a different meaning accords with the suggestion that they are independently using a common pattern rather than either being dependent on the other; and Paul's use of the noun *dokimē*, approved character, as the third link in his chain, further indicates that a word, or words, of that root played an established part in the pattern of teaching on which all three authors variously drew.

The testing of faith, then, brings about **endurance**, *hupomenē*, a word which indicates rather an active steadfastness in, than passive submission to, circumstances (cf. on v. 11). Endurance must be allowed to **do its whole work.** 4 The meaning of the phrase *ergon teleion* is unclear, and there are three main lines of interpretation. First, the *complete work* may be understood as the active steadfastness itself: this should be carried through 'completely', so that as trial should be seen only in terms of joy, it should also be met with unwavering steadfastness (thus Mayor and Hort). Secondly, the *work* may be seen as the manifestation or proof of steadfastness, which will bear fruit if put into effect (thus Ropes; AG suggests, 'let endurance show itself perfectly in practice'). Thirdly, it may be seen as the final link in the chain. The chain has thus far been specific: probation leads to hope, hope to endurance; and the expectation is that the outcome of endurance will also be specified. The following clause suggests that the outcome of endurance would be seen as completeness of character, but James has departed from the simple sequence of 'endurance produces perfection' to introduce an imperative note. The sequence is not automatic; it demands effort and decision (thus also Dibelius; the imperative serves to underline the fact that endurance is active rather than passive). The sense could be brought out in a paraphrase: endurance 'must do its work of perfecting'.

Having thus reached the final term of his sequence, James typically elaborates on it, adding a synonym and then a negative definition (cf. vv. 5b, 6a): the aim is **that you may be whole and complete, lacking in nothing**. To be *teleios*, whole or perfect, is not a matter of having achieved a higher standard (contrast *Did.* vi. 2, where those who can bear the whole yoke of the Lord are 'perfect', while others must do as much as they can). Paul may, in 1 Cor. ii. 6, reflect and reject a claim of some in Corinth to be 'the perfect' over against ordinary believers (a claim with a history in gnosticism), but in Col. i. 28, iv. 12 his hope is 'perfection' for all his readers. Similarly, Matt. v. 48 does not present perfection as either an impossible or an extraordinary demand. The adjective can carry the sense of 'mature'; the phrase *teleios anēr*, used in Jas

iii. 2 meaning 'a mature man' (cf. Eph. iv. 13), but this sense is not uppermost in James here. As the negative definition makes clear, to be *teleios* is to be a complete person, having integrity, unlike the divided man of vv. 6–8. In iii. 2, perfection is seen in exercising control over the tongue: clearly not something for an élite only to attempt but for all to strive for in order to avoid that disunity that is most blatant in sins of speech (iii. 9 f.). (This may well be the sense of the word uppermost for Matthew too, for the demand for perfection in v. 48 is a demand for consistency of behaviour like that of God, while the rich young man is offered the prospect of perfection in relation to what he lacks, xix. 20 f.) Both *teleios* and its synonym *holokleros* can also carry connotations of moral completeness, and thus blamelessness, and this sense is undoubtedly present for James (cf. *teleios* in Gen. vi. 9;[1] Deut. xviii. 13; Ecclus xliv. 17; and *holokleros* in Wisd. xv. 3).

5   Moral integrity is a matter for exhortation, and lack of it may correspondingly be a matter for blame, but James now turns to consider the lack of **wisdom**, a lack that cannot be made up by human effort, for it is a gift of God and must therefore be asked of him (cf. Prov. ii. 6; 1 Kgs iii. 9 ff.; Ecclus i. 1; Wisd. ix. 17). The sequence of vv. 4–5 is not an obvious one. Mayor quotes Bede's suggestion that the linking idea is that wisdom is necessary in order to see suffering as a joy (referring back to v. 2), a suggestion adopted by Chaine; but this very precise connection is not indicated. It is possible that there was a familiar association of perfection and wisdom (e.g. Wisd. ix. 6 asserts that though a man may seem perfect, he is worthless if he lacks the wisdom that comes from God; cf. also 1 Cor. ii. 6 f. and Col. i. 28 for the conjunction). Structurally, the sequence is established by a 'stitch-word', the verb *leipo* used in both verses, but this is not merely an artificial link, for a loose train of thought may be observed. To move from a desire for completeness to consider a lack which only

---

[1] In Gen. vi. 9 Noah is described as *teleios*. Philo expounds this in terms of completeness: the man who is *teleios* is *holokleros ex arches*, that is, complete in virtue (*De Abr.* 47, cf. 34, where Noah is *teleios* in acquiring not one virtue, but all).

God can supply is not extraordinary, and the theme of integrity introduced in v. 4 continues in the following verses in the contrast of God and man. When James refers to wisdom again, in iii. 13, 17, and attempts some definition of it, it is seen as the ground of action and the sum of virtues, so perhaps here too it is thought of as a unifying bond, conducive to the desired wholeness.

As the gift of God, it comes from him **freely**, *haplōs*. The usual meaning of the noun *haplotēs* is singleness or simplicity. As contrasted with duplicity, it may convey a lack or reservation or of guile, and as, further, this might be expressed in magnanimity or generosity, the word can also carry this latter meaning (cf. Dibelius, excursus pp. 77–79). Thus Issachar, the exemplar of *haplotēs* in the Testaments, as the man of integrity, is generous (Test. Iss. iii. 8), and neither covetous (iv. 2) nor meddlesome (v. 1). James's idea, then, may be either that God gives without hesitation or second thoughts, or that he gives generously. The latter could be suggested by the contrast immediately following: he gives generously *and without grudging*; the former by the next verse: God's lack of hesitation in giving would contrast with man's hesitation in asking. Quite probably the author is conscious of both meanings and intends both contrasts to be made.[1] The same ambivalence is found in Paul's use of this language, of human giving, in Rom. xii. 8, where 'let he who gives do it generously' or 'wholeheartedly' would make equal sense in context; though in 2 Cor. viii. 2, ix. 11, 13 it is clearly of generous giving that he writes. Hermas, also writing on the theme of human giving, inclines to the former sense: 'Give wholeheartedly, without doubting', i.e. as to the object (*Mand.* ii. 4. 6; cf. *Did.* iv. 7; Barn. xix. 11). Hermas's language is strikingly similar to James's, and as there are other echoes of the epistle in this *Mandate* (see on i. 27, iii. 8), he may be adapting the present passage to his own argument. The contrast between giving and **grudging** is familiar from the aphorisms of Ecclesiasticus (e.g. viii. 15–18, xx. 15, xli. 22), and is probably

---

[1] A discussion of the contrast between *haplotēs* and doubleness is given by J. Daniélou. *The Theology of Jewish Christianity*, ET London 1964, pp. 362–365.

proverbial; cf. also Sextus, *Sententiae* 339 and Pss Sol. v. 15 f., where a contrast between grudging human and generous divine giving is made: 'Man's goodness is (bestowed) grudgingly . . ., And if he repeat (it) without murmuring, even that is marvellous. But Thy gift is great in goodness and wealth, And he whose hope is (set) on thee shall have no lack of gifts'.

It is in the light of this known characteristic of God that James advises, **let him ask . . . and it will be given him**. There is an obvious similarity to the command of Jesus in Matt. vii. 7, Lk. xi. 9: 'Ask, and it will be given to you'. In the gospel passage the command is followed by a comparison between imperfect human fathers who yet give their sons appropriate gifts, and 'your father in heaven' who 'will give . . . to those who ask him'. James similarly attributes 'every gift that is good' to 'the Father of lights' (i. 17). It seems quite possible, then, that James draws on the tradition of the teaching of Jesus, but if so it is clear that that teaching has been absorbed without differentiation into the general stock of ethical instruction. He will have drawn on it independently of its literary fixity in either gospel, since in contrast to Matthew's general 'good gifts' he specifies the gift of God, but as the gift of wisdom rather than Luke's 'Holy Spirit'.

6   James has further elaborated on the gospel theme by introducing the idea of unanswered requests. He turns from the quality of God's giving to the quality of man's asking. An interest in prayer, its character and its power, is a marked feature of the epistle (see Introduction, pp. 27). Prayer must be made **in faith** (cf. v. 15; and Mk xi. 24, Matt. xxi. 22) and **without doubting**, otherwise its request will not be granted. The problem of apparently unanswered prayer is taken up again in iv. 3; in both places it is clear that the explanation is in terms of man the asker and not God the giver. The nature of the *doubt* is not here defined. It could be doubt about the object of the request, and what is really desired, as in iv. 3 requests are not granted as they are for an inappropriate object (SB cites as a parallel here *Tanchuma* 23b, 24a on Deut. xxvi. 16, ' When you make your prayer to God, do not have two hearts, one for God and one for something else').

More probably it is doubt about the outcome of the request, of God's ability or willingness to give. This theme is echoed in a precept in the 'Two Ways' section of the *Didache* and epistle of Barnabas: 'Thou shalt not doubt whether a thing shall be or not be' (*Did.* iv. 4; Barn. xix. 5); and by Hermas in *Mand.* ix, which again seems to draw upon the language of the epistle but develops the theme so that the doubt is specifically that of a sinner about what he can hope to receive (ix. 1), and apparent delay in granting requests is due to some sin of which the petitioner is ignorant (ix. 7 f.). The nature of *doubt* is related to the nature of *faith.* Undefined in v. 3, *faith* here will be not simply a general confidence in the proposition that prayer will be answered, but a confidence based on the belief that the God addressed is a God who gives freely (cf. also ii. 19, where the demons' acceptance of the proposition that 'God is one' is also an acceptance of the implications for them of that fact). Prayer, then, should be an expression of man's integrity: he should be wholehearted in his approach to God.

The man who lacks such integrity is **like a wave of the sea**; *kludōn*, wave, often carries in the LXX the sense of 'tempest', as in Jonah i. 4; 1 Macc. vi. 11; cf. Lk. viii. 24; but the classical use as meaning surf or rough water makes better sense in an image of one who wavers and hesitates, tossing about like the surface of water thrown up by passing gusts of wind (Wisd. xix. 7; and cf. Eph. iv. 14, where the verb *kludōnizomai* is used). The suggestion that the image is drawn specifically from the inland 'sea' of Galilee with its sudden storms (D. Y. Hadidian, 'Palestinian Pictures in the Epistle of James', p. 227 f.) is distinctly far-fetched. The verbs giving the translation **blown about and tossed by the wind**, *anemizō* and *ripizō*, are virtually synonymous, and the former may be of James's coining since it has not so far been found in earlier documents. He is fond of such alliteration, which gives a certain cadence to his style (cf. Introduction, p. 5).

That man, the man who prays in doubt, need not expect to 7 **receive anything from the Lord.** *The Lord* is here clearly not Jesus, but God the Father, the giver of gifts in i. 5, 17.

Some MSS, including Sinaiticus, omit the pronoun *anything*, so that the specific case of prayer for wisdom remains in the foreground, but it is more likely that James intends his warning to be applied to prayer in general. The punctuation of the end of this verse, and its relation to the following verse, is uncertain. The two verses may be seen as two sentences containing propositions about (a) the doubting man, and (b) the double-minded man, that are distinct, though thematically related (so AV). Alternatively v. 8 may be seen as part of the predicate of the sentence begun in v. 7: 'the doubter should not think that a double-minded man ... will receive anything' (RSV); or, thirdly, the second verse may be seen in apposition to the first, with the statement about the double-minded man providing a further and pejorative description of the doubter (NEB; JB; GNB). This last interpretation has been adopted in the above translation, on the analogy of similar two-fold descriptions in the epistle, the second often being, as here, compressed and more direct (e.g. ii. 4, iii. 2, iv. 2).

8   James's stigmatising of the doubter as **a double-minded man** accords with and no doubt derives from the idea of doubleness as the essence of sin, as found in the OT (e.g. Ps. xii. 2; 1 Chron. xii. 33; Ecclus i. 28) and later Jewish literature, especially the Testaments (e.g. Test. Asher i. 3–vi. 2; Test. Benj. vi. 5–7) and Qumran documents (e.g. 1 QS iii. 17–18, iv. 23). This idea was developed in the Rabbinic theory of the 'two impulses' in man, the good and evil impulses which struggle for control of the individual, an idea for which 'proof texts' were found in Gen. vi. 5, viii. 21, and which is sometimes seen to be reflected in Paul's analysis of his moral conflict, in Rom. vii.[1] This way of characterising man as sinful is reflected in other early Christian literature: in Hermas, especially *Mand.* ix on 'double-mindedness' (Light-

[1] For illustration of the idea in Jewish documents, see SB IV. 1, Excurs 19, 'Der gute u. der böse Trieb', pp. 466–483; and a series of articles by O. J. F. Seitz, 'Antecedents and significance of the term δίψυχος', *JBL* 66, 1947, pp. 211–219; 'Afterthoughts on the term δίψυχος', *NTS* 4, 1957–58, pp. 327–334; 'Two spirits in man: an essay in biblical exegesis', *NTS* 6, 1959–60, pp. 82–95.

foot's translation is 'doubtful-mindedness') and *Mand.* xi–xii.
3 on the evil and good desires; and in the 'Two Ways' of
Didache and Barnabas, where for both 'doubleness of heart' is
a mark of the way of death (*Did.* v. 1; Barn. xx. 1). (There is
no suggestion that James associates this division with the activity of cosmic, angelic or demonic, forces such as the Prince
of Light and the angel of darkness of 1 QS iii. 20–24; the
angel of peace and Beliar in Test. Benj. vi. 1, 7; the two spirits
of Hermas *Mand.* ix. 11, xi. 1–17; or the 'black one' of Barn.
xx. 1.)

The general theme of doubleness or division as a
characteristic of man to be distrusted, indeed deplored, and
controlled, is not confined to Jewish literature. It is not
without analogy in the common Hellenistic attitude towards
man as unhappily compounded of body and soul, or to the
Platonic theory of divisions in the soul itself.[1] The former attitude comes to be characteristic of gnosticism, and the theme
of doubleness emerges strikingly in the Gospel of Thomas log.
22: 'Jesus said to them, "When you make the two one, and
when you make the inside like the outside and the outside like
the inside, and the above like the below, and when you make
the male and the female one and the same, so that the male
shall not be male nor the female female . . . then will you enter
(the Kingdom)" '[2] (cf. log. 106). It is not suggested that James
reflects such speculative or philosophical ideas, but that this

---

[1] For the body-soul dichotomy see, e.g., *Phaedo* 67, and cf. Philo, *De Vita
Mos.* ii. 288. For a concise account of the development of Plato's un-
derstanding of the composite nature of the *psuchē* in the *Phaedo,
Phaedrus* and *Republic*, see W. K. C. Guthrie, *A History of Greek
Philosophy* IV, Cambridge 1975, pp. 346 f., 421–5, 476–8; also *Timaeus*
69 c-e. Philo assumes the tripartite nature of the *psuchē* in *Leg. Alleg.* i.
70–73, iii. 115; *De Spec. Leg.* iv. 92. For both lines of thought, see also E.R.
Dodds, *The Greeks and the Irrational*, California 1951, chapters V and
VII; *Pagan and Christian in an Age of Anxiety*, Cambridge 1968, pp.
29–36.

[2] ET by Thomas O. Lambdin in James M. Robinson, ed. *The Nag Hammadi Library in English.* The saying is substantially quoted in 2 Clem.
xii, where it is expounded in ethical terms, and it was also known to Clement of Alexandria, who ascribes it to the Gospel of the Egyptians, *Strom.*
iii. 13. 92.

idea of doubleness was widely current in his world and variously developed, and would thus make sense in other than a purely Jewish context. (For the pervasiveness of the theme of doubleness and singleness in the epistle, see Introduction, pp. 29–32.)

In Jewish documents the idea of doubleness on which James draws would most probably be conveyed through use of the idiom of the heart as representing the person. The 'double heart' is condemned in Ps. xii. 2; 1 Chron. xii. 33; Ecclus i. 28; 1 Enoch xci. 4; 1 QH iv. 14; as also the 'Two Ways' passage cited above; contrast the importance attached to the 'whole heart' in, e.g., Deut. vi. 4, xi. 12, xiii. 3; 1 Kgs ii. 4, xiv. 8; 2 Chron. xii. 38, xxxi. 21. James's adjective *dipsuchos, double-minded*, used here and again in iv. 8, is unparalleled in the LXX, NT, or any other known earlier literature, though with the noun *dipsuchia* and verb *dipsucheō* it appears in other early Christian literature: 1 and 2 Clement, the 'Two Ways' of *Didache* and Barnabas, and very frequently in Hermas, who uses James's own phrase, *dipsuchos anēr*, in *Mand.* ix. 6. Mayor suggests that the word was introduced by James himself, but it is unlikely that 1 and 2 Clement and the 'Two Ways' can be seen to derive it from him, and although Hermas knows the epistle the frequency of his use of the word-group (over forty occurrences) is unlikely to be accounted for by that knowledge alone. In 1 and 2 Clement the adjective appears in an apocryphal quotation (1 Clem. xxiii. 3 f.; 2 Clem. xi. 2 f.), and O. J. F. Seitz argues that this is the source for James and Hermas as well ('The relationship of the Shepherd of Hermas to the Epistle of James', *JBL* 63, 1944, pp. 131–140, cf. on iv. 8). It is probably, however, mistaken to seek to identify a single source from which all the known authors derive their language, and most likely that the background is an idiom current in Greek-speaking Judaism. Its coining is not remarkable; in the LXX *psuchē* is the usual rendering of *nephesh*, which denotes the individual, the self, as does 'the heart' (e.g. Gen. ii. 7; and cf. Jas v. 20), and indeed *psuchē* occasionally appears as the LXX rendering of *lēb*, heart (e.g. Ps. lxviii. 21, 33; Is. vii. 2, 4; Jere. iv. 19). To convey the Jewish idea of doubleness through a use of *psuchē* rather than the idiom of the heart may have seemed especially appropriate in view of the rôle of *psuchē* in expressing apparently congruous Greek ideas about the composite self. It is however worth noting that of those authors who use the language confidently outside quotation (thus Hermas, who uses it very frequently independent of any apparent quotation; 1 Clem. xi. 2, xxiii. 2 and 2 Clem. xi. 3 outside their apocryphon; in contrast with *Didache* and Barnabas for whom it is confined to the 'Two Ways' maxim which both include, *Did.* iv. 4; Barn. xix. 5), Hermas and 1 Clement are of certain Roman origin, and 2 Clement is also arguably Roman (see Robert M. Grant and Holt H. Graham, *The Apostolic Fathers*, Vol. 2, *First and Second Clement*, New York and Toronto 1965, p. 109). The word may, then, be a local idiom, and thus a straw in the wind in identifying the provenance of James.[1]

The double-minded man is further described as **unstable in everything he does**. This adjective, *akatastatos*, is also confined to James in the NT (here and in iii. 8), as is the noun *akatastasia* (iii. 16), but both have precedent in the LXX and classical literature. It may mean 'restless', as in iii. 8, or 'unstable', and as the phrase *en pasais tais hodois autou* is literally 'in all his ways', the whole might conjure up the image of a stumbling walker (cf. Jn x. 10). However, 'ways' and 'walking' are familiar biblical idioms for conduct (e.g. Pss xxix. 1, cxlv. 17; Jere. xvi. 17), and James's language is here more probably literal than figurative. (Once again Hermas may be seen to echo the epistle: the *dipsuchoi* are susceptible to being led astray by evil spirits, and a man so controlled 'is unstable in his every deed', *akatastei en pasē praxei autou, Mand.* v. 2. 1, 7.) The man who is divided in himself, then, will show himself as such in his doubtful prayer, and also in his inability to act firmly or reliably.

---

[1] For a fuller discussion of this question, see Sophie S. Marshall, 'Δίψυχος, a local term?', *Studia Evangelica* VI, 1973, pp. 348–351.

3. THE POOR AND THE RICH

i. 9–11

(9) Let the brother in humble circumstances boast of his exhaltation, (10) but let the rich man boast of his humiliation, for he will pass away 'like a meadow flower'. (11) For the sun rises with burning heat and 'dries up the grass and its flower falls' and its loveliness perishes. Just so the rich man will wither away in mid-career.

A loose train of thought was followed through the previous section: probation leads to wholeness; a lack of wisdom may be remedied through prayer; but prayer must be without doubt; the doubting man is 'double-minded' and this affects everything he does. There is no apparent connection between this and the contrast between humble and rich in the present passage. It could be seen to take up an idea from the beginning of the sequence: poverty is one of the perennial trials which must be endured (so Ropes), and the humble man's boasting therein is equivalent to the rejoicing of v. 2; but the link is not in any way obvious, and it is best to see these verses as introducing a new theme which, like those of prayer and doubleness, will recur from time to time in the epistle.

9 The antithetical structure of the verses requires that **the brother in humble circumstances** should be seen in contrast to *the rich man*, and his humility be understood as not a matter of spiritual or moral attitude but of social and material circumstances: he is *humble* in being poor. The character of

10 **the rich man** is more debatable. The author may see both the figures whom he contrasts as 'brothers' within his community, as in ii. 2 a rich man may be present at a meeting of the community as a member or at least a welcomed visitor; or he may contrast the humble brother with the rich outsider, as in v. 1–6 the rich as a class receive unqualified condemnation. Several modern translations (NEB, JB, GNB) and the majority of commentators adopt the former alternative. The phrase *ho plousios* contains no noun, and it is natural to supply the

one in the previous verse, *adelphos*; similarly v. 10 lacks a
main verb, and if this too ('boast') is supplied from the
preceding verse it is reasonable to take it that it will have the
same sense. The poor brother and the rich brother both have
cause to boast in their situation, as Christians; it is the content of their boast which differs, not its character. Their
boasting may be in view of the future, in the prospect of the
coming new age with its attendant blessings: the poor boasts
in the promise that his situation will be reversed, that he will
inherit the kingdom, as in ii. 5b; the rich Christian will have
to face social stigma and probable loss, but can rejoice in spite
of that, looking to the reward he knows will follow. Similarly,
their boast may be understood as in the prospect of death,
which renders all present conditions irrelevant, because of
what they as Christians expect beyond it. Alternatively, their
boasting may be in the present: for the poor in his new-found
status in the Christian community (cf. Gal. iii. 28); for the
rich in what he has gained, despite apparent losses, through
conversion (cf. Heb. x. 34). Such a boast may be in an understanding of the reality underlying present circumstances:
the poor boasts of his exaltation as 'rich in faith' (cf. ii. 5a);
the boast of the rich is not in his transitory possessions, but in
being 'poor in spirit' (Matt. v. 3).

The difficulty of this line of interpretation, in whatever
form, is that the boasting of the two is not really analogous.
There is exaltation for the poor, but no expression of either
future promise or present blessing for the rich; and it is not
his riches which are said to *pass away*, but he himself. It is
logical to understand this 'passing away' as an explanation of
what is meant by the rich man's *humiliation*, and as a threat.
The poor brother may expect a future reward (the future
tense of the verb in v. 9 indicates that the *exaltation* should
be understood in terms of future hope rather than present
experience), and boast in that hope, but the encouragement to
the rich man to boast is a bitter irony, for he has no such
future. The reversals are like those of Dives and Lazarus in
Lk. xvi. 25. The difficulty, that the verb expressed in v. 9 is
understood with a different sense in v. 10, must be accepted;
nor need the noun, 'brother', of v. 9 be understood in v. 10:

James uses *hoi plousioi* without accompanying noun for the rich he castigates in ii. 6 and v. 1. The contrast, then, is between the poor brother and the rich man, who is here almost by definition *not* a brother. The reversal motif in humility and exaltation is reminiscent of the aphorism found in various contexts in the synoptic gospels: 'He who exalts himself will be humbled, and he who humbles himself will be exalted' (Lk. xiv. 11, xviii. 14; Matt. xxiii. 12), but its general terms are applied by James to the specific situations of wealth and poverty.

The passing of the rich man is **like a meadow flower**: the image is that of flowers like poppies or anemones which grow wild among the sown wheat or grass pasture, cf. Matt. vi. 28–30, an image evoked in the OT phrase, 'flower of the field' (e.g. Ps. ciii. 15). The fate of evil-doers is likened to the withering of grass in Pss xxxvii. 2, cxxix. 6, but James rather than using a conventional simile repeats here a unique mistranslation in Is. xl. 6 of *sis ha-sādeh* as *anthos chortou*, 'flower of grass', rather than *anthos agrou*, 'flower of the field'. The Isaiah passage is taken up again, more loosely, in the

11 following verse: the sun **dries up the grass and its flower falls**, cf. Is xl. 7, 8. There is no formal quotation, but a deliberate allusion which adds point to James's threat to the rich. The image in Isaiah is of the transitoriness of humanity, 'all flesh', and its glory, before God; and James's application of it to the rich man sets him in that context. Further, by couching his threat in the language of prophecy, James adds the suggestion that it is in some sense fore-ordained. A similar allusive and pointed use of the OT in relation to the rich may be found in v. 4. Isaiah xl. 6–8 is also used in precise quotation in 1 Peter i. 24 f., but for a different purpose: in order to identify the word of God of which Isaiah goes on to speak with the word of the gospel.

Isaiah ascribed the wilting of the meadow flower to the blowing of the wind or breath (*ruach*) of the Lord; James explains it as due to the rising of **the sun with burning heat**. The noun *kausōn* is frequently used in the LXX for the strong, hot wind of Palestine, the desert Sirocco (e.g. Job xxvii. 21; Jere. xviii. 17; Hos. xii. 2), and Chaine and Cantinat

argue that James identifies two agents here, the sun and this
hot wind, the latter being his version of Isaiah's 'breath of the
Lord'. It is not, however, certain that that phrase appeared in
the LXX translation of Isaiah from which James has drawn
his allusion: Origen marked Is. xl. 7b–8a as a passage which
he had supplied from the Hebrew in his edition. The noun
makes good sense here in its general meaning of strong heat
(cf. Matt. xx. 12), and it is probable that James is simply
developing Isaiah's image in his own, and a perfectly natural,
way (cf. the image of a flower withering in the heat in 2 Esd.
xv. 50). If he were to be referring to the Sirocco, though, such
a reference could come through the literary medium of the
LXX rather than necessarily from any personal knowledge of
the Palestinian climate (as Hadidian, *art. cit.*). He rounds off
his image of the falling flower with a poetic periphrasis,
probably semitic in idiom: **its loveliness perishes**, lit. 'the
beauty of its face'.

As the flower falls, so the rich man will **wither away in
mid-career**. Like *hodos* in v. 8, *poreia* can carry the sense of
a way of life or conduct (Dibelius cites the LXX of Prov. ii. 7;
and 1 Clem. xlviii. 4; Hermas, *Sim.* v. 6. 6), though it more
usually retains its literal sense of walking or journey. Such
business trips as are planned by the merchants of iv. 13 might
be in mind in the use of the plural noun here, but a more
general sense is probably to be preferred: the rich man will
disappear 'in the middle of his affairs'. On the analogy of the
flower dropping in fierce heat, this disappearance is not a
gradual process but a sudden, unexpected end. This could be
the crisis of death, as suggested in iv. 14, and as for Luke's
rich fool and Dives (Lk. xii. 16–21, xiv. 19–25), but the coming of the Day of the Lord is similarly seen in the NT as an
unheralded interruption of everyday affairs (Lk. xvii. 26–31;
Matt. xxiv. 37–42), and it is this that appears as the threat to
the rich in v. 1–7. Here, as there, the threat to the rich is unqualified by any consideration that there might be a righteous
or reformed rich man (cf. on iv. 15). Yet whereas in the Lukan
parable no more is said of the blessed Lazarus than that he is
a beggar, and the Lukan beatitude on the poor is on them
simply as poor (Lk. vi. 20), the poor to whom James promises

exaltation is explicitly a *brother* (cf. on ii. 5). His contrast is not quite a simple black-and-white antithesis between rich and poor; though his emphasis is firmly on the fate of the rich (cf. Introduction, pp. 7–9).

4. THE GIFTS OF GOD

i. 12–18

(12) Blessed is the man who endures trial, for when he is proved he will receive the crown of life which he has promised to those who love him. (13) Let no-one under trial say, 'I am being tempted by God', for God is not tempted by evil and himself tempts no-one. (14) Each man is tempted when he is drawn out and lured away by his own desires. (15) When desire conceives, it bears sin, and when sin is mature it gives birth to death. (16) Make no mistake, my beloved brothers; (17) every gift that is good and every present that is perfect is from above, coming down from the Father of Lights, with whom there is no variation nor shadow cast by change. (18) Of his own will he gave us birth by a word of truth, so that we should be a kind of firstfruits of his creatures.

The general theme of this section is of what may or may not be said to come from God, in terms of future reward or destiny, present experience, and formative past events. Within this overall theme the sequence of thought is again a loose one, dependent on association of ideas through verbal links rather than the development of a logical argument.

12   James's exposition of his image of the flower for the rich man has been concluded, and he returns to the interlinked ideas of trial, probation and endurance, now seen not in relation to the present perfecting of character, as in i. 2–4, but to the prospect of a future reward. The macarism **blessed is the man** is a form familiar in the OT, e.g. Ps. i. 1; Prov. viii. 34;

Job v. 17; Ecclus xiv. 1. (James uses the LXX style of
denoting the recipient of blessing by noun and adjectival
clause rather than the participial phrase used in other NT
macarisms, e.g. Matt. v. 3 ff.; Jn xx. 29; Rev. i. 3.) The
blessing of one **who endures** is also familiar: Dan. xii. 12;
Zech. vi. 14, LXX; 4 Macc. vii. 22; cf. the promises of Mk
xiii. 13; Rev. ii. 2 f., ii. 10; Hermas, *Vis.* ii. 2. 7; however,
while these relate in context to the endurance of suffering or
persecution seen by most as the eschatological tribulation,
James again gives no indication of the nature of the **trial** he
envisages. It might be argued that the verse relates to the
previous section, and that endurance is of the *trial* of poverty,
the promise taking up the indication of future reward in v. 9.
The promised crown is here for *those who love him*; and in ii.
5 the promise of the kingdom to *those who love him* is inherited explicitly by the poor. James's idea would then be that
of Pss Sol. xvi. 14 f.: the testing to be endured by the
righteous is 'the affliction of poverty'; and this would be consistent with his interpretation of tribulation and endurance in
terms of everyday problems, in i. 27 and v. 7 ff. However,
James does not make such a link between this and the
preceding section at all obvious, and it can only be conjec-
tural. The phrase **those who love him** is itself conventional
as a description of the faithful, as in Ex. xx. 6; Deut. v. 10; Ps.
cxlv. 20; Ecclus i. 10; Rom. viii. 28. In some late Jewish
literature there is evidence that 'those who love him' were
thought of as a special class in the new age, pre-eminent in
virtue and therefore first in rank and glory (so G. H. Box,
commenting on *The Testament of Abraham* iii, *ad loc.*, and in
the introduction to his edition, London 1927, p. xxiii); and it
may well have become an especial definition of the martyrs
who loved God with all their life 'even though he takes it
away' (a comment on Deut. vi. 4 discussed by B.
Gerhardsson, 'The parable of the Sower and its Interpretation', *NTS* 14, 1967–68, p. 169). James, however, does
not work with such a specific definition, as is shown by his
application of the term to the poor in ii. 5.

'Those who love him' also expect a future reward in the unidentified quotation of 1 Cor. ii. 9, which appears in early

Christian literature variously as a promise made by God or by Jesus (1 Clem. xxxiv. 8; 2 Clem. xi. 7; Gospel of Thomas log. 17; Acts of Peter xxxix). Here the promise is of **the crown of life**. The image of a *crown* has a wide range of possible associations: the bay or olive wreath of a victor in battle or in the games (e.g. 1 Cor. ix. 27; 2 Tim. ii. 5), the gold crown of royalty (e.g. Ps. xxi. 3; Wisd. v. 16), the flower garland worn at weddings, festivals, or other times of rejoicing (e.g. Wisd. ii. 8), or even the wreath of the initiate in the mysteries (Apuleius, *Met.* xi. 24). Figurative uses of the term may also be found in, e.g., Prov. iv. 9; Wisd. iv. 2; Ecclus i. 11; 1 Thess ii. 19; 2 Tim. iv. 8; the ideas evoked being variously of reward, honour and celebration, and since James gives no more precise definition of his image, any or all of these may be in his mind. (See Ropes for a full account of literal and figurative meanings for the word *crown*.) The *crown* here is further described as **of life**. The genitive could be one of quality: the crown is an enduring, living one, in contrast to crowns that fade or tarnish (cf. 1 Cor. ix. 25; 1 Pet. v. 4; *Mart. Poly.* xix. 2), but is more probably epexegetic: the crown promised is in fact life itself, the life of the age to come or, on analogy with ii. 5, of the kingdom. (A close parallel may be found in 2 Bar. xv. 7 f.: 'As regards what thou didst say touching the righteous, that on account of them has this world come, so also shall that, which is to come, come on their account. For this world is to them a strife and a labour with much trouble; and that accordingly which is to come, a crown with great glory'.)

The subject of the main verb, the giver of the promise, is not expressed in many MSS (thus 𝔭 23, 74, ℵ AB, and the Coptic and Armenian versions). This is most probably the correct reading, the supplying of 'The Lord' by a large number of Greek MSS and of 'God' by some others and by the majority of the old Latin MSS being scribal guesses. The latter is most likely to represent James's intention, if we may rely on the content, in which he is concerned with what comes from God (vv. 13, 17), and the analogy of God's promise to 'those who love him' in ii. 5. In Rev. ii. 10 the same promise is held out to the Church of Smyrna by the exalted Jesus. This Church is to be exposed to trial, clearly severe trial, and faithfulness to death will be rewarded with 'the crown of life'; obviously there the reward is of life itself. The coincidence between James and the Apocalypse led Resch to identify the promise as an 'unwritten' saying of Jesus (A. Resch, 'Agrapha', *Texte und Untersuchungen*, 14. 2, 1896, p. 253). If so, the verse in James would provide evidence of the absorption of such sayings without differentiation into the stock of Christian teaching. However, in view of the familiarity both of the macarism on those who endure and of the image of a crown, any connection between the two authors is an unnecessary hypothesis: they can rather be seen as independently reproducing a popular theme in a popular image; and it is characteristic of the christology of the Revelation that its author should present the promise as pronounced by the exalted Christ.

In v. 12 *peirasmos* denoted *trial*, an external pressure to be 13 endured; in v. 14 the cognate verb *peirazō* denotes the internal experience of temptation, a drawing towards sin which is to be resisted. (Both noun and verb can be used in either sense; the context is determinative.) The sequence of vv. 12–14 can be seen (as by Dibelius) as purely artificial: the saying on trial is self-contained, while in vv. 13 f. a new theme is opened up and explored; the two are juxtaposed only because *peirasmos/peirazō* acts as a 'stitch-word'. By contrast, Hort and Cantinat see the exposition of a single theme: trial may be an occasion for reward, but may also be the occasion of failure, and such failure will be seen as a moral failure for which the individual must be held responsible. A purely verbal link seems unsatisfactory, but a looser sequence of thought may be suggested. The author reiterates the conventional blessing on those enduring *peirasmos*, but he will be conscious of the ambiguity of the word he uses, and this suggests to him a further theme of trial to be explored. The experience of trial carries with it the possibility of failure; it may thus be apprehended as the experience of being tempted. This is the more probable if the trial envisaged by James is not the great ordeal of persecution, but the perennial struggle of everyday life. James supposes a man who reacts to trial in this way, to correct a misapprehension. The shift in the meaning of *peirazō* will thus come within v. 13: **let no-one under trial say, 'I am being tempted by God'**. It is not clear if James would deny God any rôle in the process of trial; he could hardly ignore OT references to God's testing of, for instance, Abraham, to whom he refers in ii. 21, even though in later parts of the OT this testing is increasingly attributed to the Satan as a permitted (Job i. 12, ii. 6), or even as apparently a free agent (2 Chron. xxi. 1, cf. 2 Sam. xxiv. 1; and compare the rôle of Mastema in testing Abraham in Jubilees xvii. 16, cf. Gen. xxii. 1). James's concern is simply to deny that God has any interest in producing in man a state of sin as the outcome of trial, so that he might be seen as a tempter.

That man responds to his own failure by blaming God or the gods is a theme with ample parallels in both Greek and Jewish literature. (There is certainly no need to suggest, with Reicke, that the attitude is more comprehensible in a converted gentile, used to the capriciousness of his former gods.) Ropes and Dibelius cite passages from classical literature; a striking example is the complaint of Zeus in *Odyssey* i. 32 ff.: 'What a lamentable thing it is that men should blame the gods, and regard us as the source of their troubles, when it is their own wickedness that brings them sufferings worse than any which Destiny allots them'. Within Jewish literature, Mayor begins his list of parallels with the attempt of Adam to shift blame in Gen. iii. 12! Other examples are Prov. xix. 3 and Ecclus xv. 11 ff. Ben Sira uses the same rhetorical form as James, that of quoting a supposed claim in order to rebut it: 'Do not say "I fell away because of God"; for he will not create what he hates. Do not say "He made me err"; for he has no need for a man to be a sinner'; but the wording is not so similar as to suggest that the epistle alludes to this passage. The ground for James's assertion that God **himself tempts no-one** is that God **is not tempted by evil**. The adjective *apeirastos* is virtually without precedent in biblical or secular Greek, and its meaning is therefore uncertain. Hort sees it as representing the familiar *apeiratos* in the sense of 'inexperienced in'; i.e. God has no contact with evil and so cannot be seen to tempt to it. However, as derived from *peirazō* (and as thus again showing James's fondness for playing with words), the adjective will mean 'without temptation', either in the active sense, God is 'un-tempting to' evil, or the passive, God is 'un-tempted by' it. The former would make the two halves of the statement merely tautologous, and syntactically the passive is more probable. (This is the sense in which it is used in later literature, both of man, 'an untempted man is untried', *anēr adokimos apeirastos, Const. Apost.* ii. 8; and of God, *Acts of John* lvii.) God, then, cannot be seen as the author of temptation since he himself cannot be tempted. The logic is not immediately obvious: God's imperviousness to temptation could be seen as an aspect of his power; he is impervious because there is no other able to put pressure upon him, and this need not bar his action on men. What must be understood is that temptation is an impulse to sin, and since God is not susceptible to any such desire for evil he cannot be seen as desiring that it be brought about in man.

The source of temptation is to be found in man himself, **14** and more particularly **in his own desires**. As in iv. 2, *desire* is for James a force for evil (though there is no suggestion that *epithumia* is used by him in the specific sense of sexual lust, as with the seductive 'desires' of 2 Pet. ii. 18). Its action is described in two participles, *exelkomenos* and *deleazomenos*, perhaps used simply in the author's fondness for alliteration as in i. 6, or with a consciousness of their different nuances: desire may affect the initial stage of temptation when a man is **drawn out**, and carry the process through as he is **lured away**; or its promptings may be seen as both violent and seductive, so that a man may be 'dragged off' or 'enticed away' by them. The consequence of desire is vividly described **15** in terms of the image of dreadful progeny: **when desire conceives, it bears sin; and when sin is mature** (understanding the participle *apotelestheisa* within the framework of the image rather than in its general sense of 'being complete') **it gives birth to death**. Different verbs are used for the two births, *tiktō* and *apokueō*: Hort suggests that the latter indicates an abnormal birth (cf. the monstrous progeny of sin in Milton's *Paradise Lost* ii, lines 777–802), but this is unlikely in view of its use for God's gift of birth in v. 18; the variation is stylistic only. The inevitable sequence of desire, sin and death presented here is found also in Paul's self-analysis in Rom. vii. 7–11: the commandment *ouk epithumēseis* in fact occasions desire, and then 'sin revived and I died'.

The impossibility of finding in God the origin of this sequence leading to death is further underlined by James in drawing attention to what in fact comes from him, both gifts in general and birth in particular (Philo draws the same contrast in *De Fuga* 79 f.: 'the treasures of evil things are in

16 ourselves, with God are those of good only'). He enforces this with the warning, **Make no mistake, my beloved brothers**. The formula *mē planasthe* has no LXX background (save in some MSS of Is. xliv. 8), but is used by Epictetus and by Paul (1 Cor. vi. 9, xv. 33; Gal. vi. 7) and may be regarded as an idiom of Hellenistic rhetoric. It can be taken as the conclusion of the preceding remarks: the readers should *make no mistake* about the origin of temptation; but more probably serves as in 1 Cor. vi. 9 to mark the transition to a new stage of the argument, the readers should make no mistake about either the origin of temptation or the true gifts

17 of God. As in 1 Cor. xv. 33, the formula introduces what appears to be a line of verse (as the translation jingle is intended to suggest, cf. GNB): **every gift that is good and every present that is perfect** represents a slightly imperfectly quantified hexameter. If this is a quotation, its source has not been identified, and its alliterative quality may reflect again James's own playing with words. The pair *pasa dosis* and *pan dōrēma* are probably simply synonymous; if there is a distinction it could lie either in the fact that *dosis* may be translated as a verbal noun (cf. Phil. iv. 15), so that it is 'all good giving and every perfect gift' (NEB) that may be attributed to God; or in Philo's distinction between *dosis* as a moderate and *dorēa* as a special grace (*Leg. Alleg.* iii. 70; Paul uses *dorēa* and *dorēma* interchangeably for God's gift of saving grace in Rom. v. 15 f.). In any event, every such good gift **is from above, coming down from the Father** (or, 'comes down from above, from the Father', reading *anōthen estin katabainon* as a periphrastic present with NEB). Such

gifts will, of course, include that of wisdom which is 'from above' (iii. 15), and given by God to those who ask (i. 5).

The *Father* who gives good gifts from above (cf. Matt. vii. 11; Lk. xi. 9) is here described as **the Father of Lights**. No certain precedent for this title has been found in Jewish literature. It is read by Charles in the Apocalypse of Moses xxxvi, following MS D and the Armenian version: the sun and moon are shown as unable to shine 'before the Light of the Universe, the Father of Light', but the expression is absent from most Greek MSS and therefore from Tischendorf's edition (L. F. C. Tischendorf, *Apocalyses Apocryphae*, Leipzig 1866). Similarly, the *Testament of Abraham*, in the later recension, B, of the Greek and in the Arabic versions of chapter vii describes the archangel Michael as shining brightly 'as if he were the Light which is called the Father of Light', i.e. he appears with the glory of God (M. R. James, *Texts and Studies* 2. 2, 1892; James's edn of the Greek texts is reprinted with a new translation by Michael E. Stone, *The Testament of Abraham*, Missoula, Montana 1972). Both these references may, however, have come into the texts during their history in Christian transmission. In both, the reference to God as 'Father of Light' is to him as creator of the heavenly bodies, cf. Gen. i. 14–16; Ps. cxxxvi. 7; Jere. iv. 23 (LXX). The stars could be identified with, or personified as, angels; as in Job xxxviii. 7, 'the morning stars sang together and all the sons of God shouted for joy'; hence Qumran's title for Michael, 'Prince of Lights', is in virtue of his status as leader of the heavenly host (1 QS iii. 20; cf. CD v. 18, where Charles suggests the title is that of Uriel; certainly it is that of an archangel and not, as Dibelius suggests, God). James's use of astronomical terms in v. 18 shows, however, that he is thinking of the *lights* simply as heavenly bodies.

God is the *Father* of the stars in being their creator, but he does not share the characteristics of his creation, for with him **there is no variation nor shadow cast by change**. The general point that James is making is clear: it is a further insistence upon the consistency of God as only and always the giver of good (an idea complementary to that of God as the single, i.e., ungrudging, giver of i. 5); but the precise form in

73

which it is made is uncertain. The translation reflects the reading *parallagē ē tropēs aposkiasma*, found in the majority of MSS and described by Metzger as the 'least unsatisfactory' of an army of variant readings at this point.[1] The likelihood is that James is using loosely words which could bear a technical meaning in astronomy (as he uses loosely certain philosophical tags, cf. on i. 21, iii. 6), and this has left his language open to confusion. Thus *parallagē* has some currency as a technical term (AG), probably as equivalent to *parallaxis*, the change in angles of observation, but here it carries its general sense of variation or alteration, although in an 'astronomical' context; similarly *tropē* may mean specifically 'solstice' (as in Deut. xxxiii. 14; Wisd. vii. 18), but that would make no sense in this context, and again the general meaning of turning or change is being carried, in relation to the heavenly bodies. ('Shadow of change' must not be understood, as in JB, as the English idiom, i.e. 'no trace of change', a metaphorical sense the Greek *aposkiasma* cannot bear.) While heavenly bodies can be seen to change, then, either through their own movement or when shadows are cast upon them by the movement of others, God is both himself unchangeable and unaffected by change in anything outside himself (as in v. 13 he is both untempted and untempting). A similar comparison between the changelessness of God and the variability of the heavenly bodies is made by Philo (*Deus Immut.* 20–32; cf. *Leg. Alleg.* ii. 33; *De Cherub.* 88–90), for that the divine is immutable, *atreptos*, is an axiom of Platonic thought; but a closer parallel in thought to James may be found in the assertion of divine changelessness as part of the

---

[1] B. M. Metzger, *A Textual Commentary on the Greek New Testament*, London/New York 1971, *ad loc.* The reading adopted is that adopted in all major editions of the text and by the majority of commentators, with the notable exceptions of Ropes, who follows p 23, ℵ and B in reading *hē tropēs aposkiasmatos*, and thus giving the translation '... none of the variation that belongs to the turning of a shadow'; and Dibelius, who proposes an emendation to the text. A detailed note on the variants would be inappropriate in this commentary, especially as the general sense of the passage is not materially altered by any of them; such notes may be found in Ropes and Dibelius.

picture of relationship between God and man in Mal. iii. 6.

There follows a further description of God as Father, in 18 reference to one in particular of his gifts, that of birth and of a particular status *vis-à-vis* his creation: **of his own will he gave us birth by a word of truth, so that we should be a kind of firstfruits of his creatures.** It is sometimes objected that the verb used here, *apokueō*, more properly denotes the female's part in giving birth and is thus inappropriate for God the father, but it is the verb used of the breeding of death by sin in v. 15 and its repetition is probably intended to point the contrast and continue the same loose train of thought. From sin comes death; but God is the giver of all, and only, good gifts, and from him comes life. The difficulty of the passage is that there are three possible ways of interpreting James's reference to God's gift of birth. First, it may be understood as a reference to the creation of man, 'Adam, the son of God' (Lk. iii. 38; and cf. Paul's appeal in Acts xvii. 28 f.), on the divine decision 'let us make man' (Gen. i. 26) and by the creative word of Gen. i; and to the giving to man of dominion over the rest of creation, Gen. i. 28. The **firstfruits** was the sacrifice offered at the beginning of harvest (Lev. xxiii. 10 ff.; cf. Ex. xxii. 29 f.; Deut. xviii. 4); taken from the harvest as a whole it served to represent it. By its offering the sovereignty of God over the harvest was acknowledged. As an image for man in creation it would denote not priority, since man was in order of time the last to be created, but primacy: man stands in special honour as the head of creation and its representative before God. (When Paul describes Christ as 'the firstfruits of the dead' in 1 Cor. xv. 20–23, his resurrection is of course first in time, but the point of the image is that he is identified with those who belong to him so that his resurrection represents, and forms the hope for, theirs.)

Secondly, the reference could be taken to be to the creation of Israel, God's son (Hos. xi. 1) whom he begat (Deut. xxxii. 18), and who has a special status over against other nations because of the divine choice (e.g. Deut. vii. 6, xxvi. 19; Jub. ii. 19–21). Philo writes of Israel as a 'firstfruits' for God among the nations (*De Spec. Leg.* iv. 180), as Jeremiah had also described her as God's firstfruits (ii. 3; not LXX). Again the image would express a primacy of honour rather than a priority in time. The creation, *ta ktismata*, would be the human creation, mankind; and the *word of truth*, the instrument of begetting, would be identified as the Law, so described in Ps. cxix. 43, cf. Test. Gad iii. 1, 'words of truth'.

Thirdly, James may be seen to echo the familiar description of Christian converts as, on divine initiative, re-born and become the children of God (e.g. Jn i. 12 f., iii. 3 ff.; 1 Jn iii. 9; 1 Pet. i. 3, 23; Tit. iii. 5; cf. also Paul's description of Christians as God's sons, Rom. viii. 14 ff.; Gal. iv. 5 ff.; and Justin Martyr's association of rebirth and baptism, I *Apol.* lxi. 3, 10, lxvi. 1). This idea of conversion as rebirth may be argued to be derived either from the language of Jewish proselytism (for references and discussion see J. Jeremias, *Jerusalem in the Time of Jesus*, ET London 1969, pp. 323–5), or from Hellenistic initiation (e.g. *Corp. Herm.* xiii); in any event it had a wide currency. Particular Christian converts are described as 'firstfruits' by Paul in Rom. xvi. 5; 1 Cor. xvi. 15; and in many MSS of 2 Thess. ii. 13; probably not simply because they were in fact the first in their area to be converted, but because Paul regarded them as signifying his offering of their region to God (cf. Rom. xv. 16; Clement takes over Paul's image and sees these 'firstfruits' converts as becoming bishops and deacons, thus having a primacy in honour, 1 Clem. xlii. 4). In Rev. xiv. 4, the 144,000 have been purchased from mankind as a firstfruits to God and the Lamb; it is not clear if they are regarded as exclusively the redeemed, the firstfruits taken away from the rest, or whether the image should be pressed and they be regarded as representing also mankind yet to be redeemed. James's thought would similarly be of Christian believers as having a special relationship to the rest of creation, whether the human creation as in Revelation, or the total cosmos, as in Rom. viii. 19–23, for whose redemption theirs provides a hope. The *word of truth* would now, of course, and despite the absence of the article, be the gospel, so described in Col. i. 5; Eph. i. 13; 2 Tim. ii. 15; perhaps also 2 Cor. vi. 7; the gospel being the word that is the seed of rebirth in 1 Pet. i. 23 and 1 Cor. iv. 15.

Of these three alternatives, the least likely is the second. Despite the parallels for individual elements in James's picture, there is no parallel for the idea of the Law as the instrument of Israel's sonship. More generally, such an appeal to the status of Israel in relation to the rest of mankind would only make sense in a document that could otherwise be seen to attach importance to a Jewish identity or heritage. It could perhaps be suggested that the language has become that of the 'new Israel', as in 1 Clem. xxix. 3 the Church is seen as the subject of the unidentified quotation, 'The Lord taketh for Himself a nation out of the midst of the nations, as a man taketh the firstfruits of his threshing floor'; but then there would have had to be a two-fold translation of terms: from Israel the firstfruits to the Church as the new Israel and so the firstfruits; and from the word of truth as the Law to that word as now the gospel. The main alternatives are the first and third interpretations. With the exception of Hort, most older commentators adopt the latter, though among modern commentators both Blackman and Sidebottom do so with considerable reservation. When the language of birth is used of Christian conversion, it is usually expressly defined as *new* birth, or as being born *again*: thus Jn iii. 3 ff.; Tit. iii. 5; 1 Pet. i. 3, 23 (though not 1 Jn iii. 9); and in Paul's comparable idea of the new creation (2 Cor. v. 17) or of the new man (Col. iii. 10). It is doubtful if the image of the firstfruits would convey this sense of specifically *new* beginning; and in the syntax of the verse the image rather describes the intention of the divine begetting than its character. Moreover, there is no preparation in the immediate context of James for the introduction of a reference to Christian regeneration, which would appear with surprising abruptness; although it could of course be argued that to a Christian this would be the supreme gift and keystone of any argument on what comes from God, and, further, that the following reference to the word as 'saving' (v. 21) indicates what has been in mind.

So far as the context goes, the first interpretation fits most readily. It is easy to imagine a movement of thought from God the father, as creator, of the heavenly bodies, to God as the father and creator of man, the head of his creation. (A comparable connection may be observed in iii. 9, where the ideas of God as father and of man as he has created him are linked.) Ropes objects that the image of begetting is nowhere in the OT applied to creation, but L. E. Elliott-Binns, arguing that this is James's reference, provides an example from Philo: 'with his knowledge God had union, not as men have it, and begat created being' (*De Ebr.* 30; see art. 'James 1. 18: Creation or Redemption?', *NTS* 3, 1956–57, p. 148–161). Further, this interpretation allows *ta ktismata* to carry its more usual sense of the non-human creation. However, there is no parallel to the word of creation being called the word *of truth*, and no obvious reason why it should be specifically so defined.

The language of James may, then, be coherently interpreted in terms of either creation or conversion, but in neither case is his language wholly familiar in expression of the idea. This may indicate that there should not be an absolute choice between them. A possible solution is that James indeed moves naturally from thinking of God as father and creator to thinking of him as father and creator of man, but the language of sonship and birth is now so entrenched as the language of Christian conversion that this is inevitably brought to mind, and the creative word thus associated with that other creative word, the gospel. Thus the language of the second idea inter-penetrates the expression of the first, and both are indeed in mind. (This is the more plausible if it may be supposed that there would anyway be a conceptual link between the work of creation and redemption, the latter being thought of as the completion or re-establishment of the former; an idea brought to developed christological expression in Jn i. 1–14 where the same Word is active in both, cf. Heb. i. 1–4. James, of course, shows no indication of such christological reflection: the birth of creation and the birth by the gospel would both be seen as gifts of God.) Creation remains, though, the primary and dominant idea, and the image of the *firstfruits* relates to the God-given primacy of man in his creation.

5. RELIGION IN WORD AND DEED

i. 19–27

(19) Understand, my beloved brothers. Let every man be quick to listen, slow to speech, slow to anger; (20) for man's anger does not produce God's righteousness. (21) Therefore lay aside all vulgarity and the great mass of malice, and humbly accept the implanted word which is able to save your souls. (22) But be doers of the word and not just listeners, deceiving yourselves. (23) For if anyone is only a listener to the word and not a doer, he is like a man who takes a good look in a mirror at the face he was born with; (24) he considered himself carefully, and went away and forgot what he was like. (25) But he who has caught a glimpse of the perfect law, that of freedom, and stayed (with it), being not a forgetful listener, but a doer of (its) work, he is blessed in what he does. (26) If anyone thinks he is religious, when he does not bridle his tongue but deceives his heart, this man's religion is worthless. (27) Pure and unstained religion before God the Father is this: to visit orphans and widows in their affliction, and to keep himself undefiled by the world.

The last nine verses of the chapter contain a variety of material, elements of which would make their own sense in detachment from the rest. There is no clearly developing argument, and hence some commentators divide the section, Cantinat, for instance, separating vv. 19–25 from 26–27, and Blackman vv. 19–21 from 22–27. However there is again a sufficient association of ideas within the passage to argue the connection of a train of thought rather than simply a series of 'stitch-word' links. Thus James turns from the word of God to strictures on human speech. Behaviour should be guided by the saving word; but this word must be acted upon and not merely listened to. It has the character of, and may be spoken in terms of, a law. Finally, the behaviour of the truly religious man is outlined in terms of control of speech and performance of specific action.

19 The verb in the opening sentence, *iste*, could be read as indicative or imperative, and consequently as the conclusion to
the previous section rather than the introduction to the present one (thus NEB, 'Of that you may be certain, my friends').
Some copyists, feeling the abruptness of the clause, alter to
hōste, therefore; thus making the whole of v. 19 read as a
deduction from v. 18. On the analogy of similar expressions in
i. 16 and ii. 5, however, the imperative reading is to be
preferred: the author calls for particular attention to what he
is about to say (though, as with the other two passages, there
is some connection with his preceding remarks).

Of his three-fold admonition here, he develops the theme of
listening in the following verses, vv. 22–25, returning to
extensive warnings about speech in iii. 1–12, and anger in iii.
13–18, cf. iv. 2, 11. Such encouragement to ready listening,
and strictures on unconsidered or passionate speech, are commonplace in ethical teaching. Parallels may be found in the
wisdom literature of the ancient Near East, e.g. the Instruction of Ani: 'Do not talk a lot. Be silent and thou wilt be
happy' (4. 1, *ANET* p. 240; cf. Ptah-hotep 535 and Amen-em-
Opet chapters 9–10); in Israelite wisdom, e.g. Ecclus v. 11,
'Be swift in your listening, and with patience give your
answer' (cf. xx. 5–7; Prov. x. 19, xvi. 32); in Rabbinic
literature, especially in *Aboth* (e.g. i. 15, 17, ii. 10); and in
Hellenistic moral teaching (e.g. Dibelius cites the advice in
Lucian, *Demonax* 51, to those in authority, 'Don't lose your
temper ... Do little talking and much listening'; cf. also
Seneca's *De Ira*). Comparison may also obviously be drawn
with the teaching of Jesus in Matt. xii. 36 f. Cantinat sees the
instructions as addressed especially to those who are
preachers, as in iii. 1 (the anger being that which might flare
up between rival orators), but there is nothing to indicate that
they are being given other than the most general reference.
They are commonplace precepts, but the author insists on
serious attention being paid to them by all his readers.

It is only the prohibition of anger that receives a particular
rationalé, but this is probably more because it is the last of the
trio than because James is addressing an especially conten-
tious community. The reason for avoiding anger is that

man's anger does not produce God's righteousness. 20
The phrase *dikaiosunē theou* can be interpreted in three ways,
since the genitive may be seen as subjective, objective or a
genitive of origin.[1] It may thus be understood as the quality of
God's character, as a righteous or just God, which may be im-
itated like his perfection or his mercy (cf. Matt. v. 48; Lk. vi.
36); God does not indulge in anger, therefore man should not.
Alternatively, *God's righteousness* could be seen as that which
he demands, his standard set for men to attain, cf. Matt. vi.
33; to be angry is not to measure up to that standard. Thirdly,
dikaiosunē theou could be that which God gives, his justification, the verdict of acquittal or acceptance, effectively his
salvation (cf. Rom. iii. 24, v. 16 f.); in these terms James's
warning would be that an angry man cannot hope to win this
favourable verdict. James is certainly familiar to some extent
with Paul's use of the language of justification, as is clear from
the polemical passage ii. 21–25, but it is probable that he here
uses the expression in the second sense, that of the standard
God sets for man and which he cannot achieve if he gives way
to anger. Hermas clearly understood James in this way when
he also warns that 'angry temper' (his idiosyncratic word
oxucholia) leads men astray from righteousness (*Mand.* v. 2.
1; for the use of James in this *Mandate* see Introduction
p. 23).

What is required is restraint, indeed absolute renunciation, 21
of **all vulgarity and the great mass of malice** (*pasan
ruparian kai perisseian kakias*). The two nouns *ruparia* and
kakia are fairly general in meaning, carrying the sense of
physical dirt and by analogy moral uncleanness, and
wickedness or viciousness respectively. Since James is con-
centrating in context on warnings about speech it is probably
fair to particularise his condemnation as of vulgar and
malicious talk. His fondness for cadence and alliteration has
produced a difficulty in translation. The noun *perisseia* normally means an excess or surplus: James is hardly counselling

---

[1] Cf. the analysis of the possible interpretations of the same phrase in
Rom. i. 17, iii. 21, by J. A. Ziesler, *The meaning of righteousness in Paul*,
Cambridge 1972, pp. 9–14.

merely the discarding of surplus malice! Chaine and Cantinat
think of the final elimination of any malice that remains in the
character of the Christian convert; NEB of excess as what
malice produces, paraphrasing 'the malice that hurries to
excess'. James's meaning is clear, as in i. 17, although he uses
his words imprecisely: as he wants *all vulgarity* abandoned,
so he wants all malice, which he sees as a *great mass*,
eradicated. Both these his readers must **lay aside**. This
represents the idiomatic use of the verb *apotithēmi*, which
normally refers to the taking off of clothes, found in similar
passages of ethical instruction in other epistles: Col. iii. 8–10.;
Eph. iv. 22–26.; 1 Pet. ii. 1; *kakia* appearing in all three passages.

The act or renunciation is to be balanced by an act of
acceptance, made **humbly**. The phrase *en praütēti* could
qualify either verb, and may be intended to cover both.
Renunciation and acceptance alike require the quality of
humility which will later be seen as a mark of life ordered by
wisdom (iii. 13). What is to be accepted is **the . . . word
which is able to save your souls** (the soul, *psuchē*, not of
course denoting a higher part of man, but the man himself, cf.
v. 20). This *word* would most naturally be understood as the
preached word of the gospel, with both its promise of salvation and its ethical demand, and to 'receive' or 'accept' the
word is a familiar description of conversion in the NT, e.g.
Acts viii. 14, xvii. 11; 1 Thess i. 6, ii. 13; cf. Lk. viii. 13. The
exegetical difficulty arises from James's description of this
word as **implanted**. The adjective *emphutos* usually means
'implanted from birth', i.e. innate (as wickedness is innate in
the inhabitants of Canaan, according to Wisd. xii. 10), though
it can also describe a subsequent ingrafting, like that of gifts
of God in Barn. i. 2, ix. 9. Yet whether the implanting is of
nature or of subsequent gift, there is a logical difficulty in a
command to receive what is already within; and the command cannot as it stands be understood to be to receive the
word 'so that it becomes' innate. The NEB translation
suggests a progressive acceptance: 'quietly accept the
message planted in your hearts' (cf. JB, 'accept and submit to
the word . . .'); and both Chaine and Cantinat support such an
interpretation, the latter arguing that the difficulty is removed

if 'accept' is understood as 'obey', and the thought as of obedience to the inner law, as in Rom. ii. 14 f. It is improbable that James's language can bear that interpretation. The verb *dechomai* indicates an initial reception, whether of a gift, a proposition or a person (it can mean 'welcome'); and James uses the aorist imperative, carrying the sense of a single rather than a progressive action.

Three factors should be borne in mind in interpreting this difficult verse. First, the balance of '*lay aside . . . accept*' may well represent an established pattern of teaching which James adopts deliberately to reaffirm and recall for his readers their undertakings at conversion. Secondly, the difficulty of a command to accept what is already within depends on the identity of what it is that is both to be received and yet is already possessed. In i. 18 the 'word' to which James referred was seen to be the word of creation, yet because for him reference to the word of creation suggests also the word of the gospel, the language of the latter has come into reference to the former. Here, conversely, it may be said that the reference is primarily to the word of the gospel, yet because of this interaction of ideas, and because the creation word of v. 18 is still in mind, the word of the gospel is described in terms of the word of creation, part of the nature of man from his birth. James is concerned with ethical exhortation not metaphysical speculation about the nature of the word of God, but the idea behind his imperative could be that the call to accept the word of the gospel is a call to man to be what he properly is, what he was created to be. A call to receive this word, already 'natural' to man, would not then be a meaningless one. Thirdly, James's phrase *emphutos logos* is reminiscent of the Stoic notion of the *logos spermatikos*; the Reason that is the principle of the universe as macrocosm is seminally present in man as microcosm. Stoic ideas of the *logos* were drawn on in Hellenistic Judaism in discussion of the Torah, which might be seen as the pattern for creation as well as a demand to be obeyed (a notion developing in the later wisdom tradition, cf. Ecclus xxiv. 23). Thus Philo associates the Stoic term 'right reason', *ho orthos logos*, with the law of Ex. xvi. 4 (*De Virt.* 127, and cf. the discussion by P. Borgen, *Bread from Heaven*,

Leiden 1965, pp. 136–141); 4 Macc. tells the story of the
Maccabean martyrs in terms of the Stoic virtue of *apatheia*,
and Eleazer argues that living according to the Law is living
according to reason and nature (4 Macc. v. 22 ff.); and Paul
asserts that the gentiles do the Law by nature because it is
'written on their hearts' (Rom. ii. 14 f.). The Stoic idea comes
into specifically Christian discourse with the claim of Justin
Martyr's second *Apology* that 'all writers, through the
engrafted (*emphuton*) seed of the Word which was planted in
them were able to see the truth darkly' (II *Apol.* xiii. 5, cf. viii.
1); all truth is thus 'Christian' truth. James may be familiar
with this sort of language in the context of popular
philosophy, whether or not through the medium of Hellenistic
Judaism, and the notion of the natural word might seem congruous with his interest in the word of creation. Very
probably he has chosen as he does elsewhere (iii. 6) to adopt a
philosophical tag as a form of expression, without intending
to import its full technical meaning, even if he were conscious
of it.

Jas i. 18, 21 and 1 Pet. i. 23–ii. 2 are strikingly similar in
sequence and language. In both there is a reminder of birth by
a word of God, followed by a call to renunciation (including in
both a renunciation of *kakia*), and then an encouragement to
receive a word, with the hope of salvation (if Peter's phrase in
ii. 2, *to logikon gala* is properly translated 'the milk of the
word', on the basis that the adjective must in context refer
back to the *logos* of i. 23 ff.). James interrupts the sequence
with his three-fold admonition in v. 19 f.; and the two writers
use different verbs for the giving of birth, Peter using *anagen-
naō*, beget again, and developing the idea with his image of
the newborn infants. Peter has no hint of James's interest in
the word of creation; his 'word' is expressly 'the word which
was preached to you', and he cites Is. xl. 6–8 (a passage to
which James alluded for a different purpose in i. 10) for its
testimony to that word. It is unlikely in view of these
differences that the similarity can be explained in terms of
either author's direct dependence on the other, but highly
likely that they are drawing on a common pattern of instruc-

tion, most probably for new converts (see Introduction, pp. 18–20).

The word that can save carries with it an imperative. It is 22 important to be swift to listen (v. 19; now the general admonition is related to a more developed and specific argument) but listening alone is not enough. Because the word demands response and action, ideas of obedience and so of law are associated with it, and in v. 25 James shifts from talking in terms of *word* to talking in terms of *law*. (Some miniscules introduce this shift earlier, reading 'doer of the law' in v. 23.) This does not mean that the word and the law are identified, but that the former involves the latter. James's phrase **doers of the word**, like his 'doers of the law' in iv. 11, represents apparently a Jewish idiom: in ordinary Greek *poiētēs logou* would be 'a word-maker', i.e. an orator, as *poiētēs nomou* would be 'a law-maker'. Paul uses the latter phrase in the same way as James, in Rom. ii. 13, for one who observes and practises the law, and the background may be found in the idea of 'doing' the commandments, Deut. xv. 5; cf. Ecclus xix. 29; 1 Macc. ii. 67.

The idea that hearing the Law is valueless apart from its acting out was a subject of debate in Judaism, for the reverence accorded to the Torah was such that only to hear it might be accounted a blessing. The relative merits of hearing and doing are discussed in *Aboth*, i. 17 and v. 14, and Paul alludes to such discussion in Rom. ii. 13. A midrash on Ex. xxiv. 7 pictures Israel as crowned by six thousand angels when, at Sinai, she gave precedence to 'we will do' over 'we will hearken' (*Shabbat* 88a). Such debate may well have been familiar to James and, translated into his own terms, his position in it is clear. There is also, of course, a parallel in thought with Jesus' condemnation of those who merely listened to his words, Matt. vii. 24 ff.; Lk. v. 47 ff., but James shows no knowledge of the illustrative parable of the two houses, and any dependence is unlikely.

James's own parable is of a mirror, an image rare in biblical 23–25 literature (Job xxxvii. 18; Ecclus xii. 11; Wisd. vii. 26; cf. 1 Cor. xiii. 12; 2 Cor. iii. 18). The man who looks at himself in a

mirror is contrasted with the man who looks at the law, and the verbs used in the two cases heighten the contrast. For the former, the verb is *katanoēo*, to notice carefully or con-
23 template: the man with a mirror **takes a good look** and
24 **considered himself carefully**; for the latter it is *parakuptō*, to bend over, and hence to contrive to steal a glance (cf. Jn xx. 5, 11; 1 Pet. i. 12): for the man who has just **caught a glimpse** of the law, this is enough to cause him to stay with it and remember it. (The NEB surprisingly reverses this sense, so that the look in the mirror is fleeting and that at the law careful, but this seems both inaccurate and to weaken the force of the contrast.) The function of the parable is disputed. Dibelius and Blackman regard it as simply illustrative, a simile for looking at the law. Hort draws attention to the od-dity of the phrase *prosōpon tēs geneseōs*; had the intention been to give simply the metaphor of a man looking at his face, *prosōpon* alone would have been enough. Hort therefore argues that *genesis* should be taken to mean not 'birth' but 'nature', as it does in iii. 6. The man who hears the word recognises his 'invisible face', his self as God created him to be; but, hearing only, he forgets. In iii. 6, however, *genesis* is part of a stereotyped phrase; its meaning there cannot be determinative elsewhere. The translation **the face he was born with** (NEB, 'the face nature gave him') is adequate for the sense of the passage, but the deliberate qualification of *prosōpon* may be intended to suggest that there is more to be seen of a man than that, and that another, or fuller, image of him may be found in the law. It may be suggested that the law shows man as he was created to be, which is also his re-born self (cf. the interaction of the 'word' of i. 18, 21), but this suggestion comes rather from the context than from being built in to the image. Philo uses the image of a mirror rather similarly when he comments on the record that the basin in the Temple was made of mirror glass (1 Kgs vii. 23 ff.; 2 Chron. iv. 2 ff.): this was to remind the priests as they washed their bodies to wash their consciences in the Torah, the mirror of the soul (*De Vita Mos.* ii. 11; in the Christian *Odes of Solomon* xiii. 1 f. the Lord is the believer's mirror in which he sees and learns his face, cf. 2 Cor. iii. 18).

The law that the man looks at, and which it may be **25** suggested shows him his true self, is described as a **perfect law** (cf. Ps. xix. 7; Aristeas 31). Again, as in i. 4, the central idea of perfection is of wholeness: the law is itself a whole and therefore demands integrity; it must be kept in full (ii. 10) and be both listened to and acted upon. It is also **the law . . . of freedom**, a seemingly paradoxical description that would however be familiar to Jew and Greek alike. 'He that takes upon himself the yoke of the law, from him shall be taken away the yoke of the kingdom and the yoke of worldly care' (*Aboth* iii. 5, cf. Matt. xi. 29 f.; cf. also *Aboth* vi. 2 and Ps. cxix. 45). Jewish scholars speculated on the exegesis of Ex. xxxii. 16: the writing of the Law was 'graven', *haruth*, on the tablets; but one might instead read *heruth*, 'freedom' (*Aboth* vi. 2; the same point may have been taken at Qumran, cf. 1QS x. 6–8, which refers to an ordinance 'engraved' for ever, with the same ambiguity). For the Stoic, 'only the wise man is free', since he acts according to nature keeping his passions under control through the law, the Reason of the cosmos (Dibelius cites many examples, e.g. Seneca, *De vita beata* xv. 7; Epictetus, iv. 1. 158). Philo adopts the Stoic dictum, applying it to the Torah (*Quod Omn. Prob.* 45 f.; *De Vita Mos.* ii. 42 ff.). For Paul too there is 'the law of the spirit of life in Christ Jesus that has freed me from the law of sin and death' (Rom. viii. 2; cf. Barn. ii. 6, 'the new law of our Lord Jesus Christ which is without the yoke of compulsion'; and later Irenaeus, *Adv. Haer.* iv. 34. 4, the gospel is the law of freedom). James is then reiterating a familiar idea, probably in a familiar phrase; the existence of Jewish parallels does not decide the question of the identity or content of his *law*, of which he gives here no further indication.

The man who is not a **forgetful listener** (lit. 'a hearer of forgetfulness', *akroatēs epilēpsmonēs*, balancing *poiētēs ergou*, lit. 'a doer of work', in James's familiar love of cadence and alliteration), but one who puts the law into practice **is blessed in what he does**. There is here the same ambiguity as in i. 9–10. The *blessing* may be a promise for the future: the man is, i.e. will be, blessed *for* what he does; or it may be inherent in the obeying of the law, to perform which carries its own experience of blessing with it. Very probably the author would consider both interpretations correct.

The terminology now changes but the general line of thought continues, with a warning of the need for restraint in speech (including no doubt angry, v. 19, or vulgar and malicious, v. 21, speech), and a statement of the necessity also 26 for action. If a man **thinks he is religious**, but lacks that control of speech, he **deceives his heart** and his **religion is worthless**. (The first clause could be translated as 'if anyone seems to be religious', but the judgment of self-deception would seem to follow rather on what he seems to himself than what he seems to others.) The noun *thrēskia* is rare in biblical Greek (and James provides the first literary evidence for the adjective *thrēskos*). It denotes the worship of a deity, usually as expressed in cultic form (though not always; AG cites a passage from *Corp. Herm*, xii. 23 that is strikingly similar to James's thought: 'the worship, *thrēskeia*, of God is one thing only: not to be evil'), and is used of idolatrous worship in Wisd. xiv. 27; of the worship of angels in Col. ii. 18.; but also of Judaism in Acts xxvi. 5 (so also Josephus *Ant.* xii. 253; 4 Macc. v. 7); and of Christianity in 1 Clem. lxii. 1. The *religious* man must **bridle his tongue**; James's verb *chalinagōgeō* is not found elsewhere in the NT or LXX used either literally or metaphorically (his metaphor appears in Ps. xxxix. 1, but in different language in the LXX). He uses it again in iii. 2, of the 'perfect man', and his language is adopted and adapted by Hermas in relation to the 'evil desire' (*Mand.* xii. 1. 1 f., see Introduction p. 23). Without this control the man *deceives his heart*, perhaps because he fails to recognise the inconsistency of his words to God and to man (iii. 9 f.); and his *religion is worthless, mataios*, an adjective often applied to pagan religion (e.g. Jere. viii. 19, x. 3; Acts xiv. 15; 1 Pet. i. 18), which may give an extra pejorative thrust to James's condemnation.

This religion is ineffective or inconsistent (cf. on ii. 14–17); by contrast James supplies a description of **pure and un-** 27 **stained religion**, in terms of action. Such religion is that addressed to **God the Father** (lit. 'the God and Father', cf. 1 Cor. xv. 24; Eph. v. 20; and see on iii. 9); it is not here further defined in terms of a reverence for Christ (contrast the development of the description of God as Father in Rom. xv. 6; 2 Cor. i. 3, xi. 31; 1 Pet. i. 3). It is expressed in the performance, first, of a duty to **orphans and widows**. This could be because their plight was particularly prominent in the situation to which the epistle was addressed, as it would seem the plight of widows was a matter of special concern in some Christian communities (cf. Acts vi. 1; 1 Tim. v. 3–16), or more probably because in the OT tradition widows and orphans are especially the object of God's concern and man's charity (e.g. Ex. xxii. 22 ff.; Deut. xxvii. 19; Ps. lxviii. 5; Is. i. 17; Ezek. xxii. 7; Zech. vii. 10; Ecclus iv. 10, xxxv. 14). This tradition is continued in Hermas's listing of the care of widows and visiting of orphans among good works (*Mand.* viii. 10); Justin's putting this first in his examples of Christian charity (I *Apol.* lxvii. 7); and the stigmatising of sinners as those neglectful of it by Ignatius (*Smyrn.* vi. 2) and Barnabas (xx. 2). James's reiteration of this duty may have more to it than simply traditionalism or archaism: inasmuch as God is known to have an especial care for orphans and widows, a worship of him should naturally be expressed in a similar concern. To **visit** orphans and widows (the verb is *episkeptomai*) may be literally to go to see and spend time with them (cf. Ecclus vii. 35; Matt. xxv. 36, 43); but certainly is also to do so in order to make provision for their needs.

Their **affliction** would be that of poverty, and the lack of protection and legal status that came with the death of the head of the family. That this defenceless condition should be called *affliction* is an interesting use of language, since elsewhere in the NT the noun *thlipsis* has almost the status of a technical term for the sufferings that precede the End, the 'Messianic Woes', e.g. Mk xiii. 19; 2 Thess i. 4; Rev. ii. 22; cf. Dan. xii. 1; Hermas, *Vis.* ii. 2. 7. In Col. i. 24 Paul seems to see his own sufferings as contributing to the *thlipseis tou Christou*, the 'Messiah's affliction' which his people must bear. Schlier concludes that in the NT *thlipsis* 'is inseparable from Christian life in this world, ... it is the suffering of Christ, who is afflicted in his members, ... this is eschatological tribulation' (*TDNT* III, p. 144). If James is aware of this connotation of the word (even without Schlier's christological dimension), his own adoption of it is of some significance. For him, the everyday, commonplace suffering of the socially disadvantaged is to be described in terms of the woes that precede the End. It could be that he is trying to dispense with the old eschatological ideas, finding them no longer appropriate (perhaps in reaction to the 'delay of the Parousia'), and one way of doing this is to generalise the technical language. Alternatively James may be trying to keep the expectation alive and real in a situation where the traditional 'signs' are conspicuously lacking, and in that attempt he carries out a deliberate re-interpretation of the nature of the signs (cf. on v. 7 ff., above on i. 2, 12, and Introduction p. 28 f.).

The further demand of pure religion is that the religious man should **keep himself undefiled by the world**. This is the reading of the majority of MSS, though some miniscules read 'keep them undefiled . . .'; i.e. a further definition of the duty to orphans and widows, while the early papyrus p 74 has a different verb and reads '. . . to protect them from the world'. As James began with a consideration of the would-be religious man in himself, it is appropriate that he should return to that point in conclusion, and the expression of a duty to avoid defilement is congruous with the description of religion as 'pure and unstained'. (For an argument in favour of the second variant, however, see D. J. Roberts, 'The definition of "Pure Religion" in James 1²⁷', ExT LXXXIII, 1972, p. 215 f.)

Religion, then, involves keeping oneself undefiled by **the world**. The noun *kosmos* as meaning 'world' was used by Greek writers from Pythagoras onwards to denote the universe in its perfect order and arrangement, and it is used generally in the NT also of the created universe, the world in which men live, and of the world of mankind itself. James's counsel to avoid contact with the world shows, however, that his use of *kosmos* corresponds to that found sometimes in Paul (Rom. xii. 2; 1 Cor. ii. 12), and especially in John (e.g. xv. 18 f., xvi. 33; cf. 1 Jn ii. 15–17): the world is that which is separate from, and indeed at enmity with, God. In John the hostility is primarily that of men, and 'the world' means 'mankind in opposition to God' (as Jn i. 10–11 indicates); in 2 Peter i. 4, ii. 18–20, as in gnostic thought, the separation is that of the physical (including especially sexual) and material aspects of human existence from the divine nature. There is some similarity between the language of James and 2 Peter (cf. the use of *aspilos*, undefiled, here and in 2 Pet. iii. 14), but James's meaning will be deduced from other contexts in which he uses the word. In iv. 4 the enmity towards God is that of men who seek their own pleasures and thus 'the friendship of the world'. This produces divisions among them (iv. 1), and ineffective prayer (iv. 3). In iii. 6 it is the tongue which represents the world and effects the defilement of the body: the enmity towards God would be seen in the human speech which blesses him while cursing his image (iii. 9). 'The world' for James would seem to be mankind in its false values, self-seeking and self-assertion, and in that dividedness that is for him the essence of sin (cf. iv. 8). It is congruous, then, that a *pure religion*, which demands avoiding the defilement of *the world* thus understood, will necessarily also involve control of the tongue and acts of charity.

It might be argued by contrast that in his definition of religion James shows his Jewish affinities. Religion is addressed to God the Father; practical piety is expressed in that form of charity traditional in Judaism; while the avoidance of the world's defilements might seem to be most obviously achieved through maintaining the Jewish laws of cleanness and separation. However, the first two would be part of the heritage of any Christian group that used the OT (and indeed the term 'the God and Father' would seem to be a stereotype in Christian rather than Jewish literature); while there is no specific reference in the epistle to any Jewish rule of ritual purity to give cogency to the third suggestion. James's first two adjectives, *katharos* and *amiantos*, pure and unstained, might well lend themselves to use in connection with ritual cleanness, but he uses them explicitly for the expression of religion in charitable action (and Hermas takes them over in a similar connection, *Mand.* ii. 7). The third, *aspilos*, undefiled, has no LXX background and does not therefore of itself naturally suggest an allusion to the laws of cleanness contained there. In other passages where James uses similar language, iii. 6 and iv. 8, it is clear that no cultic associations are involved. O. J. F. Seitz in examining this question rightly concludes that, 'although our author makes occasional use of words which, in the vocabulary of the LXX may be said to have acquired some cultic associations, in no case does it appear that he is consciously alluding to any specific Jewish cult practice, or that he shows any noticeable concern with cultic defilement or purification from it' ('James and the Law', *Studia Evangelica* II, 1964, p. 483).

On the other hand, James's appropriation of the language of purity for the exposition of religious duty in ethical terms cannot be seen as therefore implying a polemic against Judaism and its ritual law. Such a polemic is found in the prophetic tradition of Judaism itself, e.g. Is. i. 1–11, lviii. 3–7; Jere. vii. 21 ff.; Hos. vi. 6; Amos v. 21ff.; Micah vi. 6ff. and Ps. li. 1–17; cf. also the teaching of Jesus in Matt. xii. 7, xxiii. 23; Mk vii. 14–23; but the absence of specific contrast with ritual prescriptions, as in those passages, tells against polemical intention on the part of James. He should rather be compared with passages where 'cultic' language is used of the right conduct of daily life, without the edge of controversy: e.g. Rom. xii. 1; 1 Pet. ii. 5; and within Judaism cf. Ps. xxvi. 6 and the famous observation of R. Johanan b. Zakkai after the destruction of the Temple that 'we have an atonement . . . the doing of loving deeds' (*Aboth R. Nathan* iv. 11a, cit. C. G. Montefiore and H. Loewe, *A Rabbinic Anthology,* London 1938, p. 430 f.). James's language is neither Jewish nor anti-Jewish; that is not the issue. His target is the would-be religious man who does not control his speech or (by implication) put his religion into practice. The form in which such a man might himself express his reverence for God is not criticised, nor indeed is it defined further than being a reverence for God the Father; what is at issue is the inconsistency of his accompanying behaviour, an issue that greatly concerns this author and which he will raise again (cf. ii. 14–17, 19, iii. 9 f., iv. 3 f.).

6. THE SIN OF DISCRIMINATION

ii. 1–9

(1) My brothers, do not hold the faith in our Lord Jesus Christ, the glory, together with discrimination between people. (2) If there should come into your meeting a gold-ringed gentleman wearing splendid clothes, and there should also come in a poor man in filthy clothes, (3) and you should look at the man wearing the splendid clothes and say, 'You sit here, in a good place', and say to the poor man, 'You stand there, or sit here under my footstool', (4) would you not have made distinctions in your own minds and have become judges who make corrupt decisions? (5) Listen, my beloved brothers. Did not God choose the poor of the world to be rich in faith and to be heirs of the kingdom which he has promised to those who love him? (6) But you have insulted the poor man. Do not the rich oppress you, and drag you into the courts? (7) Do not they slander the good name which was called upon you? (8) If you are indeed fulfilling the royal law according to the scripture, 'Thou shalt love thy neighbour as thyself', you are doing well; (9) but if you are showing discrimination you are committing sin, and stand convicted by the law as transgressors.

James continues with his theme of consistency, giving it a new reference, for now the issue is of conduct compatible with faith in Jesus Christ. The argument of this section is much tighter than any in chapter one: a single theme is introduced and explored at length. The profession of Christian faith is inconsistent, indeed incompatible, with an attitude towards other men that discriminates against some and in favour of others. It should be unthinkable to **hold the faith, 1** and exercise **discrimination between people**, 'respect of persons', an attitude frequently condemned in the OT (e.g. Lev. xix. 15; Ps. lxxxii. 2; Mal. ii. 9), and seen to be wholly uncharacteristic of God (Job xxxiv. 19; Ecclus xxxv. 13; cf.

Acts x. 34; Barn. xix. 7). The Hebrew idiom *nāsār pānim* is rendered literally in the LXX as *prosōpon lambanō*, 'receive the face'; an idiom retained in the 'Two Ways' sections of the *Didache*, iv. 3, and Barnabas, xix. 4. Compound words derived from this apparently did not appear before the NT, where the noun *prosōpolēmpsia* appears in Rom. ii. 11; Col. iii. 25 and Eph. vi. 9 as well as here in James (the compound verb *prosōpolēmpteō* is found only in James ii. 9; the adjective in Acts x. 34; and the adverb, with negative prefix, in 1 Pet. i. 17). MM describes the group as 'among the earliest definitely Christian words', but if they are so, they were clearly not coined to express a distinctively Christian idea but in a logical development of Christianity's heritage of Jewish biblical language. James uses the noun in the plural; this may be because he begins with a general condemnation of all forms of discrimination before giving a specific example, or even because it is felt that the exercise of discrimination is not a single exercise: to discriminate in favour of one is to discriminate against another; to give special treatment to the rich is to deny it to the poor.

The opening verse of this section contains the second of the two explicit references to Jesus in the epistle, for the faith with which discrimination is incompatible is **the faith in our Lord Jesus Christ, the glory**. The whole phrase is syntactically extremely awkward, being a string of genitives of which the last, *tēs doxēs*, reads like an appendage without any clear connection with what precedes it. It has been suggested, therefore, as with i. 1, that the reference to *Jesus Christ* is an interpolation to Christianise the document, and that originally the definition of faith was that of the Jew in 'the Lord of Glory', Yahweh (cf. 'the God of glory', Acts vii. 2). It is axiomatic that discrimination between people is foreign to his nature, and it is therefore intolerable in those who profess faith in him. There is again no textual warrant for omitting the reference to Jesus, and the title 'Lord of Glory' is not in any case so common a title for God in Judaism as to argue its being the natural original reading for the verse. (The main evidence for its currency is found in 1 Enoch, e.g. xxv. 2, xxxvi. 4, xl. 3, and it may be from an apocalyptic background that Paul derives it as, in fact, a title for Christ in 1 Cor. ii. 8.) It seems best, then, to retain the phrase in full as an original part of the epistle, and to attempt to explain the connection of *tēs doxēs* with what precedes it.

There is a wide variety of suggestions for such an explanation. The final phrase may be seen as adjectival, qualifying one of the preceding nouns: 'the glorious Lord', or 'the glorious Christ'; but this would be to disrupt the self-contained phrase 'our Lord Jesus Christ'. Ropes and Dibelius see it as qualifying the whole phrase, 'our glorious Lord Jesus Christ'; but for that one would expect a different word order, with *tēs doxēs* intervening between the first noun and its article. Alternatively, the genitive might be seen as objective, describing the content of the faith as *in* 'the glory of our Lord ...'. This is the solution of Chaine, who finds support in the Peshitta, and cites for comparison Acts iv. 33, the witness of the apostles *tēs anastaseōs tou kuriou* (comparison may also be made with similar constructions in 2 Cor. iv. 4 and Rom. v. 2). Again, the objection to this suggestion is that the genitive phrase is at some distance from the noun, *faith*, which it is said to define; even granted the self-contained character of the long intervening phrase. A third approach is to admit that *tēs doxēs* cannot be attached to any one word in the preceding phrase; rather it stands separate from it to supplement or complement it. Thus it could be taken as giving a second title of lordship to Christ: 'our Lord Jesus Christ, (the lord) of glory'; though one would expect that second 'lord' to be expressed rather than understood. GNB adopts that translation, and NEB paraphrases, 'our Lord ... who reigns in glory'. Hort and Mayor see the relation of *tēs doxēs* to the preceding as one of apposition: 'our Lord Jesus Christ', i.e. 'the glory' (Mayor compares a similar use of the genitive in apposition in 1 Tim. i. 1; Jas i. 12 would provide a comparison within the epistle itself).

This solution seems best to take account of the structure of the verse, but the question would remain of what it means to describe Christ as **the glory**. In the LXX *doxa* as the regular translation of the Hebrew *kābōd* is part of the language of theophany denoting the splendour, sometimes actual light,

that is both a sign and an effect of the presence of God.[1] So
the presence of God in the wilderness is demonstrated by a
'glory' (Ex. xvi. 10); the entry of the glory into Solomon's new
temple is a sign of God's presence in it (2 Chron. vii. 1–3), as
its departure is a sign of his abandoning it (Ezek. xi. 23); glory
is part of the context in which the prophet meets with God
(Is. vi. 1; Ezek. viii. 4), and in which the shepherds receive a
message from heaven (Lk. ii. 9). The eschatological hope of
the future enjoyment of the presence of God may be expressed
as a hope for the return of glory, as to the temple, in Hag. ii.
7–9; Zech. ii. 5 (and thus there is no need for any other light
in the New Jerusalem of Rev. xxii. 5). In the NT Jesus is
frequently associated with, or described in terms of, glory.
The synoptic transfiguration narrative has clear associations
with the Exodus theophany (Mk ix. 3; Matt. xvii. 2, 5; Lk. ix.
32), and may reflect the hope expressed in 2 Macc. ii. 8 that at
the last days 'the glory of the Lord shall return, with the
cloud'. 2 Pet. i. 17 describes the transfiguration as Jesus'
receiving 'honour and glory'. Paul, John and the author of
Hebrews all speak of his glory in terms of his relation to God:
Paul, contrasting the revelation in Christ with that through
Moses, asserts that God has given 'the light of the knowledge
of the glory of God in the face of Jesus Christ' (2 Cor. iv. 6);
John described the glory of the Word as 'glory as of the only
begotten of the Father' (Jn i. 14), and records the Son's prayer
to the Father to 'glorify thou me with thine own self' (xvii. 5);
while in Hebrews the Son is 'the effulgence of his glory' (i. 3).
These writers develop the idea of glory in their individual
ways, but in their common use of it there may be reflected one
early form in which the Church expressed its understanding
of Jesus. In him it experienced the presence and activity of
God (however precisely or imprecisely this might be defined);
a revelation of God that was perhaps his final revelation. A
natural framework of language in which to express this belief
would be the OT language of theophany, of which 'glory' was

[1] See L. H. Brockington, 'The Septuagintal background to the New Testament use of δόξα', in *Studies in the Gospels*, ed. D. E. Nineham, Oxford
1955, pp. 1–8.

an important element. So when James calls Jesus *the glory*, he may be seen to reflect this understanding of Jesus as 'theophany'; a manifestation of the presence of God.[1]

James differs from the other NT writers quoted above in not providing any further definition of the *glory* he associates with Jesus.[2] This absolute use of the noun probably led to Hort's taking it as a more specific title, identifying Jesus with the divine hypostasis, the Shekinah or the Presence. It is not, however, certain either that 'the Presence' was thought of as an hypostasis in the NT period, or that 'glory' be an obvious or appropriate term for it. The more general idea already presented is probably as far as we can go in defining James's christology. We have, as in i. 18, a passing reference to an element of faith whose full content we can only guess at. James is not here concerned with the definition of christology but with the relation between faith and behaviour; he does not explain why this particular element of faith should seem to him to be relevant to the particular subject of discrimination. Perhaps the underlying thinking might be that faith in Christ is a faith in the Christ who provides a revelation of God, the God whose opposition to discrimination is well known, and with faith in this Christ the operation of a double-standard in dealings with men must be unthinkable.

After this opening statement of the incompatibility of faith with an attitude or exercise of discrimination, James proceeds to give an example of what he is condemning. Dibelius warns against pressing the example into service as evidence for the actual circumstances of James's community. James is not here attacking an actual, flagrant offence within that community

[1] Justin Martyr takes up this general idea, developing it within his much more sophisticated scheme of thought, when he refers to the presence of the Logos in theophanies, and to his consequently bearing the title of 'Glory' (*Dialogue*, cxxviii. 2).

[2] It is sometimes suggested that James's use of 'the glory' without further definition as a term for Jesus can be paralleled in 1 Pet. iv. 14: *to tēs doxēs kai to tou theou pneuma* could be translated as 'the spirit of the glory and the spirit of God', but in this much simpler construction the function of the genitive phrase is more obviously adjectival, giving 'the glorious spirit of God' or 'the glorious and divine spirit'.

(contrast 1 Cor. v. 1, for example); he is concerned to attack a general attitude or mode of conduct, which he illustrates in an artificially contrived picture. Yet for the example to convey his message it must presumably bear some relation to his readers' experience, and portray a situation which either has or could obtain for them (he appeals directly to their experience in v. 6b–7). The illustration may have an element of exaggeration or caricature, but it may still shed some light upon the setting of the epistle (cf. the way that the parables of Jesus develop in extraordinary terms from situations familiar to his hearers, C. F. Evans, *Parable and Dogma*, London, 1977, p. 16 f.; and Introduction p. 7).

Certainly the present illustration depicts an extreme situation: two dramatically different persons are shown as treated in sharply contrasted ways (cf. Jesus' pharisee and publican, Lk. xviii. 9–11). The **gold-ringed gentleman** may be something more than simply a typical rich man: James's coining of the adjective *chrusodaktulios* may be to indicate his social status, for the gold ring was part of the insignia of the equestrian order, the second rank of the Roman aristocracy (so E. A. Judge, *The Social Pattern of Christian Groups in the First Century*, London 1960, p. 53; the suggestion was also made by B. H. Streeter, *The Primitive Church*, p. 196). Equestrians were customarily wealthy, for there was a property qualification for the rank, and this could be achieved through trade and commerce as would not have been thought appropriate for members of the senatorial order. Equestrian rank was somewhat debased under the Empire, when it could be bestowed upon freedom (like Claudius's Pallas and Felix), but it was still the road to careers in the civil service, perhaps leading to procuratorial office such as Felix and Pilate held in Judaea. A further opportunity was open to equestrians to increase their wealth through holding posts in the tax-collection system. Such a person would provide a particularly striking example of 'the rich man'; and would also be a covetable patron for a minority group. It may be over-pressing the idea to see his *splendid clothes* and the *angustus clava* of the equestrian, the *tunica* with its narrow purple border, but the picture is meant to be impressive. The adjective *lampros* literally means bright, shining, and is used of the clothing of an angel in

Acts x. 30, of the clean linen of the angels of Rev. xv. 6 and of the bride of the Lamb in xix. 8. It need not suggest just white garments, for it is used of the garment with which Herod's soldiers robe Jesus in Lk. xxiii. 11; not the purple of Pilate's soldiers in Mk xv. 20, but presumably something comparable to the royal garments of Herod in Acts xii. 21. James may picture a figure whose clothes have a gleam of colour or texture, or one whose spotlessly clean robes contrast forcibly with the **filthy clothes** of the **poor man**. The noun *ptōchos* in classical usage denotes a beggar or utterly destitute person, as distinct from *penēs*, a man who had not property and therefore had to earn his own living. This distinction is not strictly maintained in the LXX and NT where the words are virtually interchangeable, but the full force of *ptōchos* is no doubt intended by James in this context.

To these contrasted persons correspondingly contrasting 3 treatment is given. The *gold-ringed gentleman* is ushered to **sit . . . in a good place** (*kathou hōde kalōs*; Ropes, Dibelius and RSV prefer to render the adverb as the request, 'sit here, *please*'). There is some confusion in the textual tradition as to what alternative is offered to the *poor man*: **stand there or sit here** represents the longest text; others omit the preposition 'here' and read either 'stand there or sit under my stool' or 'stand, or sit there under . . .'. MSS evidence is pretty equally divided; it may be that as the UBS editors decided, the longer reading arose to create a neater parallelism (Metzger, *Textual Commentary, ad loc.*), but it represents the probable alternatives offered plausibly enough: the *poor man* should most properly *stand over there*, well away, but if he must sit it should be in an equally appropriate, inferior position, *here, under my footstool*, i.e. on the floor. The main verbs of v. 3 are plural in form, following the opening address of v. 1; in terms of the illustration one person would presumably do the directing of people to their seats (though he would no doubt do so as reflecting the usual practice of the meeting), but James is concerned with a general warning to his readers against the attitude thus illustrated.

The occasion for this exercise of discrimination is when the 2 two persons come **into your meeting**. They should most probably be understood to come as visitors rather than as regular members of the community: this would follow from the fact that they need to be directed to their places, and from the hypothetical nature of the introduction, **if there should come** ... rather than 'when there come'; it is a possibility rather than a regular occurrence. They come *eis sunagōgēn humōn*. *Sunagōgē* is familiar as the term for the Jewish place of worship, the synagogue, which had come to form in practice the centre of the religious life of Jews outside Jerusalem since some time after the exilic period. The word is found with this specific meaning in Josephus, e.g. *BJ* ii. 285, 289, vii. 44; in Philo, *Quod Omn. Prob.* 81; and frequently in the NT, Mk i. 39; Lk. iv. 16; Jn xviii. 20; Acts xiii. 14. Support for identifying James's *sunagōgē* with the Jewish building is sometimes found in the details of his picture: the presence of *good seats*, cf. Matt. xxiii. 6; Mk xii. 39, and of the **footstool**, as a footstool would be provided for the president of a synagogue. Such arrangements might however figure in any meeting place. Nor need a 'synagogue' denote simply a Jewish building: the Jewish Christian sect of the Ebionites used the term for their meeting places, according to Epiphanius, *Haer.* xxx. 18, and Jerome, *Ep.* cxii. 13. Moreover, it could apparently be sufficiently detached from Jewish connotations for the Marcionites to use it: MM cites an inscription from Lebaba *c.* A.D. 318 which records the existence of a *sunagōgē Markionistōn*. It is presumably in the light of this that NEB adopts the neutral translation 'place of worship'.

The word may, however, function even more generally. It may be used for an assembled company rather than the place of their assembly, and is probably so used of Jewish congregations in Acts vi. 9, ix. 2; Rev. ii. 9, iii. 9; of a Christian, and not certainly Jewish Christian, congregation in Hermas, *Mand.* xi. 9, 13, 14; and of a patently non-Jewish Christian congregation by Justin, *Dialogue* lxiii. 14. It is unlikely that it is in this sense that James uses it, since he takes *ekklēsia* to denote his community in v. 14. A further meaning, though, is that of the occasion of a meeting or assembly (as distinct from those who constitute it or the place where it is held). So it is used in secular Greek of an assembly of the town council or other public body; of a meeting of Jews for

67989

worship in Acts xiii. 43; and of Christian meetings (or lack of them) in Ignatius, *Poly.* iv. 2, cf. Heb. x. 25. This broadest sense of the word seems adequately to fit the context of James, and does not prejudge the question of the character of the community he envisages. In any case, even in its more specific uses, *sunagōgē* has not such inescapably Jewish associations as to be unambiguous evidence of the Jewish or Jewish Christian character of the setting in which it is used. The meeting which James envisages can only be said to be a meeting of Jews or of Jewish Christians if the character of the epistle as a whole supports such an identification; and indeed only then if it be thought justifiable to relate James's example to his own or his readers' situation.

The nature of the *meeting* is not defined. It is usually assumed to be a meeting for worship, which strangers might attend (cf. 1 Cor. xiv. 23 ff.). R. B. Ward, however, points to the oddity in that context of the condemnation of the discriminators as unjust judges in v. 4 ('Partiality in the assembly: James 2: 2–4', *HTR* 62, 1969, pp. 87–97). Ward shows striking parallels between the details of James's picture and Rabbinic passages regulating the administration of justice. In the Jewish court the judges sat while litigants stood: to allow one litigant to sit and keep the other standing is to show prejudice (*Shebuoth* 30a, cf. v. 3 here); similarly to admit one splendidly dressed litigant and another in rags is to allow the possibility of prejudice, so both should be dressed alike (*Shebuoth* 31a, cf. v. 2). Thus Ward sees the picture as one of the exercise of judgment in and by the community. Undoubtedly Christian communities evolved judicial procedures (cf. Matt. xviii. 15 ff.; 1 Cor. v. 3 ff., vi. 5 f.), and in doing so took over much from the judicial practice of Judaism. The difficulty is that Ward's reconstruction involves seeing the two as members of the community coming to it for judgment (he argues that the gold-ringed gentleman is deliberately not called *plousios*, which is a term for the outsider as in ii. 6), while it is more probable that they are visitors. Ward's parallels are striking, but it is doubtful if the terms in which James sketches his supposed situation will allow for so precise a definition of it (and of course the overall question of whether

Jewish institutions can be appealed to to explain references in James is begged).

4 Another explanation for James's condemnation of the discriminators as unjust **judges** can in fact be found, and it lies rather in OT associations than in the details of the image. In v. 8 f. James appears to invoke Lev. xix. 18 as the ultimate sanction against discrimination, though the argument from loving one's neighbour as oneself to treating all men alike is not immediately obvious. If however Lev. xix. 18 is related to its scriptural context, the connection may be made, by a simple exegetical procedure. Lev. xix. 18 provides the norm for conduct and must thus be related to the theme in question. That norm is love of neighbour, and the word 'neighbour' provides a link with another precept in which it occurs, Lev. xix. 15: 'Ye shall do no unrighteousness in judgment: thou shalt not respect the person of the poor, nor honour the person of the mighty: but in righteousness shalt thou judge thy neighbour'. To love the neighbour is, then, to treat him without discrimination; to discriminate is to break that law of love. Lev. xix. 15 treats of discrimination in the particular form of discrimination between poor and influential persons, and this pattern is taken up, in his own terms, in James's example. Those who exercise discrimination, then, **make distinctions in your own minds**; *diekrithēte en heautois* should be taken as having a middle force, for it is the personal, internal dividedness that is the target of James's attack. They are also *judges* **who give corrupt decisions** (*kritai dialogismōn ponerōn; dialogismos* here functions as the term for a legal decision rather than meaning thought or motive, as in NEB's 'judges by false standards'); and they are described as such because their conduct in their own situation is to be seen in the light of the scriptural precept.

James's community, then, might find itself visited by persons as disparate as the splendid gentleman and the filthily dressed beggar. They are seen as possible visitors rather than as regular members of the community, but as such they would presumably be seen as potential members. In this respect James's emphasis is clearly on the reception of the poor man. The condemnation of discrimination is not equally of

toadying to the rich and disparaging the poor, but the stress is
that *you have insulted the poor man* (cf. Ecclus x. 23).
The rich and the poor have now ceased to be simply figures in
a parable, and are seen as typical of groups with whom
James's readers have to do. It would seem that for James the
poor are to be seen as the natural members of the community
(cf. i. 9). Yet he stops short of an unqualified idealisation of
poverty as the distinguishing mark of membership. **The poor of** 5
the world are chosen to be **rich in faith**, and it is surely this
faith that is the mark. Materially poor, they are spiritually rich by
virtue of their faith, cf. Rev. ii. 9, iii. 17; and Test. Gad vii. 6.
(Hermas describes the poor as 'rich in intercession', *vis-à-vis* the
rich, and expounds this in quantitative terms to argue the interdependence of the two in the community of faith: the poor
makes up the rich man's lack of prayer, and the rich the poor's
lack of goods, *Sim.* ii. 4–7.) The poor are not only thus rich in the
present, but also have the prospect of future reward, since they
are **heirs of the kingdom**; but the kingdom is that **which he
has promised to those who love him**, and this love of God is
demonstrable not only in the situation of poverty, but also, in
i. 12, in the enduring of trial. James seems to take a middle course
between the Matthean and Lukan versions of Jesus' promise of
the kingdom to the poor. He neither spiritualises the idea of
poverty as Matthew does (Matt. v. 3), for his poverty is literal
poverty, but nor does he show poverty as rewarded *per se* as Luke
appears to do (Lk. vi. 20, and the rewarding of Lazarus in xvi.
19–25 apparently only because of his misfortunes; cf. on i. 11).
There is a promise for the poor, but inasmuch as their poverty is
accompanied by faith and the love of God, and as they are chosen
in order that it should be so.

The idea of the poor as the pious and as especially the
object of God's care and blessing is sufficiently familiar from
the psalms (e.g. ix. 18, xii. 5 f., lxx. 5, and see Introduction
p. 7 f.) to account for James's appeal to his readers' knowledge:
Did not God choose ...? There is certainly no indication
that this choice and promise is thought of as mediated
through the words of Jesus. Yet because the promise is
specifically of the kingdom, a knowledge of the beatitude
(found also in Thomas, log. 54) may well be in the

background. James's wording is not close enough to any of the gospel versions to argue a literary dependence (e.g. the kingdom is not defined as 'of God', Lk. vi. 20, or 'of heaven', Matt. v. 3 and Thomas), and we may therefore take this as a further example of the way the oral tradition of the words of Jesus has been absorbed into the general stock of Christian teaching (cf. on i. 5, and Introduction p. 34 f.).

Similarly, the attitude of James to the rich is not here clear-cut. Despite the harsh reminder of v. 6b, the rich do not seem to be by definition enemies. There is no hint that the rich visitor to the meeting has no business to be there, nor that his visit is a hostile one, in contrast to the poor man's; nor, strictly, is the welcoming manner of his reception condemned, but only the insulting manner of the beggar's. James does not say that his readers should not receive a rich man at all, but confine their membership to the poor, and certainly if the situation pictured bears any relation to experience, his readers did not think this. For the purposes of the illustration, at any rate, rich and poor are equally possible visitors to the assembly and are to be given equal treatment (cf. Ecclus iv. 7-8), even if the emphasis is on the poor as the more natural potential members of the community of faith.

James's condemnation of discrimination, as illustrated in his chosen example, has so far been taken to include four main considerations: the inconsistency of discrimination with faith; an appeal to the norm of Lev. xix. 18; and, in the terms of the example, a reminder first of God's choice of the poor, and secondly of the general experience of the behaviour of the rich. Two of these require further comment: the experiences alluded to in vv. 6b-7, and the status of Lev. xix. 18.

James's accusations against the rich are framed in such rhetorical and generalised terms that it is hazardous to draw very specific conclusions from them about the experiences of his readers. There appear to be two charges. First, the rich
6 **oppress you**. The verb *katadunasteuō* carries the sense of oppression or exploitation by abuse of power, and is found frequently in the LXX for the oppression of the poor by the rich and powerful, e.g. Ezek. xviii. 12, xxii. 29; Amos iv. 1; Zech. vii. 10 (the powerful man of Lev. xix. 15 is in the LXX

a *dunastēs*). The economic power of rich over poor may be abused by a ruthless insistence on legal rights such as to the exaction of taxes or the repayment of debt. So here the rich **drag you into the courts.** If James has deliberately portrayed the rich man of his illustration as an equestrian, of the order from which tax officers were drawn, then that particular form of oppression may be suggested. When he again castigates the rich for maltreatment of the poor, in v. 4, he presents this maltreatment as an abuse of economic power; though there in the 'illegal' form of the withholding of wages.

Secondly, they **slander the good name which was 7 called upon you.** In the OT Israel bears the name of her God; usually she is said to be called *by* the name, as in Deut. xxviii. 10; Is. xliii. 7, cf. lxiii. 19; Jere. xiv. 9; 2 Macc. viii. 15; but the idiom of the name being called *upon* her is found in Amos ix. 19 (quoted by James of Jerusalem in Acts xv. 17). Were the epistle to be taken as originally a Jewish writing, that idea would be understood here (and, of course, it could also be so understood by a Church that saw itself as the bearer of the rôle of Israel). Members of the Church were early called 'Christians', a term they probably did not coin but accepted (Acts xi. 26, xxvi. 28), and this appellation is called a 'name' in 1 Pet. iv. 16. They thought of themselves, however, as bearing the name of Jesus, and it is probably this to which James alludes (cf. Acts ix. 15; Rev. ii. 13; Ep. Poly. vi. 3; Hermas, *Sim.* viii. 10.3, ix. 13. 2 f. and 28. 5). The point at which they took on this rôle was baptism, which is frequently defined as baptism in or into the name of Jesus: Acts ii. 38, x. 48, xix. 5; 1 Cor. vi. 11, cf. i. 13; Hermas, *Sim.* ix. 16. 3. The use by James of the aorist participle may suggest that there is here a deliberate allusion to the specific time at which the name was received, rather than to the general character of the readers (cf. Hermas, *Sim.* viii. 6. 4). This baptismal name the rich *slander* (the verb is *blasphēmeō*). It could be that James is thinking of abuse of Christ himself, a slander that might more properly be called blasphemy, but is it more likely that he is thinking of abuse of Christ's name through abuse of those who bear it (cf. Acts v. 41)? They may be vilified for 'the name itself', solely for being Christians (as in 1 Pet. iv. 14, where being reviled 'for the name of Christ' would seem to be interchangeable with suffering *hōs Christianos* in v. 16), or be the victims of scurrilous talk which associates their profession of Christ with all kinds of crimes and vices (1 Pet. iv. 15 seems to warn against giving any justification for this tendency, which is well established by the time of Pliny, *Ep.* x. 96. 2, and Tacitus, *Ann.* xv. 44). Any such abuse of Christians is abuse also of the name they bear.

A number of constructions could be put on these two charges and their possible inter-relationship. It might be suggested that allegations against Christians are the cause of their being dragged into the courts; that the situation envisaged is one of active persecution through the processes of law, a persecution whose initiation is attributed to the rich members of non-Christian society (there is no warrant for drawing comparisons with Acts xiii. 50, xvi. 19 and xviii. 12 and suggesting that these persons are specifically rich Jews). It would be necessary then to argue that a reference to persecution here is congruous with other indications in the epistle (e.g. i. 2–4, 27; and cf. Introduction, p. 28 f.). Alternatively the relationship may be reversed: the bringing of some Christians into court, perhaps in the financial causes suggested (exaction of taxes or debt) leads to the slandering of them as a group by those who wield such power as, say, bad citizens or unreliable debtors. Again, it could be suggested that the situation is an internal one: that rich Christians have been resorting to the civil courts in suits against their brothers (cf. 1 Cor. vi. 1–8), and by this unloving litigiousness either themselves implicitly abuse the name they bear or bring it into disrepute among outsiders (as Clement sees to be the effect of the contention at Corinth, 1 Clem. xlvii. 7; and as Paul accuses the Jews of causing the name of God to be blasphemed, Rom. ii. 24). This line of interpretation would, however, strain the active form of the verb; and more direct condemnation of such behaviour would be expected if it obtained within the community itself. The second construction seems the most probable, but the two charges are framed in rhetorical questions, and their connection should perhaps not be too precisely interpreted. In general terms, though, James's readers' experience of the rich as a class in society is of them as prone to taking oppressive legal action against themselves, probably with a view to financial advantage, and as also prone to abusing the profession of Christianity. Rich and poor alike may come as visitors to a Christian meeting, but what sort of potential members are they? The readers have little cause to be optimistic about the prospects of the rich man, but they are well aware of God's promise to the poor. To give an enthusiastic welcome to the former and effectively to insult the latter is ridiculous.

It is also a transgression of *the royal law*. The conjunction 8 *mentoi* is an emphatic one: if his readers are **indeed** (as, it is implied, they claim) obeying the law; fine! It is highly improbable that, as Ropes suggests, James is countering an argument of his opponents that in honouring the rich man they are obeying the command to love. Rather, he begins with a basic common assumption. His readers, like himself, accept the importance of the command to love one's neighbour, and in this they **are doing well**. It is necessary, though, to see the implications of this acceptance, and that discrimination between people is inconsistent with it. James uses the same procedure as in ii. 19 of commending something that his readers as well as he accept, but then attacking the fact that proper conclusions are not drawn from it. It has already been suggested that the movement of thought from love of neighbour to condemning discrimination is not an immediately obvious or necessary one, and that James justifies the connection by drawing upon the context of Lev. xix. 18, and especially upon Lev. xix. 15. It might have seemed simpler just to cite Lev. xix. 15, as a precept directly opposing that form of behaviour, but it seems that Lev. xix. 18 carries a special authority.

It is disputed whether or not that special authority consists in Lev. xix. 18 being identified as itself **the royal law**, *nomos basilikos*. Several commentators, e.g. Ropes and Blackman, argue that *nomos* would not be used of a single commandment, for which *entolē* would be the correct term (as used of the command to love in Mk xii. 28; Matt. xxii. 36; Jn xv. 12; though cf. the use of *nomos* in Rom. vii. 2 for one particular dictate of the law). Moreover, *teleō*, fulfil, might seem an appropriate verb for obedience to the whole law (as e.g. in Rom. ii. 27), but for a single precept *tereō*, keep, would be expected (cf. v. 10, and Matt. xix. 17 f. for individual precepts including Lev. xix. 18). Dibelius and V. P. Furnish (*The Love Command in the New Testament*, London 1973, pp. 177–180) argue further from the context. In v. 10 f. James weighs one precept alongside another, arguing for the keeping of the law in its entirety. The force of this is that he is reinforcing his warning against discrimination by showing that if other commandments are kept but this one neglected, the whole 'royal law' is not being fulfilled. Thus Lev. xix. 18 is one precept among others, a part of the whole law. This argument is unconvincing. First, had James wished to weigh the precept against discrimination alongside others it is again surprising that he does not cite Lev. xix. 15 itself. Even granted that he wished instead to invoke Lev. xix. 18 against that sin, yet Lev. xix. 18 is not in fact one of the two precepts he weighs in order to appeal to the whole law. The supposed argument has a missing link. Moreover, v. 10 marks a new stage in the thought of the epistle. The section vv. 1–9 focuses on the sin of discrimination, and reaches its climax when Lev. xix. 18 is invoked precisely against that sin. In v. 10 a new, albeit related, idea, that of keeping the law in its entirety, is introduced and discussed in its own terms. Certainly Lev. xix. 18 is not for James everything he means by law, but nor is it simply one command among others. Mitton and Sidebottom guardedly suggest that inasmuch as it could be seen as the guiding principle for obedience to the law as a whole (the law is to be fulfilled 'according to the scripture', i.e. in the way indicated by Lev. xix. 18), and inasmuch as that whole law is 'royal', Lev. xix. 18 partakes of that character. However, it is justifiable to see the commandment as itself identified as *the royal law*. It is clearly important for James to bring his warning against discrimination into relation to this commandment, to show that it is comprehended within it, and he underlines the authority of the commandment with an honorific description. (The argument thus rests on the treatment of Lev. xix. 18 in context; there may also be something to be said for Hort's comment that 'there is no difficulty in . . .

applying so wide a term as νόμος to a single precept, since the precept itself was so comprehensive'; certainly if James is indicating the wide applicability of that precept, *teleō* could be argued to be the appropriate verb.)

Lev. xix. 18, then, is *the royal law*. The adjective *basilikos* means regal, or belonging to a king, as in its use of the king of Edom's highway in Num. xx. 17 and of Herod's territory in Acts xii. 20 (where the noun is understood). Philo comments on Num. xx. 17 that the king's highway is 'royal' both because it is his and because it leads to him, and he finds here an allegory of the Law, which is the true 'royal road' (*De Post. Cain.* 101—102; cf. Clem. Alex. *Strom.* vii. 73. 5: the deliberate choice of righteousness is the 'royal road' which the 'royal nation' travels). In relation to a law, the adjective would most naturally indicate a law promulgated by a king, and is so used of the decree of Artaxerxes in 1 Esd. viii. 24, or a law applicable in his kingdom, as probably in the Pergamum inscription quoted by A. Deissmann (*Light from the Ancient East*, p. 362, n. 5). C. H. Dodd gives examples of the use of the phrase *basilikos nomos* by Greek political writers to describe a law as given by, or worthy of, a king, and sometimes in relation to the maxim that 'the law itself is king' (*The Bible and the Greeks*, London 1935, p. 39). Hort suggests that a *royal law* could be 'a law which governs other laws, and so has a specially regal character'. We would then understand Lev. xix. 18 as the governing principle for all precepts (cf. Matt. xxii. 37–40). However, this strains the meaning of the adjective, which never seems to have been used in the sense of 'governing'; and Lev. xix. 18 is anyway not appealed to here as a key to other precepts but in virtue of its own content and authority.

The law of love would be *royal* in being promulgated by a king or as applicable to his realm, or indeed both. It is natural to compare this passage with Mk xii. 29 ff., and Jesus' identification of the two great commandments. The law is not cited here as a word of Jesus but as **scripture**, and quoted precisely; but of course Jesus himself was quoting the Law (nor was he unique in singling out this precept, for R. Akiba also saw it as the most comprehensive rule in the Law,

THE EPISTLE OF JAMES

(Moore, *Judaism* II, p. 85 f., citing *Gen. R.* 24. 7). Paul too quotes Lev. xix. 18 as the supreme command, with no explicit appeal to the authority of Jesus (Rom. xiii. 8–10; Gal. v. 14). John, by contrast, attributes a command to love specifically to Jesus, and never uses the OT form of love of the neighbour (though 1 Jn ii. 7 shows a consciousness that the new commandment is also an old one). It is reasonable to suppose that the prominence of a command to love in many of the NT documents is due to its prominence in the teaching of Jesus, even when this is not explicitly acknowledged. If so, it is probable that when James quotes Lev. xix. 18 as *scripture* he does so in the knowledge that this scripture has received the added authority of Jesus' use. It is unlikely that the description of the law as *royal* involves anything so specific as a recognition of Jesus as the king who has promulgated the law, especially as it is God who is said to promise the kingdom in ii. 5 (cf. iv. 12: there is only one lawgiver; clearly God). Lev. xix. 18 is for James the *royal law* because it is the law of the kingdom of God; but as in ii. 5 he would be conscious that Jesus proclaimed God's promise, so here he will be conscious that Jesus proclaimed God's kingdom and its law. So then, James concludes, if his readers are prey to the sin of dis-

9 crimination, they are **convicted** by the royal law of Lev. xix. 18 itself, and are found to be **transgressors** of it.

7. THE WHOLE LAW

ii. 10–13

(10) For whoever keeps the whole law, but trips up in one particular, has become answerable in respect of all. (11) For he who said, 'Thou shalt not commit adultery', said also, 'Thou shalt not murder'; so if you do not commit adultery, but murder, you have become a transgressor of the law. (12) Speak and act in every respect as people who are going to be judged in terms of a law of freedom. (13) For judgment is merciless to

him who shows no mercy; mercy boasts in the face of judgment.

James now moves from his consideration of what is involved in the keeping of one major precept to the full, to insist upon the keeping of the law in its entirety. This introduces a 10 new idea, but it is probably intended to add further seriousness to his previous warning. He has argued that by exercising discrimination between people his readers put themselves in the position of transgressing a particularly notable commandment: now he reminds them of the yet wider implications of the transgression of a single commandment in relation to the whole.

His statement that the law must be kept in every particular or it is not kept at all, finds ample parallel within all branches of Judaism. The Rabbis warned against distinguishing between 'light' and 'weighty' commandments, with the commonsense observation that 'if you become slack about one commandment, you will end by becoming slack about another' (*Derek Eretz Zuta* iii. 5, as quoted by C. G. Montefiore and H. Loewe, *A Rabbinic Anthology*, London 1938, p. 157); and the judgment of R. Johanan is often quoted by commentators, 'if he do all, but omit one, he is guilty of all severally' (*Shabbat* 70b, the comment is specifically in relation to the Sabbath regulations). Paul warns the Galatians of what they are taking on in their acceptance of Judaising, 'every man who receives circumcision ... is a debtor to do the whole Law' (Gal. v. 3); a warning derived from the principle that a proselyte must be considered 'in all things as an Israelite', i.e. he was bound to observe the whole Law (*Yebamoth* 47b, cit. J. Jeremias, *Jerusalem in the Time of Jesus*, p. 323). The Testament of Asher sees the keeping of some commands and breaking of others as a manifestation of 'doubleness', a characteristic which the Testaments hold in as much abhorrence as does James (Test. Ash. ii. 5–10). At Qumran the community ruled in regard to its own law that 'no man among the members of the Covenant of the Community who deliberately, on any point whatever, turns aside from all that is commanded, shall touch the pure Meal of the men of holiness' (1 QS viii. 16 f.) In Hellenistic Judaism,

Philo, in retelling the story of Joseph and Potiphar's wife, concludes that 'he who exercises perfect self-control must shun all sins, both the greater and the lesser, and be found implicated in none whatever', *Leg. Alleg.* iii. 241). In 4 Macc. the martyr tells King Antiochus, 'think it not then a small thing for us to eat the unclean thing; for the transgression of the Law, be it in small things or in great is equally heinous, for in either case equally the Law is despised' (v. 19). 4 Macc. is concerned to relate the Jewish religion to Stoic philosophy, and the insistence on the Jewish principle may be intended, as Charles suggests, to show a correspondence with the Stoic theory of the solidarity of virtues or vices (Augustine, writing to Jerome, *Ep.* clxvii. 4, draws a comparison between this Stoic teaching and James's). Finally, a close parallel may of course be seen between James and the warning of Matt. v. 19, following Jesus' insistence on the absolute continuity of the Law, that 'whosoever therefore shall break one of the least of these commandments, and teach men the same, shall be called least in the Kingdom of Heaven'.

A man, therefore, who **trips up in one particular** (no noun is expressed) becomes **answerable in respect of all**. The primarily legal term *enochos* has a number of functions. With the dative it denotes liability to a tribunal (as in Matt. v. 22a), with the genitive, as here, it has three possible meanings: liable for punishment; guilty of crime; or liable in respect of a person or thing against which an offence has been committed (as in 1 Cor. xi. 27). It is unlikely that James may be understood to say that the man who commits one transgression is liable to all the punishments specified for all transgressions, and to say that he is guilty of all transgressions is probably too extreme, so the third meaning is preferred. The man who commits one offence must accept that he is responsible and answerable not only in respect of the single precept he has broken, but in respect of the whole corpus of law of which that precept is a part.

In asserting this principle James would seem to stand squarely within the context of Jewish legalism. But the situation becomes less straightforward when he proceeds to give
11 an example of what he means: **if you do not commit adultery, but murder, you have become a transgressor**

of the law. Two precepts of the decalogue are balanced against each other, and the argument seems curiously inept. The decalogue was so central a part of the Torah that no one of its precepts would seem to need reinforcement by such an argument as this. Moreover, the prohibition of murder and adultery would be so generally accepted that assent to them would hardly be seen to entail assent specifically to the Jewish Law and everything else contained in it. It is improbable that these two commands are singled out in relation to the situation addressed because, as Hort suggests, the community prided itself on scrupulously avoiding fleshly sins (if the address in iv. 4 were taken literally, as he later argues, the reverse might be the case!); and nor is it likely that 'you murder' in iv. 2 is to be taken as literally describing the situation to which this argument relates. Nor is there any indication that James is enlarging the idea of murder as Jesus does in Matt. v. 21 f., seeing it as an extreme lack of love, far less that he intends to subsume under its heading the ill-treatment of the poor man in ii. 2 f. If James intended to argue for the entirety of the Jewish Law he could have done so more tellingly by juxtaposing a 'light' and a 'weighty' commandment, as some Rabbis juxtaposed Deut. xxii. 6 f., against birdsnesting, and Deut. v. 16, on honouring father and mother, pointing out that the reward promised was the same for each (Moore, *Judaism* II p. 5, cites *Kiddushin* 6lb, cf. 39b; Montefiore and Loewe, *Anthology* p. 126, quote a Rabbinic parable making this point).

It might be suggested that it is James's earlier quotation of Lev. xix. 18 that has led him to the precepts of the decalogue, because of a familiar connection between the two. In Matt. xix. 18 f. Jesus concludes a recitation of part of the 'second table' by citing also Lev. xix. 18 (the connection is also made in the version of the story of the rich man in the Gospel of the Nazarenes, perhaps independently, see Hennecke-Schneemelcher I, p. 148 f.); and in Rom. xiii. 8–10, Lev. xix. 18 is seen as the summary of these commandments in particular. K. Stendahl comments that 'the combination of the latter part of the Decalogue with a Leviticus text as well known as that of Lev. xix. 18 was certainly in accordance

with Jewish custom' (*The School of St Matthew*, London
1954, p. 63). However, even if this connection is assumed, the
terms of James's argument still raise the question of the content and extent of his 'law'. He quotes the decalogue; he
quotes Lev. xix. 18. The latter he probably expounds in relation to another precept, Lev. xix. 15, but one from the immediate context, and from the Holiness Code which could be
regarded as a unit in itself and which was a main source of the
Jewish catechetical tradition. Both these elements of the Law
have in the gospel tradition the sanction of Jesus (Mk x. 19,
xii. 29 ff. and parallels); both are affirmed by Paul (Rom. xiii.
8–10), who of course rejected the imposing of the whole Law
upon all Christians. When we further take into account
James's manner of using 'cultic' language in a non-cultic connection (see on i. 27) it would seem by no means certain that
his argument involves the whole Jewish Torah, but probable instead that he is using a familiar, originally Jewish,
principle with a different scope and application in the Christian
context.

James's citation of the two precepts of the decalogue is
different from his usual way of introducing quotations. He
normally introduces these as *graphē* (ii. 8, ii. 23, iv. 5 f.), but
here uses a masculine article and participle. This forbids an
assumed reference to the feminine *graphē*, though it might be
suggested that the reference is to the law, *nomos*, of vv. 9–10,
thought of as 'speaking' as scripture does in iv. 5, 6. However,
the use of the aorist participle suggests a single event rather
than the continuing speech of law or scripture, and the
probable thought is therefore of the definitive past speaking of
God on Sinai: **he who said . . . said also.** The point of this
form of introduction may be simply to direct attention to God
as the ultimate authority for the law, but it may reflect the
widespread Jewish tradition that the decalogue was distinct
from and even perhaps holier than the rest of the pentateuch.
Philo says that unlike the other commands of the Law, the
decalogue was revealed by a miraculously created voice (*De
Dec.* 32–35); and Josephus also records that as these precepts
were too holy to be impaired by the human voice they were
spoken by a heavenly one (*Ant.* iii. 89 f.; according to *Ant.* iii.

273 the other laws were framed by Moses).[1] It may be that some such tradition, that the decalogue is peculiarly the law that God speaks, lies behind James's form of citation here; but if so it would not for him lessen the special importance to be attached to the 'royal law'.

James quotes the two precepts in the order **Thou shalt not commit adultery** and **Thou shalt not murder**. This reverses the order found in the Hebrew (MT) text of both Ex. xx. 1–17 and Deut. v. 6–21, in which the sixth to eighth commandments prohibit murder, adultery, theft, in that sequence. The same sequence is followed by Mk x. 19; Matt. xix. 18 f., cf. v. 21, 27. In most MSS of the LXX, however, the order of commandments in Exodus is adultery, theft, murder, and in Deuteronomy, adultery, murder, theft. Although the placing of the prohibition of theft varies, this sequence adultery–murder is followed by Philo, *De Dec.* 51 and *De Spec. Leg.* iii. 2; Lk. xviii. 20 (an alteration by Luke of his Markan source); and Paul, Rom. xiii. 9. Josephus, although in *Ant.* iii. 91 he is clearly following the LXX narrative of Exodus, reverts to the 'Hebrew' order in recording the decalogue. The question of the order of the decalogue as known in the Greek-speaking synagogue is a vexed one.[2] A precise distinction between 'Hebrew' and 'Greek' or 'Palestinian' and 'Diaspora' orders should probably not be drawn. Yet it would seem probable that in areas of Judaism which had close contact with the Temple a knowledge of the daily recitation there would encourage a fixity of order, whereas in the synagogue context, where such a practice never obtained,

[1] This tradition probably gave rise to the claim of the *minim* that 'only those commandments were given to Moses on Sinai', P. *Berakoth* i. 3c; a claim that is given as the reason for the abandoning after A.D. 70 of the daily recitation of the decalogue which had formed part of the Temple service, cf. *Tamid* v. 1, lest it should give rise to a misleading concentration on it.

[2] A full discussion may be found in K. Stendahl, *The School of St Matthew*, p. 62. The problem is complicated by the existence of a Hebrew MS of disputed provenance and purpose, the Nash Papyrus, which contains the decalogue in the 'Greek' order, see S. A. Cook, 'A Pre-Massoretic Biblical Papyrus', *Proceedings of the Society of Biblical Archaeology*, xxv, 1903, pp. 34–56.

fluidity would be more understandable. As the bulk of evidence for variety in order is in Greek literature (e.g. the variation between Exodus and Deuteronomy in the LXX; the relegation of the command to honour parents from fifth position, in all the synoptic gospels) we may associate it primarily with the Greek-speaking synagogues, and take this as perhaps another pointer to James's situation, or at least to the medium through which he gained his knowledge of Judaism.

He does not in fact quote the commandments in precisely their LXX wording. It is characteristic of the LXX to express prohibitions by the negative *ou* with the future indicative, and this idiom is retained by Paul and Matthew in their quotations of the decalogue. James, like Mark and Luke, uses instead the stylistically more correct form of *mē* with the aorist subjunctive. This may be with James a stylistic improvement, or reflect the fact that he is quoting not from the text direct, but from memory or common knowledge of it.

12   After giving his example, James sums up with an exhortation that his readers should **speak and act in every respect as people who are going to be judged in terms of a law of freedom**. The translation *in every respect* is an attempt to bring out the force of the repeated *houtōs*, 'so speak and so act'; the stress is not on the observance of a sum total of minutiae, but on the maintenance of a complete integrity of word and deed. The reference to judgment makes explicit what is implicit in the idea of liability in v. 10. There is a recokoning to be made in the future, a judgment *dia nomou*. The law is not here the norm or standard by which they are measured for judgment, for that would require the preposition *kata*; *dia* with the genitive normally serves to identify the agent or instrument of action, so that the law might be seen as the agent of judgment, as in Jn vii. 51 (cf. the law as 'convicting' in Jas ii. 9). More probably, though, it here indicates the state or condition in which an action is performed; the *law of freedom*, cf. i. 25, is the framework or context within which they speak and act, and the future judgment will take account of that fact (so Ropes and Hort; the idea will be that of Rom. ii. 12).

13   Finally James adds to the idea of judgment that of mercy, in

two statements only loosely attached to the foregoing argument and seeming proverbial in form. The train of thought seems to be simply from one idea of judgment to another, 'Talking of judgment . . .'. It would be forced to see in the introduction of this new idea of mercy a reference back to the situation of James's illustration in ii. 2 ff., with mercy as the implied antithesis of discrimination and therefore as the basis for the treatment the poor man should have received. The syntactical change from second person address to third person statement suggests that what is being given is a general principle rather than a specific guide. The principle that **judgment is merciless to him who shows no mercy** is a familiar one, as developed in the parable of the unmerciful servant (Matt. xviii. 23–35). Ropes cites P. *Baba K.* vii. 10, 'Every time that thou art merciful, God will be merciful to thee; and if thou art not merciful, God will not show mercy to thee'; an argument similar to that which Matt. vi. 14 f. draws out of the petition for forgiveness in the Lord's prayer. The principle is enunciated in the positive form of blessing rather than threat in the beatitude of Matt. v. 7; cf. Ps. xviii. 25; Test. Zeb. v. 3, viii. 1–4; and with mercy seen in its concrete demonstration in almsgiving in Ecclus xl. 24; Tobit iv. 10. (James's word *aneleos*, merciless, is another *hapax legomenon* in the epistle, the usual term being *anelees* or *anēlees*, but it is formed by the regular principle of adding negative prefix to noun.)

No conjunction joins the first statement in the verse to the second to suggest their relationship. The compound verb used in the second statement, *katakauchaomai*, to boast against, or exult over, another, is rare in secular and biblical Greek, cf. only Jas iii. 14 and Rom. xi. 18 in the NT; and the aphorism **mercy boasts in the face of judgment** could be understood in either of two ways. Judgment and mercy could be seen here as two attributes of God: God, the author of judgment in 13a, delights in a situation where his mercy may over-ride his judgment. Where a man has shown no mercy, God's judgment of him is inexorable, but where there is evidence of merciful deeds, God's attribute of mercy triumphs over the dictates of his justice, and the balance is tipped in man's favour (cf. the saying of R. Eliezer, 'The scales are evenly balanced: the scale of iniquities on the one side and of merits on the other; the Holy One inclines the balance to mercy', *Pesikta* 167a). More probably, though, the focus is on man's rather than God's mercy. The merciless man may expect merciless judgment; a man, however, who has shown mercy may stand before judgment with confidence (LS offer the paraphrase 'to have no fear' for *katakauchaomai* here). James would apparently have no difficulty with the notion that man may boast before God, his judge; or that man's mercy may be made a meritorious work that boasts a claim on God's approval (contrast Rom. iv. 2–4). His aphorism could be said, though, to be not only independent of but logically inconsistent with the argument of ii. 10: there the law must be kept in full or there is liability for the whole; here the consideration of mercy may apparently serve to waive judgment.

The sequence of thought on law and judgment has therefore moved some way from its initial introduction in terms specifically of the exercise of discrimination to the enunciation of general principles of judgment and mercy. In the following section the leading ideas are of faith and works, but the note of mercy on which this section ends may provide some transition to the next subject, which is introduced in relation to the treatment of those in need.

8. FAITH AND WORKS

ii. 14–26

(14) What is the good of it, my brothers, if a man should say that he has faith, but has no works? His faith cannot save him, can it? (15) If a brother or sister is scantily dressed and lacking food for the day, (16) and one of you says to them 'Go in peace, may you be warmed and filled!' but does not give them the bodily necessities, what is the good of it? (17) In just the same way, faith, if it has no works, is dead in itself. (18) But someone will say, 'You have faith and I have works'.

Show me this faith of yours without works, and I will demonstrate to you my faith from my works. (19) You believe that God is one, do you? You do well. The demons believe that too, and they shudder.

(20) Do you wish to understand, you stupid man, that faith is useless without works? (21) Was not Abraham our father justified by works when he offered up his son Isaac on the altar? (22) You see that faith co-operated with his works and by works faith was made complete. (23) And the scripture was fulfilled which said, 'Abraham believed God, and it was reckoned to him for justification', and he was called 'friend of God'. (24) You see then that a man is justified by works and not by faith alone. (25) And was not Rahab the harlot justified by works in the same way, when she welcomed the messengers and sent them out by another route? (26) For just as the body is dead without breath, so is faith dead without works.

The contrast between judgment and mercy now changes to a contrast between faith and works. In a question that can expect no answer but an emphatic 'no', James asks of the man with faith but no works, **his faith cannot save him, can it?** 14 (*his* is not present in the Greek but may be taken as the sense of the article). It could not save him, presumably, from the judgment of vv. 12–13, for he has no deeds of mercy to boast in the face of judgment. **What is the good of it**, this faith? None, it would seem, to himself, nor, in v. 16, to those in need for whom he does nothing. He may **say that he has faith**, but that is itself an unreal claim, for the faith so isolated from works is a dead thing (v. 17). James's example of unreal faith is shown in failure to exercise charity, an argument reminiscent of Matt. xxv. 31–46, where the destiny of the 'goats' for eternal punishment and the 'sheep' for eternal life is dependent on whether or not they have performed such deeds; and of 1 Jn iii. 17–18, where the claim to have the love of God abiding in one cannot be sustained against a lack of compassion for the needy; and indeed of James's own presentation of 'true religion' in i. 27.

In both James and 1 John the situation is envisaged as
15 within the community: it is **a brother or a sister** who may
be in need. As with ii. 2–4, James is providing an illustration
for his general theme, and this one also has elements of
caricature. Those in need of food and clothing are of course
stock objects of charity (e.g. Tobit iv. 16), but presumably to
carry its point the illustration must bear some relation to
experience. It is possible for the readers to conceive of such
need existing within the community, though this should not
be taken as evidence of the character of the whole society: it is
also assumed that there will be members able to supply their
need. It is debatable how extreme a need James intends to
present; whether it is of as stark a poverty as that of the
beggar of ii. 2. The brother or sister are described as being
gumnos, an adjective that can mean literally naked, as in
Mk xiv. 51 f., or inadequately dressed, having the *chiton*
or undergarment but not the more substantial outer
himation,[1] as probably in Jn xxi. 7; Acts xix. 16, cf. in the
LXX Amos ii. 16; 1 Sam. xix. 24. MM states that this is the
familiar sense of the word in the papyri. AG and Mayor
suggest as a third meaning 'poorly dressed', but it is not clear
how this would be distinguished from the second. The
brother or sister are also in want of *tes ephēmerou trophēs*, a
phrase not found elsewhere in NT or LXX, but familiar in
secular Greek literature. This too could be taken in a more or
less extreme sense: the phrase cannot mean 'daily food', i.e. a
supply from day to day, but must mean 'food for the day', 'the
day's supply', but this could be interpreted as implying a
crisis in which the sufferers have no food *even* for that day, or
as simply a statement of the case at the time: for *that* day
they have no food. Hort wishes to press the use of the verb
huparchō and the present participle *leipomenoi* as describing a
continuous condition, habitual poverty, but it is doubtful if
that is demanded. It seems probable that James intends to
draw not a picture of utter destitution, the abject condition of

[1]For *chiton* and *himation* as the components of normal dress see the two
forms of the saying in Matt. v.40, if a man sues for the price of the undergarment he is to be given the more expensive *himation*; and Lk. vi. 29,
if sued for the outergarment, hand over the indispensable *chiton* as well!

a Lazarus (Lk. xvi. 20 f.) which only the most callous could
ignore, but rather of a poverty which, though certainly mis-
erable, might not seem to require emergency action but which
could be dismissed with hopeful remarks.

James is not concerned to portray the man he accuses as
simply callous. He is the man who says that he has faith, and
his words should be read as expressing a pious hope, if not ac- 16
tually a prayer. **Go in peace** is a semitic idiom, a form of
farewell found in the OT (Jud. xviii. 6; 1 Sam. xx. 42; 2 Sam.
xv. 9) and reproduced in the NT either as *hupagete en eirēnē*
(as here and Acts xvi. 36) or *eis eirēnēn* (Mk v. 34; Lk. vii. 50).
The two imperatives *thermainesthe* and *chortazesthe* could be
in the middle or passive voice. The middle would give the
hearty, if unrealistic encouragement to 'dress warmly! keep
fed!' (so AG); but there is little evidence that *chortazō* was
used in the middle with this active sense, and the passive is to
be preferred, **May you be warmed and filled!** This use of
the passive to express hope should further be understood as a
reverential periphrasis: the hope is not simply that somehow
or other these wants will be supplied, but that *God* will supply
them (cf. Mk v. 34, 'Go in peace, and be healed!'). In the light
of this, *Go in peace* may take on an added solemnity: 'Go in
the peace of God' (though there is no need to suppose it to be
the deacon's blessing at the close of a service of worship, as
Reicke, and cf. Trocmé, art. 'Les Eglises pauliniennes vues du
dehors', p. 663). The wording of the pious hope would not in
the circumstances seem very felicitous: *chortazō* is usually
applied to the fattening of cattle (though it can have the sense
of being well-fed, satisfied, as in Mk vi. 42). James's choice of
this verb is probably intended as a caricature of what to his
supposed man of faith would seem a wholly appropriate
response. Confronted with a case of need, he commits it with
prayer to God, who clothes the naked and feeds the hungry
(Gen. iii. 21; 1 Sam. ii. 5; Ps. cvii. 5 f.; Lk. i. 53), and sends
away his fellow-believers with expressions of confidence.

To James such a response is wholly inadequate. He cannot 17
give this expression of faith even the qualified approval that
he will give to another in v. 19. This faith is not simply inadequate or unprofitable in relation to the situation posed, it

is **dead in itself.** Ropes rightly emphasises that the contrast here is not simply between faith and works but between a dead faith and a living one. The man is presumed to have the means to supply **the needs of the body** (*ta epitēdeia tou sōmatos*; a phrase found only here in the NT, though common in classical authors), to make his pious hope a reality, and does not do so. He believes that God would wish such need to be relieved (since his prayer is that God will respond to it), yet he does not himself act in accordance with that belief. (The argument of Jack T. Sanders that in James's insistence that the needy be relieved a 'humanistic principle' operates (*Ethics in the New Testament*, London 1975, pp. 125–128), is anachronistic and inadequate. The works of charity are not for James a matter of 'mere humanity', but of live faith in God.)

18   At this point there is an interjection into the argument, **someone will say . . .**, which poses an extremely difficult critical question, discussed at length by Ropes, pp. 208–214, and Dibelius, pp. 154–158. The problem is that the interjector appears to attribute to James himself precisely the claim that he has been opposing: **'You have faith'**, and to credit himself with that which James had advocated: **'I have works'**.[1] Apart from resorting to suggestions that there has been a major corruption of an original text in which the claims were reversed, there are three main lines of approach to a solution of this problem. First, the interjector, the **someone**, may be identified as an ally of James, taking up his position in the attack on the 'man of faith' (so Mayor, who comments that this attack demands a claim to 'works' which James is too modest to make for himself); or with James himself as putting up an 'Aunt Sally' suggestion ('one might say', 'I might as well say') that works and faith might be separated, only to knock it down in the second half of the verse (so Chaine). Secondly there are attempts to make sense of the text as it stands and to suggest a content for the faith with which James seems to

[1] This is assuming with most commentators that the interjection consists of v. 18a. Some argue that it continues in 18b, some even include v. 19. But 18b is more plausibly read as an ironic demand to do the impossible, and v. 19 as an equally ironic demonstration of the meaninglessness of an appeal only to faith.

be credited and the works which his opponent claims. By dismissing one claim to faith in v. 17, James implies that he knows what real faith is, indeed that he possesses it. Be that as it may ('You have faith, do you, James?'), the man he has condemned may lay claim also to works, but not James's sort of works: works of the Law ('I have works as well as you!'; thus Hort, and cf. Reicke). Thirdly, it may be argued that the **You** ... **I** distinction should not be taken as specifically relating to James and an opponent, but may be taken more loosely as the expression of two contrasted positions: 'one has faith and another has works' (so Ropes, who cites a not wholly convincing parallel from the Cynic Teles).

The first approach must be dismissed. To introduce an ally who disappears as abruptly as he has appeared is an unlikely procedure for any writer, however modest. Moreover, as Ropes and Dibelius argue, the phrase *all' erei tis* is so standard an introduction of an objection, especially in the diatribe tradition, that it could not be used in reference to the author himself, or his 'second'. It does not seem to be clear, though, that the objection must necessarily be a hostile one; it could come from a neutral observer or an interested but perplexed listener (cf. 1 Cor. xv. 35, where the objection, 'How are the dead raised?' could be read either as a scornful attempt to ridicule Paul's proclamation of resurrection as preposterous, or as the puzzled question of one who desires to believe but finds the idea unimaginable). The second approach certainly reads the words as those of an objector, but demands a new understanding of 'works' which is neither made explicit nor taken up in the subsequent counter-attack.

The third suggestion seems to fit best into the sequence of the argument. James has stated that faith without works is dead, that the two are inseparable. But is this true? Might it not be objected that they are different activities, doubtless complementary and equally praiseworthy, but the provinces of different persons? (Cantinat and Mitton compare 1 Cor. xii. 4–11, where faith is one among the gifts of the Spirit, 'to another faith by the same Spirit; to another gifts of healing ...'; cf. also Rom. xii. 6–8, where separate instruction is given to 'he that exhorteth' and 'he that giveth'; or even Acts vi.

2–4, where the twelve require seven persons to see to the 'daily ministration' so that they can give themselves to prayer and the ministry of the word.) It is for some to devote themselves to charitable works, for others to give themselves to faith, especially if faith is seen as related to prayer in v. 16. The *someone* who puts forward this argument is not necessarily to be identified with the *one of you* of v. 16, but would be seen to give the defence of that line of conduct. Yet even this attempt to give content to the objection in terms of genuinely held positions may be too elaborate for James's rhetorical structure. He may just be putting up a straw man in order to knock him down: supposing purely artificially a separation of faith and works in order to enforce his argument for their inseparability (thus Dibelius). Faith cannot stand apart: **show me this faith of yours without works** is an impossible demand, but **I will demonstrate to you my faith from my works**, for they are its proper expression.[1]

(The objection to the third line of approach, that of taking 'you' and 'I' as equivalent to 'one' and 'another', is that it assumes that the Greek *su* and *egō* could be used as equivalent to *heis* and *heteros*, a usage which does not seem at all well substantiated. Moreover in v. 18b the pronouns would seem to revert to their normal usage, 'show me this faith of yours'; even if 'yours' means 'the faith you are talking about' rather than 'the faith you claim'; and 'I will show you . . .'. The objection is admitted. This solution to the difficulty is adopted because it seems to make the best sense in context, not because it is entirely satisfactory.)

19 To reinforce the point that it is not the content of an expression of faith that he is quarrelling with but its lack of

---

[1] Perhaps ironically, the best comment, almost a paraphrase, on this passage may be found in Luther's Preface to the Epistle of St Paul to the Romans: 'O it is a living, busy, active mighty thing, this faith. It is impossible for it not to be doing good things incessantly. It does not ask whether good works are to be done, but before the question is asked, it has already done them, and is constantly doing them. Whoever does not do such works, however, is an unbeliever. He gropes and looks around for faith and good works, but knows neither what faith is nor what good works are. Yet he talks and talks, with many words, about faith and good works.'

connection with action, James cites what must be a central
tenet both for himself and his supposed objector: **You
believe that God is one, do you? You do well**. The first
sentence can be read as a simple statement of fact; certainly
the rhetorical question is not intended to cast any doubt on
what the man believes: he believes this, and it is a good thing
to believe. There is some textual variance over the expression
of belief. A number of texts, notably B, lack the definite article
and so read the statement as *heis theos estin*: 'there is one
God', a statement of simple monotheism. This reading is
preferred by Hort and Ropes, probably because it is unusual
to find *theos* without an article. Other texts include the article
but vary the word order; the above translation is based on the
reading of p 74, ℵ and A among other Greek MSS, and supported by the Coptic, Syriac and Armenian versions: *heis estin
ho theos*. This reading is also adopted by Kilpatrick and the
UBS text, and among commentators by Mayor and Dibelius.
It gives a statement rather about God's character than simply
his existence: *God is one*. The datum of faith thus appealed to
is not specifically Christian. It is of course characteristic of
Judaism (Deut. vi. 4 makes the acceptance of it basic to
Israel's behaviour and this formed part of the twice-daily
recitation of the *Shema*, and for Philo it is the second article
of his 'creed', *De Opif.* 171); but it is equally so of Christianity in its Jewish heritage (cf. 1 Cor. viii. 4–6; Gal. iii. 20; Eph.
iv. 6; 1 Tim. ii. 5; Hermas, *Mand.* i. and *Didache* i. 1), and it
has a special place in this author's thought (see Introduction
p. 30).

It might be suggested that the statement of belief is made
not just in generally acceptable terms, but specifically in terms
of the *Shema*, whether as read in Deut. vi. 4 or as recited. The
LXX text as we have it reads *Kurios* rather than *Theos* for the
divine name in the Hebrew text, but it is not clear in what
words the *Shema* would have been recited by Greek-speaking
Jews, and it is possible that *Theos* and *Kurios* might have
been alternative substitutes for the name. Another explanation of James's choice of words will be suggested below, but it
is reasonable to suppose that any affirmation of the oneness of
God would contain, or evoke, an allusion to the central text

for its declaration, even without exact quotation; and if such an allusion were caught there might be for the Christian an additional point of connection, with Jesus' confirmation of Deut. vi. 4 (Mk xii. 29 ff.). In this tradition Jesus brought together Deut. vi. 4 and Lev. xix. 18, a conjunction that seems to be original to him (unless Test. Iss. v. 2 is certainly earlier), and which was maintained in Christian ethical instruction, cf. *Did.* i. 1, which in contrast to Barn. xix. 2 appears as a Christianising of the original 'Two Ways' material. Though this is often simplified into the double command to love God and the neighbour without the introductory doctrinal basis for the first (so Matt. xxii. 37 ff. and Lk. x. 27, editing Mark), it is unlikely that that basis was forgotten. It is notable that James singles out for approval in the same terms, *you do well*, Lev. xix. 18 in ii. 8 and the affirmation that God is one, here, and this may be because he has in mind their conjunction by Jesus and sees them as having an equal status and authority.

However that may be, the acceptance of so central a tenet of belief cannot be other than approved, and *you do well* is not ironical. The sting in the tail is in what follows: **the demons believe that too, and they shudder.** This passage is often cited to show that James's understanding of faith is of it as mere intellectual assent to a proposition,[1] which even a demon can make. This is greatly to undervalue James's argument. The demons' assent is by no means merely intellectual: in believing that God is one they believe something about him that evokes a response: that as *one* he is wholly and consistently their enemy, *and they shudder*. The picture of the demons' recognition of God is comparable to that of demons recognising Jesus in the Markan exorcism traditions (Mk i. 24, iii. 11, v. 7), where the naming should not be seen as merely identification but as a defiant attempt to gain power over the adversary whom they can see has come 'to destroy us' (Mk i. 24).

It is highly probable that James's own illustration has its background in the practice of exorcism. The verb translated

---

[1] As, for example, by H. W. Montefiore, *A Commentary on the Epistle to the Hebrews*, London 1964, p. 187.

shudder, *phrissō*, is only used in general terms in the LXX to express horror or fear (though the use for a reaction to visions in Job iv. 14 f. and Dan. vii. 15 is interesting) but has a very specific use in the papyri. It 'is constantly used of the effect that the sorceror wishes to bring about by means of his magic' (MM). The Leiden papyri contain an example similar to James, recommending the exorcist 'to say the great name (Aōth), which every god kneels to and at which every demon shudders'; and Deissmann gives, from the Paris papyri, a Jewish example contained in a phylactery (or amulet?) which is to be hung round the neck of the patient because 'it is of every demon something to be shuddered at (*phrikton*), which he fears' (A. Deissmann, *Light from the Ancient East*, pp. 256, 260). Deissmann also records an example which he calls 'A Septuagint Memorial': 'I charge you by the holy name which is not spoken ... I shall name it and the demons shall be aroused and astounded, and shall be in great fear' (*Bible Studies*, ET Edinburgh 1901, p. 288).[1] This last example may suggest an explanation for the choice by James of the 'God is one' formula of faith. In the Jewish incantation the divine name is not spoken, its pronunciation being kept as an ultimate threat. The magical papyri reveal that in this syncretistic science the Old Testament names and titles for God were frequently and often strangely employed (see, for example, J. Hull, *Hellenistic Magic and the Synoptic Tradition*, London 1974, p. 31), but it seems probable that such use would be shunned by an 'orthodox' Jewish exorcist, and the statement 'God is one' or appeal to 'the one God' would be sufficiently specific and sufficiently potent. Jeremias comments on this passage that the demons tremble 'whenever the εἰς θεός is used as an exorcist formula' (J. Jeremias, 'Paul and James', *ExT* LXVI, 1954–55, p. 370). The formula need not be confined to Jewish use though; Dibelius points out that it could appeal to Hellenistic use in the context of popular philosophy's tending to monotheism, and E. Peterson links the formula with the *Aiōn* name found in the magical papyri

---

[1] Justin Martyr describes the demons as 'shuddering' before the power of God revealed in the crucified Christ, *Dialogue* xlix. 22.

($\epsilon\hat{\iota}s$ $\theta\epsilon\acute{o}s$, Göttingen 1926, pp. 295 ff.). Further use of the language of exorcism may be found later in the epistle, at iv. 7; and cf. Introduction, p. 5 f.

James's *argumentum ad hominem* is, then, a pungent one. He is not concerned to contrast faith, as intellectual assent, with works, but to indicate the necessary outcome of faith, if it is a live faith, and the impossibility of its existing alone. For the demons, belief in the God who is one produces a response of fear (if there is indeed an exorcist background it could be said that a declaration of this faith is itself active, effecting the work of casting out the demon). The idea that belief in God as one carries implications for action is not of course a new one, but goes back to Deut. vi. 4 itself: 'The Lord our God is one Lord, and thou shalt love the Lord thy God with all thy heart and with all thy soul and with all thy might', and the Rabbis pondered the proper expression of that total love (see B. Gerhardsson, 'The parable of the Sower and its interpretation', pp. 167–169; and *Berakoth* v. 5). For Jesus, whose teaching may be in James's mind, love of the God who is one leads to love of the neighbour. The challenge to James's man of faith is to show what response his profession evokes from him.

20 The next stage of James's argument is to confront the **stupid man** with scriptural examples as authority for his position. The direct, harsh address is characteristic of diatribe style (cf. Rom. ii. 1; 1 Cor. xv. 36). James's imagined objector is characterised as *kenos*, lit. 'empty'. The faith he advocates is, without works, **useless**. Some MSS read *nekra*, dead, probably in assimilation to vv. 17 and 26; p 74 describes the faith as *kenē*, empty, like the man himself, assimilating the second half of the verse to the first; but the majority of MSS have *argē*, which as a contraction of *a-ergē*, provides a nice pun in James's typical style. Faith without works is indeed 'workless'; useless.

It is at this point that James introduces into his argument about faith and works the idea of justification, and the example of Abraham. The question is therefore raised of the relation of his argument to Paul's discussion of justification in Gal. ii. and, more fully, Rom. iii–iv; the question that makes this probably the most discussed section of the epistle (as well as the commentaries, see J. Jeremias, 'Paul and James', cited above). The apparent antithesis between Paul and James can be presented most sharply in the contrast between Paul's judgment in Rom. iii. 28, 'we reckon that a man is justified by faith without works', and James's conclusion in v. 24, *you see, then, that a man is justified by works and not by faith alone*.

On closer examination, however, the two arguments appear less closely engaged. Both writers quote Gen. xv. 6 (Jas v. 23; Paul, Rom. iv. 22; Gal. iii. 6), but whereas Paul interprets the justifying faith of Abraham in relation to the immediate context of the promises of God (Rom. iv. 18, quoting Gen. xv. 5, cf. Gal. iii. 16), James links it with the offering of Isaac (v. 21, alluding to Gen. xxii. 2, 9). In this linking of Gen. xv. with Gen. xxii, James passes without comment over the account of Abraham's circumcision in Gen. xvii, and thereby misses a vitally important point in Paul's exegetical argument: that Abraham's justification was pronounced before he was circumcised, and can therefore have no relation to the Law (Rom. iv. 9–11). This leads on to a second and more obvious difference. When Paul speaks of 'works' in relation to justification, he speaks consistently and explicitly of works of obedience to the Jewish Law (Rom. iii. 20, 28, cf. x. 31 f.; Gal. iii. 10 f.). The Law plays, however, no part in James's argument at this point, and his understanding of *works* is most naturally seen in terms of the deeds of charity demanded in v. 15 f. Paul's other deduction from the example of Abraham, that justification applies to the gentile in the same way as to the Jew (Rom. iv. 11 f.; Gal. iii. 7–9), is not considered by James. Nor does he attempt an alternative exegesis of Paul's second major proof-text, Hab. ii. 4, 'the just by faith shall live' (quoted in Rom. i. 17 and Gal. iii. 11), which one might have expected him to do if he was attempting both to engage with Paul and to establish his case from scripture. Conversely, his second scriptural example, that of Rahab (v. 25), has no place in the Pauline argument.

It is unlikely, therefore, that James's argument is developed in relation to Paul's, as that apostle systematically expounded it. Even bearing in mind E. L. Allen's warning here that 'the history of theological discussion shows that no limits whatsoever can be set *a priori* to the possibilities of misunderstanding' ('Controversy in the New Testament', *NTS* 1, 1954–55, p. 144), he misses far too many points. Yet the polemical tone of v. 24 cannot be ignored, and the majority of commentators agree that the Pauline doctrine is in some way the issue involved. Mayor, a notable exception to this general consensus, argues for the priority of James to Paul, and that Paul writes to correct a misuse of this epistle in the Judaising interest (his argument has recently been revived by J. A. T. Robinson, *Redating the New Testament*, p. 126). This takes the point that James does not deal thoroughly with Paul's argument, but gives insufficient weight to James's polemical tone.

The idea of justification is an important one in Old Testament and subsequent Jewish thought. In the forensic context to which the language originally belonged, justification referred to the judge's verdict on the individual before him, who is acquitted or pronounced 'in the right' on the basis of his proven innocence. This idea of being 'in the right' could be extended to describe the status of one person over against another in a situation where the criteria applied are not strictly those of proven virtue (Gen. xxxviii. 26; Lk. xviii. 14: Tamar and the publican are not virtuous persons in a straightforward sense). Further, the OT idea of the judge included his function of upholding the rights of persons at a disadvantage and in need of protection, like widows and orphans and the poor (Prov. xxxi. 8 f.; Is. i. 17). This understanding of justice is seen as authorised by God, and when the language is used of him, it is of him as the judge who is expected to pronounce the verdict of acquittal, and to confer the status of being in the right with him on those whose obedience (especially to the Law) merits such a verdict; as Paul reminds his readers in Rom. ii. 13; Gal. iii. 11 f. He is also however spoken of, especially by Deutero-Isaiah, as 'just' in his deliverance of Israel from oppression (Is. xlv. 21, cf. xlvi. 13 and Ex. vi. 6); probably in an extension of the idea that the judge is also the protector of those in need. Theological problems arise when God is not seen to be acting in this way: the argument of Job is worked out very much in terms of Job's right and God's apparent injustice (e.g. Job xxiii. 2–7,

xxvii. 2–6); or when the verdict of justification is pronounced
in a situation which seems wholly incompatible with it. This
is the particular paradox of Paul. In declaring both that 'all
have sinned', and yet that 'we are justified freely' (Rom. iii.
23–24), he is compelled to wrestle with the idea of the justice
of God, so central to his Jewish heritage, and to show that it
is tolerable and indeed necessary both to seem to describe
God as an unjust judge (Rom. iv. 5, cf. Is. v. 23) and yet to
continue to assert that he is 'just and the justifier' (Rom. iii.
26).

It is impossible here fully to discuss Paul's doctrine of
justification, or indeed the background of interpretation of the
idea against which he expounds his own.[1] Suffice it to say
here that in his exposition Paul distinguishes between any
suggested rôle for men's works in the forming of God's judgment, which he rules out as impossible in view of man's sin-
fulness (Rom. iii. 9–20), and the rôle of faith as the acceptance
that God in fact does the impossible, as he did for Abraham
and as he now does in justifying sinners in Christ (Rom. iv. 17 f.,
23 ff.). It is this absolute distinction between faith and
works in relation to justification that seems to have no precedent in Judaism (even in 2 Esd. ix. 7 f., xiii. 23, where works
and faith seem to be distinguished, they are seen as alternative possible means of salvation and not as opposed), and
which is the subject of James's attack. As argued above, it is
highly unlikely that his familiarity with the distinction comes
from a following of Paul's own written argument, and
probable instead that he has heard it used as a slogan by
others to support their own position. Paul himself feared that
his teaching would be twisted (indeed seems to have known
that it had been so twisted) to licence antinomianism or libertinism (Rom. iii. 8, vi. 1). It does not seem likely that James
has met it in this connection: his concern is not here with im-
morality but with quietism, the argument that confession of

---

[1] Paul's argument is of course analysed and variously interpreted in commentaries on Romans and Galatians, and in the major Theologies of the
New Testament, e.g. R. Bultmann, *Theology of the New Testament*, Vol.
1, ET London 1952, pp. 270–285; and W. G. Kümmel, *The Theology of
the New Testament*, ET London 1974, pp. 193–203.

God is all, that expressions of trust in God obviate the necessity for taking any action about human need (the same suggestion is raised rhetorically after the statement of justification by faith in 1 Clem. xxxiii. 1; cf. Introduction, p. 16 f.).

It is a further question whether James heard the 'justification by faith alone' slogan quoted as attributed to Paul. Despite Jeremias's suggestion that it is Jesus' teaching in the parable of Lk. xviii. 14 that is the origin of Paul's doctrine (*art. cit.* p. 396 f.), the NT evidence suggests that the use of justification as a term for salvation is in the Christian tradition peculiarly associated with Paul. Luke, who seems in Acts to betray little if any knowledge of Paul's epistles, uses the term only once, putting it into the mouth of Paul in the only one of his speeches (apart from his apologia under trial) that is addressed to Jews, and in relation to the question of the Law (Acts xiii. 38 f.). Similarly, the author of the Pastoral epistles, writing under the name of Paul, uses the language of justification in a summary account of salvation, probably 'paulinising' a stereotyped confessional or credal formula (Tit. iii. 4–7). The likelihood is, therefore, that when James heard the slogan 'justification by faith alone' used (or misused) it was as carrying the authority of Paul. (For the implications of this for reconstructing James's situation, see Introduction pp. 16–19.)

Attempts to harmonise James and Paul and thus produce an apostolic consensus, are probably fruitless. Certainly they have more in common than the bald juxtaposition of their key statements might suggest. It has already been argued, on ii. 19, that faith is not for James simply assent to a proposition. It is for him as for Paul a matter of relationship with God, and it is striking that James's references to faith outside this context connect it with prayer (so i. 6, v. 15) or with trust in face of adversity (ii. 5, poverty is faced in assurance of God's promise; i. 3, trials are to be seen as having a purpose). Paul, too, outside the tight arguments of Gal. iii and Rom. iii–iv, assumes the necessity of good works as the expression of or response of faith (cf. the 'fruits of the Spirit' of Gal. v. 22, and the logic of Rom. xii. 1 ff.), and even writes of a future judgment on the basis of works (1 Cor. iii. 13; 2 Cor. v. 10). True, too, they address themselves to different aspects of salvation: Paul to the initial experience of acceptance by God; James to the continuing life of faith. Yet Paul could surely never have tolerated James's explicit assertion that justification is *not by faith alone* nor his lack of attention to an initial saving act of God that makes faith and consequent good works possible. However much one may modify the superficial contrast, a basic lack of sympathy must remain.

It is doubtful, too, if James could have followed Paul's 21 highly original exegesis of the example of **Abraham**, for his own appeal to that example is simple and traditional. He refers, like Paul, to Abraham as **our father**. This would of course be a familiar claim for a Jew (e.g. Matt. iii. 9; Lk. iii. 8; Jn viii. 33, 39; *Aboth* v. 3), but Paul claimed Abraham also for gentile Christians (Rom. iv. 11–12, 16; Gal. iii. 7 f., 29), perhaps following precedent in proselyte theology, cf. on v. 25. Clement also describes Abraham as 'our father', in addressing a Christian community that is certainly not exclusively, if at all, Jewish Christian (1 Clem. xxxi. 2). In fact, as he cites them, neither of James's examples explicitly makes the point that he wishes, for the 'work' of Abraham seen to complete his faith was not actually performed, since Isaac was not in the end sacrificed, and conversely although Rahab's 'work' is described in v. 25, there is no mention of her faith! In both cases, however, familiar ideas are being drawn on. Whether v. 22 is read as a statement or as a rhetorical question, James appears to assume that his interlocutor, and his reader, will follow him in his association of Abraham's justification with both his faith and his deeds. The scripture which connects Abraham's justification with his faith requires to be *fulfilled*, and such fulfilment is to be seen in terms of Abraham's works. The justification of Abraham by God rests on God's recognition of something proven or provable in Abraham's faith.

Such an idea, clearly alien to Paul, finds many parallels in Jewish sources. Abraham's faith, understood as trust in God or fidelity, might be seen as itself achieved and so as a meritorious work: 'Abraham our father inherited this world and the world to

come solely by the merit of faith, whereby he believed in the
Lord' (*Mekilta* on Ex. xiv. 31 referring to Gen. xv. 6). Where
faith is necessarily understood in relation to the Torah,
Abraham's was seen as consisting in his having fulfilled the
whole Law before it was written (*Kiddushin* iv. 14). At a less
sophisticated level, and more familiar, is the idea that Abraham's
faith was demonstrated in his trials, of which the requirement to
sacrifice Isaac was the final and most crucial test: 'Was not
Abraham found faithful in temptation, and it was counted to him
for righteousness?' (1 Macc. ii. 52; cf. Ecclus xliv. 20); 'With ten
temptations was Abraham our father tempted, and he stood
steadfast in them all, to show how great was the love of Abraham
our father' (*Aboth* v. 4; cf. Jubilees xvii. 17 f., xix. 8, where the
death of Sarah is the final trial). For the authors of Hebrews and 1
Clement, too, the movement of thought from Gen. xv. 6 to Gen.
xxii is a natural one, since it is the child of the promise who is to
be sacrified and therefore the faith of Abraham in that promise
that is being put again to the proof (Heb. xi. 17 f.; 1 Clem. x. 6–7).
While setting James's argument in the context of familiar ideas
(and for further discussion and illustration of the Jewish interpretation of the faith of Abraham, see Dibelius, pp. 169—172
and Lightfoot, *Galatians*, pp. 155–164), his characteristic
emphasis should also be noted. The relation between Abraham's
22 faith and his works is not properly one of consequence,
demonstration or confirmation, all of which terms assume a
measure of distinction between the two: for James they go
together in a necessary unity, **faith co-operated with his
works, and by works faith was made complete.**

Some commentators find a discrepancy between the use of
the plural **works** in vv. 21 and 22 and the appeal to the single,
and unperformed, act of the offering of Isaac. Thus R. B.
Ward draws attention to the similar conjunction of Abraham
and Rahab as exemplars in 1 Clem. x–xii, where they are
examples of faith and of hospitality, *philoxenia* ('The Works
of Abraham', *HTR* 61, 1968, pp. 283–290). It is Rahab's acts
of hospitality that demonstrate her faith in Jas ii. 25 and so,
Ward suggests, the *works* of Abraham to which James refers
should be understood in the same way, with both James and
Clement reflecting the strong tradition of Abraham as an

hospitable man (deriving from Gen. xviii, and seen in *Aboth R. Nathan* i. 7 and the midrash on Ps. xxxvii. 7, where Abraham is an innkeeper, the conversion of whose guests is his payment). The sacrifice of Isaac, since it did not take place, was not a justifying work; rather its being averted is the sign of the justification Abraham had received for his hospitality to the three angels. This seems to require a network of allusion more complicated than James's usual use of scripture suggests, and as he seems clearly to define Rahab's works in v. 25, so he may be taken to do so with Abraham in v. 21. Should the plural noun seem to need any explanation, it would more probably lie in the idea of the offering of Isaac as the culmination of Abraham's tests. But the plural is really no more appropriate in the case of Rahab, for the reception and safe-conduct of the messengers is a single event rather than two distinct actions; and the use of *erga* in both examples surely derives from the contrast between *faith* and *works* throughout vv. 14–26, the language being imposed on both illustrations of the theme, rather than emerging from a strictly literal consideration of their content.

Apart from his conjunction of Gen. xv. 6 with Gen. xxii, which, although it is not indicated in Genesis itself and is alien to Paul, has been shown to be a familiar one, James's use of the passage is straightforward. There is no trace in his reference to the offering of Isaac of the increasing Jewish interest in Isaac's own participation in the event as willing victim (see G. Vermes, *Scripture and Tradition in Judaism*, Leiden 1961, pp. 193–218); Abraham remains the central 23 figure. The citation of Gen. xv. 6 derives from the LXX, which differs from the Hebrew text in expressing the subject of the first verb, '*Abraham* believed', and in replacing the active of the second, 'he reckoned it', by the passive, 'it was reckoned'. James differs slightly from the LXX in his opening conjunction, making a stylistic improvement, and in giving the name *Abraham* rather than the LXX 'Abram'. The latter is of course correct, since Abram is not given his new name until Gen. xvii. 5, but the new name is the more familiar, and the slip, as it most probably is, is easily explained if the quotation is made from memory rather than a consultation of the text. (Paul, incidentally, shows the same differences from the LXX in his quotation in Rom. iv. 3 and Gal. iii. 6).

The final clause of v. 23 is more problematical, since although it seems to be included under the citation of *scripture*, the description of Abraham as **friend of God** does not derive from Gen. xv. 6. In the Hebrew text of Is. xli. 8 God is seen to speak of Abraham as 'my friend' and in 2 Chron. xx. 7 Jehoshaphat refers in prayer to the seed of Abraham 'thy friend', but in neither case does the LXX translate with the noun *philos* but paraphrases with the verb *agapaō*: Abraham 'whom I loved' (Is. xli. 8), or 'who was loved by you' (2 Chron. xx. 7; cf. Dan. iii. 35, LXX, and 2 Esd. iii. 14). This might seem to indicate that if James's reference is indeed 'scriptural', then it must derive from the Hebrew scripture. However, the designation of OT saints as *philoi theou* in Greek-speaking Judaism can be seen in Wisd. vii. 27 and Philo, *De Vita Mos.* i. 28, and there is some suggestion that epithets implying the divine affection found their way into Greek versions of the Abraham saga itself. Gen. xviii. 17 in the Hebrew reads 'shall I hide from Abraham the thing which I do?', and the LXX as we have it adds 'from Abraham *tou paidos mou*', 'my child' or 'my servant'. Philo quotes the passage in this form in *Leg. Alleg.* iii. 27, but in *De Sobr.* 56 he quotes the same verse in the form *tou philou mou*, 'my friend'. As it is relatively certain that Philo read his bible only in Greek, and certain that he based his exegesis on the Greek text, it would be justifiable to conclude that he knew a text that gave that reading; and as James refers to two parts of the Abraham saga, it would be more likely that he derived his third reference from that context than from Isaiah or Chronicles. However, it is perhaps more probable that the Hebrew passages originally supplied the title for Abraham, which became popular (e.g. Jubilees xix. 9; CD iii. 2; it is found frequently in targums on the saga and in Rabbinic literature, cf. J. Bowker, *The Targums and Rabbinic Literature*, Cambridge 1969, pp. 209, 212), and passed into Greek-speaking Judaism without direct dependence on the biblical text, but rather intruding glosses into it. Philo's variant quotations of Gen. xviii. 17 may be seen as evidence of such glossing. James, then, is not strictly quoting scripture at this point but echoing a familiar description of Abraham which ultimately has a scriptural background. The continuing popularity of the description of Abraham as *friend of God* can be seen in early Christian literature (1 Clem. x. 1, xvii. 2; Tert. *Adv. Jud.* ii. 7; Iren. *Adv. Haer.* iv. 14. 4, 16. 2; all passages surely independent of James), and ultimately in its passing into the language of Islam (Ropes cites the *Quran, sura* iv. 124 and the description of Abraham as *el khalil*).

Before citing his second example, James states his general **24** conclusion from his first. It is ironically he and not Paul who gave Luther his term **by faith alone**, and this is a vital part of his argument. He is not concerned to set faith and works against each other and deny the former any rôle in justification; what he is contrasting is 'faith without works' and 'works inseparable from faith'.

Abraham is *our father* and the *friend of God*; **Rahab** is *hē* **25** *pornē*, **the harlot**. James and Hebrews, xi. 31, show no hesitation in following the OT and so describing her, whereas Josephus, *Ant.* v. 7 and the Palestinian targum on Josh. ii. 1 make her an innkeeper (see note *ad loc.* in the Loeb edn of *Ant.* v). The two figures, the holy patriarch and the sinful foreign woman, stand as sharply contrasting illustrations of the same theme, as James emphasises with his introductory **even**. Rahab is a comparatively minor character in the hexateuch, appearing only in Josh. ii and vi, but later legends gathered about her. With Sarah, Abigail and Esther, she was one of the four chief beauties, she married Joshua, and became the ancestress of eight priests who were also prophets, including Jeremiah and Ezekiel (*Megillah* 14b–15a). Josephus, *Ant.* v. 12, and Clement, 1 Clem. xii 8, describe her (for different reasons) as herself a prophetess. In the Matthean genealogy, Matt. i. 5, she is (by a union with Salmon) one of the ancestresses of the Christ, singled out for mention with Tamar, Ruth and Bathsheba, all four women whose sexual unions were, initially at least, irregular, and who serve therefore as in some measure types of Mary whose apparently shameful conception was in fact blessed.

Most of the later interest in her was focused on two

elements of the biblical narrative: her confession in Josh. ii. 11 that 'the Lord your God is he who is God in heaven above and on earth beneath', a statement of faith that is also the climax to Moses' preamble to the commandments in Deut. iv. 39; and the note in Josh. vi. 25 that after her rescue from Jericho she dwelt in Israel 'to this day'. She therefore came to be seen as the archetypal proselyte, the foreigner who makes the confession of Israel's faith and enters the community of Israel. Daube quotes Joshua b. Levi's account of the prayer of Hezekiah in his illness: he 'turned to the wall of Rahab, saying, Lord of the Universe, Rahab saved only two souls for thee ... (the spies she helped to escape), and how many souls hast thou saved for her ... (all her family were spared); my fathers gathered for thee all the proselytes ... how much the more shouldest thou spare me!' (D. Daube, *The New Testament and Rabbinic Judaism*, London 1956, p. 354). It is perhaps because she has this character that she is paired with Abraham here, for he also could be thought of as a proselyte: Paul's appeal to him as the father of the gentiles who have faith (Rom. iv. 11) has parallels in Philo's account of his conversion from astral religion (*De Virt.* 211–216; 'He is the standard of nobility for all proselytes', *De Virt.* 219), and in the description of him in *Mekilta* on Ex. xxii. 20 as the first proselyte, on the basis of his words in Gen. xxiii. 4, 'I am a stranger and a sojourner with you'. The conjunction of Abraham and Rahab by James, then, may be not simply because they provide a dramatic contrast, but because they already belong together in Jewish preaching in their character as ideal proselytes. Clement probably draws independently on the same ideas when he couples them together as examples of 'faith and hospitality' (1 Clem. x. 7, xii. 1; the intervening example of Lot being of 'hospitality and piety', *eusebia*). It would seem then that the idea of Rahab's faith would be sufficiently familiar for James to assume that when he referred simply to her *works*, they would be seen to be works in which faith also was operative.

Granted this assumption, James's appeal to the example of Rahab is as straightforward as to that of Abraham. He includes none of the legendary developments referred to above, nor does he find hidden meanings in the events as does Clement in her 'scarlet thread' (1 Clem. xii. 7–8; cf. Justin, *Dialogue* cxi. 10). The window through which she let them down is simply the **other way** by which they left, without further elaboration. The only oddity lies in his description of the two spies as *angeloi*. In Josh. ii they are described simply as men, LXX *andres* or *neaniskoi*. Josephus, Hebrews and Clement follow this, or refer to them as *kataskopoi*, spies, which derives from the character of their mission and the use of the verb *kataskopizō* in the LXX. There is no evidence of a midrashic tradition that gave these figures the character of angels and thus made of Rahab one who 'entertained angels unawares', and it would seem a rather unlikely development of the story. Yet neither were they really 'messengers', except in the sense that they were to report back to Joshua. James is obviously only alluding to the story in general terms.

Finally, James reiterates his statement of v. 17, with an **26** analogy: **just as the body is dead without breath, so faith is dead without works**; *pneuma* is here used of the animating principle of life (cf. Gen. ii. 7, vi. 17; Ezek. xxxvii. 8 f.; Eccles xii. 7). Again it is clear that James is not drawing a simple contrast between faith and works, but between *faith alone*, which is dead, and faith active in and completed by deeds, which is only thus alive.

9. THE POWER OF THE TONGUE

iii. 1–12

(1) Do not many of you become teachers, my brothers, because you know that we shall receive a stricter judgment. (2) For we all err in many ways. If anyone commits no error in his speech, he is a perfect man, able to bridle the whole body also. (3) Look, we put bits in horses' mouths so that they will obey us, and we guide their whole body. (4) Look at ships, too, which big as they are and driven by strong winds are guided by a tiny rudder where the impulse of the steersman directs.

(5) In the same way, the tongue is a little limb which
boasts a lot. See how small a fire kindles how great a
forest! (6) The tongue is a fire as well; the tongue appoints itself as the wicked world among our members
and defiles the whole body; it sets light to the wheel of
life and is set alight by Gehenna. (7) Every kind of beast
and bird, of creeping thing and of sea creature, is
tamed and has been tamed to humankind, (8) but no-
one can tame the tongue; it is a restless evil, full of
deadly poison. (9) With it we bless the Lord and Father,
and with it also we curse men, who are made 'in the
likeness' of God. (10) Out of the same mouth come
blessing and curse. My brothers, these things should
not be so. (11) Surely a spring does not gush forth fresh
and bitter water from the same opening? (12) Surely,
my brothers, a figtree cannot produce olives, or a vine
figs? No more can salt water produce fresh.

This passage, with its highly rhetorical and dramatic accounts of the evils attributable to the tongue, takes up and
develops themes introduced in i. 19, 26 and ii. 12. The self-
contained nature of the section and its parallels in Hellenistic
literature have led some to suggest that an independent
diatribe on the tongue has been incorporated, but there are
sufficient links in language, thought and style with the rest of
the epistle to make it clear that, whatever in his environment
he may have drawn upon, this section also is James's composition. There is however no obvious connection with the
preceding passage; it is artificial to suggest that the warning
against becoming teachers is related to James's attack on the
purveyors of the Pauline slogan. This initial specific warning
stands itself in some isolation from the passage as a whole,
which is of general application; it is surely not only teachers
who may mix blessings and curses in their speech! The first
verse should not however be treated as a separate saying, but
seen as introducing the general topic by reference to a particular instance. Teachers being men of words *par excellence*
are particularly exposed to the danger of sins of speech.

1   James seeks to discourage **many** of his readers from

becoming **teachers**, and his warning is therefore different in content from Matt. xxiii. 7 f., where it is the use of titles of honour which is forbidden, not the exercise of the teaching function. It may be presumed that it was the status given to the teacher that was the attraction in James's community. Jeremias (*Jerusalem in the Time of Jesus*, pp. 233–245) provides illustrations of the enormous respect accorded to teachers within Judaism ('Let . . . the fear of thy teacher be as the fear of heaven', *Aboth* iv. 12), and if James's community had some links with or background in Judaism, this may have been to some extent transferred to its Christian teachers. There is no suggestion that James is opposing exponents of false teaching, as with 1 Tim. i. 7; 2 Pet. ii. 1 (unless one were to make a close connection with the following passage on wisdom, iii. 13–18, and detect here an implicit attack on a false claim to 'heavenly wisdom'). Rather he seeks to dissuade those inadequate for the proper task. Hermas, in his vision of the twelve mountains, saw on the fifth mountain self-appointed teachers who had taken on the rôle from pride and misplaced confidence, but who because they were only foolish and lacking in understanding had a chance of repentance (*Sim.* ix. 22. 2). This is no doubt a perennial temptation in a community where teaching and hence the teacher is given an important place, enough for it to be the object of ambition. There is no warrant for associating James's warning specifically with an unregulated Pauline Church, in whose meetings many speakers, more or less qualified, might intervene at will (as Trocmé, 'Les Eglises pauliniennes vues du dehors', p. 665 f., cf. Introduction, p. 17).

By thus seeking to limit the number of teachers, James shows that he views teaching as the function of particular members of the community rather than of the community as a whole (as might seem assumed in Col. iii. 16; Heb. v. 12). The relation of these teachers to the 'elders' of v. 14 is undefined; rather than being distinct groups, the former might be members of the latter group, as with the elders 'who labour at . . . teaching' of 1 Tim. v. 17; cf. Tit. i. 9. Further reference to teachers is found in other early Christian literature. Acts xiii. 1 lists 'prophets and teachers' at Antioch, without it being

clear if these are different classes. Paul distinguishes in 1 Cor.
xii. 28 between apostles, prophets and teachers, as does Eph.
iv. 11 (further distinguishing 'evangelists and pastors'), and
Did. xi. 1–3, cf. xiii. 1 f., xv. 1 f. This distinction is blurred in
Mart. Poly. where Polycarp is described as 'an apostolic and
prophetic teacher' (xvi. 2). It is not wholly clear on what the
distinction rested, and what was the specific function of the
Christian teacher. It is probable that whereas apostles were
itinerant preachers, connected with the foundation period of
the Churches (though retaining some personal authority over
the Churches of their own founding), most prophets and certainly teachers were resident members of their local community, working within its continuing life. So in Acts xiii the
prophets and teachers are members of the Antiochene
Church; 1 Cor. xiv may be seen to assume the regular
presence of prophets in the Church of Corinth (thus C. K.
Barrett, commenting on 1 Cor. xii. 28 in *The First Epistle to
the Corinthians*, London 1968); and the *Didache* requires
that true apostles must be on the move, but prophets may settle
and be supported, as teachers are (xi. 4 ff., xiii. 1 f.).

As between the latter two, again a precise distinction is
difficult. K. H. Rengstorf's definition of prophets as
'pneumatics' and teachers as 'non-pneumatics' (in article
διδάσκαλος, *TDNT* Vol. II, p. 158) is unsatisfactory, since he
himself qualifies it in a footnote by saying that teachers would of
course also have the *pneuma*, and since Paul is clear that teaching
is a *charisma* (Rom. xii. 7), and that teachers are provided by
God (1 Cor. xii. 28, cf. v. 8). The common distinction between
kerygma and *didache* is also probably unhelpful, if it is used to
suggest that prophets were the proclaimers of the gospel, while
teachers (*didaskaloi*) were concerned only with the moral
education of the community. J. D. G. Dunn, though warning
against the drawing of too sharp a distinction between the two,
proposes as a general one that 'prophecy would express a new
word from God as such', though that new word might come from
the interpretation of earlier sayings, 'whereas teaching would
tend to denote more *a new insight into an old word from God*', i.e.
into traditions already accepted as authoritative: the Old Testament, expounded in its Christian reference, sayings of Jesus, and

the gospel initially received (J. D. G. Dunn, *Jesus and the Spirit*, London 1975, p. 237, cf. pp. 186 and 282 f.). The Christian teacher would thus be heir to the rôle of the Jewish teacher as guardian and interpreter of the tradition he shared with his community (cf. the role of the 'guardian', *mebakker*, or 'master', *maskil*, at Qumran, as instructor and interpreter: CD xiii. 7 f.; 1 QS ix. 12–20; and Vermes, *Dead Sea Scrolls in English*, pp. 19–25). The teacher might be much occupied in study, and expect some material support from the Church, and his work could therefore be seen more than that of the prophet as the exercise of an 'office' (Gal. vi. 6; 1 Tim. v. 17; *Did.* xiii. 7).

This theory of the teacher's function is supported by those documents which may be associated with 'teachers'. The epistle of Barnabas, whose author's insistence that he addresses his readers 'not as a teacher but as one of you' (i. 8, cf. iv. 9) should be read as a modest disclaimer rather than, as by Cantinat, as an actual refusal to assume the teaching office without warrant, contains the ethical material of the 'Two Ways' (xviii–xx), but is also characterised by its reinterpretation of the Old Testament: allegorical interpretation of the ritual laws (x), and exposition of the Old Testament prefiguration of Christ (v–ix, xi–xii). The *Didache* too, inasmuch as it warns against teachers who teach contrary to its own instruction (vi. 1, xi. 1 f.), may be taken as an example of Christian 'teaching'; it also includes the 'Two Ways' (i–vi. 1), with instruction about the Christian liturgy and ministries (xii–xv). James, who by his use of the first person plural in iii. 1 would seem to class himself among teachers, may provide in his own epistle the best example of the exercise of the Christian teacher's task: his primarily ethical instruction is at various points linked with the interpretation of his law (ii. 8 f., 10 f.); the re-application of the Old Testament (i. 10 f., iv. 5, v. 4); of the teaching of Jesus (i. 5, 17, iv. 3, v. 12); and of the received doctrine of God (i. 13, ii. 5, ii. 19, iii. 9).

The teacher would, then, be responsible for passing on the various traditions accurately and thoroughly, for their legitimate re-interpretation and application, and hence to a large degree for the guidance of the community in many aspects of its life (intellectual, spiritual and liturgical as well as moral). It is important that aspirants to that position should be fit for it, though James supplies no criteria for assessing this and makes no mention of a spiritual gift for teaching any more than he does for healing (v. 14). Those who so aspire should be conscious that with responsibility goes accountability: **we shall receive a stricter judgment.** The noun *krima* can mean the process of judging, and also the judicial verdict, usually of condemnation. It generally carries the latter sense when found, as here, with the verb *lambanō* (cf. Mk xii. 40; Rom. xiii. 2). However, it seems unlikely that James would hold out to all teachers, and indeed himself, only the prospect of greater or lesser punishment,[1] but rather that of particularly rigorous scrutiny at the final judgment (cf. 1 Cor. iii. 10–15). The warning is similar to that of Matt. xii. 36f., and the principle that of Lk. xii. 48b (comparison may also be made with Paul's especial severity to the Jew who purports to be a *didaskalos*, in Rom. ii. 17–23, and with the warning to Ezekiel as the watchman, Ezek. xxxiii. 1–9). If, however, the more usual sense of *krima* were to be adopted, the argument would presumably be that the prospect of punishment must

2 be accepted because the likelihood of failure is so strong: **we all err in many ways.** This clause forms the transition from the special case of the teacher to the general topic of the use (or abuse) of speech.

The special case James raised was also his own case, and he continues to use the first person plural in speaking now of a general human condition. Error in speech may be particularly crucial for the teacher, but it is not a problem for him alone. In view of the destructive power James attributes to the tongue it is surprising that he should use here only the verb *ptaiō*, to trip or make a mistake. If the choice is deliberate, it may be in order to associate with the danger apparently trivial failures as well as blatant offences (cf. ii. 10). The first half of the verse asserts a universal failure, *we all err*; the second shows this to be a warning couched in hyperbole, for it immediately introduces the qualification, **if anyone commits**

---

[1] The Vulgate reads the second person plural, *sumitis*, rather than the first, *sumimus*, presumably to avoid any suggestion that the author might himself be open to condemnation.

no error in his speech, he is a perfect man, able to bridle the whole body also. Ben Sira similarly both asks 'Who is he that hath not sinned with his tongue?' (Ecclus xix. 16), and also pronounces blessing on the man 'that hath not slipped with his mouth' (xiv. 1); a close coincidence, but not identity, of language on a common theme. The metaphor of bridling, used in i. 26 of the tongue, is here re-introduced, with a straining of the image, in relation to *the whole body*. The argument could be that if a man can control his tongue he can *a fortiori* control the rest of his body, but a better interpretation might be that in that the tongue produces instability and disunity (vv. 8, 9), the man who is master of his speech is *ipso facto* in total control of himself. The following image of the horse would bear out this interpretation: the man who puts a bit in a horse's mouth by so doing achieves control over its whole body. As in i. 4, *perfect* relates not to a higher standard of virtue for some only to attain, but to the completeness and wholeness that is the ideal for *anyone*.

The re-introduction of the metaphor of bridling leads in to 3 the first of three examples of an exercise of power like that of the tongue: those of horse and bit, ship and rudder, and fire in the forest. Of the first two, there is no parallel in biblical literature for the image of the ship; though the image of the rudder for the tongue is, interestingly, found as early as Amen-em-Opet 8: 'Steer not with thy tongue (alone). If the tongue of a man (be) the rudder of a boat, the All-Lord is its pilot' (*ANET* p. 423 f.). The nearest parallel to the image of the horse is found in Ps. xxxii. 9: horse and mule must be controlled by bit and bridle; such control should not be necessary for man. The images are however commonplace in Hellenistic literature, and thus serve to demonstrate James's familiarity with Hellenistic idiom. (His image of the ship is no indication that the author lived in some coastal town, any more than that of the horse indicates his equestrian skill!) Ropes cites some examples of the two in similar combination, as by Plutarch: '"It is the character of the speaker which persuades, not his speech." No, rather it is both character and speech, or character by means of speech, just as a horseman uses a bit, or a helmsman uses a rudder, since virtue has no instrument so human or so akin to itself as speech' (*Quom. adul. poet. aud. deb.* 33 f). Dibelius explores the images at length, their deriva- tion, association and application, and the correspondence in detail between James's use of the metaphors and that of Greek and Latin authors (pp. 185–190); it is unnecessary to duplicate or summarise his examination. It may however be noticed that the metaphors are found together three times in Philo: *De Agric.* 69; *De Opif.* 86–88, in expounding the con- trol of man over the rest of creation, both animals and plants; and *Leg. Alleg.* iii. 223 f., where the control of charioteer and helmsman is compared with that of the mind: if irrational sense takes control 'the mind is set on fire and is all ablaze'. The coincidence of ideas in these last two contexts with James in vv. 6, 7 is of course only evidence of their familiarity in Hellenistic thought. Reicke indulges here in a flight of fan- cy in reading the verses as a warning to preachers, the leaders of the Church, to control the Church itself, as the 'body' (understood as Paul's 'body of Christ', 1 Cor. xii. 27), and the 'ship' (as in the Petrine image, 1 Pet. iii. 20).

Many miniscules, and the bulk of the old Latin tradition, in- troduce the example of the horse with the conditional phrase 'if we put . . .', but the sentence would lack a correctly formed apodosis in answer to this protasis. The reading *ei de* is thus a more difficult reading than the imperative *ide*, **look**, found in other MSS including A, B, C and P, and the introduction of the latter could be explained by itacism and by harmonisation with *idou* in vv. 4 and 5b (thus Metzger, *Textual Commen- tary, ad loc.*; the reading is also adopted by Hort and Can- tinat). However, *ide* would clearly make better sense in con- text, and the rise of *ei de* from it equally be explained by itacism, and by harmonisation with the *ei* of v. 2b. On balance, therefore, it is read here, as also by Mayor, Ropes and Chaine.

4   The image of **ships** is more elaborate than that of the **horses** (where it was not even explicit whether the control thought of was that of a rider or a charioteer). The size of the ships is emphasised in contrast to the smallness of their **rudder** (the superlative *elachiston* is used), and they are **driven by strong winds**. The point of this detail might be

either that the rudder exercises control even when the winds are contrary, or that the movement of ships requires a strong favourable wind yet the real directive force is not the obviously powerful one. The rudder guides the ship **where the impulse of the steersman directs** (lit. 'wishes'). The *impulse, hormē*, could be a physical pressure or a mental decision; neither fits very well with the verb, the idea of physical pressure 'wishing' being odd, and that of a decision wishing tautologous. The former would further develop the image by introducing the idea of the control of a great ship by a man's hand; the latter would indicate the fact that behind the control exercised by the small object, whether rudder, bit or tongue, lies a human decision (so Cantinat and Dibelius).

The illustration that these images provide of the power of 5 the tongue is summarised before the introduction of the third image: the tongue is similarly **a little limb that boasts a lot** (the translation reflects alliteration in the Greek, the stylistic device for which James has such fondness, cf. i. 2, i. 17, i. 21). This boasting is not just vainglory, for the tongue's power is real, and the use of the phrase *megala auchei*, 'it boasts great things', rather than the verb *megalaucheō* (cf. Ezek. xvi. 50; Zeph. iii. 11; Ecclus xlviii. 18) may be to make that distinction. A further play on words is found in the use of the same adjective, *hēlikos*, for **fire** and **forest**, with the opposite sense understood from the context. The image could be that of fire consuming 'a huge stack of timber' (NEB), for *hulē* may mean cut wood as well as woodland, but Ropes and Dibelius illustrate the popularity of the metaphor of the forest fire in both classical and biblical literature (e.g. Ps. lxxxiii. 14; Is. ix. 18; and Philo, *De Dec.* 173 of the spread of desire like a flame in a forest). As the image of fire is used in v. 6 of the destructive power of the tongue, the idea of a devastating conflagration is more appropriate here than that of the bonfire or the hearth (for which cf. Ecclus xi. 32).

Many commentators draw attention to the dissimilarity, indeed incongruity, of the three images. Ropes observes that no note is taken in v. 3 of the size of the bit, the point there being of the exercise of control on the mouth, whereas in vv. 4 and 5 it is the small size of rudder and flame that is stressed, and these two images thus go together to illustrate the great power that can be exercised by a small object. This is hardly a convincing division in view of his own demonstration of the familiar pairing of horse and ship images, and of the presence of James's summary observation between ship and fire images in v. 5b. Mitton draws attention instead to the contrast between the images of control, the positive exercise of power, in the case of horse and ship, and the image of fire as a destructive force. Cantinat thinks that there is here a deliberate indication that the tongue can be a force for good as well as evil; it can, after all, utter blessing (v. 9). Yet such a reasonable balance is hardly present in this section, where the stress is patently on the tongue as evil in its character and its effects (vv. 6–8); and even the blessing of v. 9 is given in a situation which 'should not be so'. The images should be seen neither as alternative illustrations of a single point, nor as making different points, but as building up an argument through a chain of associated ideas: to control the tongue is to control the whole body (v. 2b), as a bit (which it is taken for granted is a small object) in a horse's mouth controls the whole body of the horse (v. 3); in v. 4 the idea of control remains, and now it is explicitly the control of a small object over a great one; in v. 5b this small/great contrast is stressed, but the idea of control gives way to that of destructive power. The very difference of the images serves to make James's point clear: control of the tongue is imperative, because the tongue is a force for evil; and the statement in v. 6 of this destructive force takes up a link from the beginning of the chain, for the power of the tongue is exercised over 'the whole body'.

6   The general sense of the statement is clear enough, but as with i. 17 it is made in a verse which is extraordinarily difficult for the translator and exegete. In the first place, the syntactical structure of the verse is obscure, and some commentators suggest that the text is corrupt. The subject, the tongue, is (a) connected with a noun in the nominative case acting as its complement, 'fire'; (b) it is the subject of the verb in the clause 'appoints in our members'; and (c) it is described in a series of three relative clauses formed with participles, it

'defiles', 'sets aflame', and 'is ignited'. Between (a) and (b) intervenes a further phrase, (d), with article and noun in the nominative case, 'the wicked world', whose function in the verse is a major difficulty. Most editors and translators of the text (including RV, RSV, NEB and JB) isolate (a) from the rest of the verse, seeing it as a comment by the author on the image of the forest fire: 'the tongue is a fire as well'. It is possible to read (d) as a further such gloss: '. . . a fire as well; it is the wicked world'; though the relation of that comment to the image would be obscure (the Peshitta provides an allegorical explanation: 'the tongue is the fire, the wicked world the forest'). To adopt this solution would leave (c) as the predicate of (b): the tongue 'appoints (itself)' as that which 'defiles' etc.; a construction which Hort judges to be impossible. Dibelius regards (b) and (d) as a composite gloss on an original sequence of fire imagery in (a) and (c), but the two may be more strictly related. The verb used in (b), *kathistēmi*, has in iv. 4 a reflexive force: he who seeks to be a friend of the world 'makes himself an enemy of God', and it can be seen to have the same force here, with the phrase (d) acting as its predicate. The tongue *appoints itself as the wicked world among our members*.

Such a decision about its structure does not, however, immediately clarify the meaning of the verse. That **the tongue is a fire** is a familiar analogy, deriving no doubt from the visual image (cf., for example, Ps. cxx. 3 f.; Prov. xvi. 27; Ecclus xxviii. 22 f.; Pss Sol. xii. 1 ff.; and *Lev. R.* 16, where R. Jose b. Zimra remarks on the inflammatory power of the tongue, despite its prone position with a water channel beneath it!). Much more problematical is the statement that the tongue appoints itself as *ho kosmos tēs adikias*. The noun *kosmos* may bear a number of possible meanings. First, it may mean 'ornament', cf. 1 Pet. iii. 3, the sense it usually carries in the LXX, except in those books originally written in Greek. The tongue would thus be 'the ornament of wickedness', i.e. that which puts a fair outward appearance on wickedness. This interpretation is adopted by Chaine, appealing to the authority of Isidore of Pelusium, *Ep.* iv. 10. A second possibility is that it means 'sum-total' (cf. Prov. xvii. 6a; *Mart. Poly.* xvii. 2), the meaning suggested by the Vulgate's rendering, *universitatis iniquitatis*, and by AG, which suggests the translation 'the tongue becomes (or proves to be) the sum total of iniquity'. Either of these interpretations would require *kosmos* to carry here a different sense from that in i. 27 and iv. 4, in spite of apparent links between the passages in the reference to defilement in both i. 27 and iii. 6 and to the members of the body in iii. 6 and iv. 1. In both i. 27 and iv. 4, *kosmos* means 'world', with the connotation of 'the world of men as hostile to God' (see on i. 27, and cf. also ii. 5). James's meaning here might thus be that the tongue, with its destructive and disuniting power, is in the individual a microcosm of that hostile macrocosm: it is 'an unrighteous world among our members' (RSV), or 'a whole wicked world in itself' (JB). Both these translations, however, disregard the presence of the article in the clause, which is an oddity of the syntax. It is presumably there to point a quite specific reference to **the wicked world** (lit. 'the world of wickedness', the genitive having an adjectival function, cf. 1 Enoch xlviii. 7; Mk xvi. 14, W; Lk. xvi. 9). It is the tongue that brings the individual man into relation with 'the world'; indeed brings the world within him, **among our members**. NEB translates: 'it represents among our members the world with all its wickedness' (cf. Ropes, and Dibelius on the meaning of the text as it now stands). As representative it is to be seen as an active agent. The tongue effects in a man the defilement that is inherent in the world (cf. i. 27, with the warning already in i. 26 that the religious man must bridle his tongue), and its effect is total: it **defiles the whole body**. The idea is presumably that it is in his speech that a man identifies himself with that total hostility to God, and shows that it is part of his inner character (cf. Mk vii. 20 ff.).

Nor is the influence of the tongue confined to the individual, for in addition **it sets light to the wheel of life**. Again the general sense is clear: the baneful effect of the tongue is felt not only on the individual but throughout the realm of human experience. The point is made, though, by the use of an expression which has no biblical background, *ho trochos tēs geneseōs*, lit. 'the wheel of birth'. (Ps. lxxxiii. 13, even granted the coincidence of the image of the forest fire in v. 14, presents only a very general similarity, and Hort's suggested links between James's expression and the wheels of Ezekiel's vision, Ezek. i. 15, 16b, 19 f., are far too tenuous.) The obvious background for the phrase is its use, with similar expressions such as the 'circle' of life, fate or necessity, to express the originally Orphic and Pythagorean theory of metempsychosis, the eternal transmigration of souls from one body to another with little hope of the desired escape. (A full citation and translation of references in classical literature to this theory, which was also adopted by Plato, is given in Dibelius, p. 196, n. 79 and 80.) James is hardly to be credited with so pessimistic and fatalistic a view of human existence, and his use of the phrase here is a further example of his adoption of a popular philosophical catch-phrase without adopting, maybe without understanding, its connotations (cf. i. 21). That this particular expression had already passed into common use as a term for the course of human life, whether or not pessimistically regarded, is demonstrated by Philo's allegory of Pharaoh's gift of a necklace to Joseph as 'the circle and wheel of unending necessity' in contrast to Tamar's pledges to Judah which represented the 'natural order' (*De Somn.* ii. 44, referring to Gen. xli. 42 and xxxviii. 25). Another Hellenistic Jewish writer judged that 'sufferings are common to all; life is a wheel; happiness is uncertain' (Pseudo-Phocylides, 27). Interestingly, the expression is also found in Rabbinic literature, thus illustrating the absorption of Hellenistic terms into so-called Palestinian Judaism: 'There is an ever rotating wheel in this world, and he who is rich today may not be so tomorrow, and he who is poor today may not be so tomorrow' (*Shabbat* 151b, cf. *Ex. R.* 31). It is unnecessary to suppose that James's knowledge of the phrase came *via* Jewish usage; what is demonstrated is its wide currency outside the strictly technical context.

As *the tongue is a fire*, the destructive effect it has on the course of human life is described in the same imagery: it *sets light* to it. Pythagoreanism taught the periodic destruction of the universe by fire (an idea adapted in 2 Pet. iii. 7, 10), but the background of James's language now becomes unambiguously Jewish, for the *wheel* is **set alight by Gehenna**. (Once again James's fondness for alliteration is demonstrated in the alternation of active and passive participles of *phlogizō* and the sequence of *geneseōs* and *geennēs*.) *Gē Hinnōm*, the valley of the son(s) of Hinnom, a ravine to the south of Jerusalem once used for pagan fire sacrifices (2 Kgs xxiii. 10; Jere. vii. 31), was portrayed in Jere. xix as the place of slaughter and divine punishment for Jerusalem. Its traditional character as the place of burning is variously derived from its being the place where the fire sacrifices had been offered, and from its being the place where refuse from Jerusalem was burned (so Mitton). By New Testament times the corruption 'Gehenna' becomes the term for the place of punishment after the last judgment, and so appears in the synoptic gospels, especially Matthew (Mk ix. 45 and parallels; Matt. v. 22, x. 28, cf. Lk. xii. 5 and 2 Clem. v. 4, and xxiii. 15; cf. the 'accursed valley' of 1 Enoch xxvii. 1 ff., lvi. 1 f., xc. 26 f.; 2 Esd. vii. 36). The word is only otherwise used in the NT at this point. James's use can hardly be derived from the LXX for, except in Josh. xviii. 16, the translation *pharagx huiou Ennom* is preferred to transliteration; but this is not therefore necessarily a pointer to Palestinian origin as the word was probably part of the general stock of Jewish vocabulary in the first century. The sense of the phrase might derive from Gehenna as the place of punishment: the tongue directs human life towards inevitable retribution, and the course of life has about it already this doomed character; or from Gehenna as the abode of its 'prince', whose evil power lies behind that of the tongue, Gehenna therefore giving it that fire with which it inflames the human realm. (In *Arakhin* 15b, God is said to summon the Prince of Gehinnom to join him in punishing the slanderer with the evil tongue.) The language is rhetorical and allusive, with an evocative force rather than a meaning to be precisely spelled out.

7   Having thus indicated the destructive potency of the tongue, James takes up another image of control: that of man over the animal kingdom. The image is similar in character to those in vv. 3 and 4. The images of horse and ship indicated the need for control of the tongue; the image of the order of creation serves to accuse men of their lack of this control. As with the earlier images, reflection on man's control of the

animal kingdom is a commonplace of Hellenistic, especially
Stoic, philosophy (e.g. Cicero, *Nat. Deor.* ii. 60. 151; Seneca,
De Ben. ii. 29. 4; cf. also Philo, *De Somn.* ii. 152 ff. and *De
Opif.* 88, cited on v. 3 above). In this case, however, there is
also a biblical background to the idea, in the account of man's
being given dominion over the beasts at creation (Gen. i. 26,
28–30, with Adam's naming the beasts in Gen. ii. 19 f.; Ps.
viii. 6–8; Ecclus xvii. 4; cf. Jubilees iii. 1–2, 15 f.). It is
probable that James's claim that every creature **is tamed and
has been tamed** is made in this two-fold form not simply
for rhetorical effect, but to indicate that the present
situation was established in the past, at creation (there is an
explicit allusion to the creation narrative in v. 9). That the
creatures are tamed **to humankind** (the construction is more
readily understood as the usual dative of advantage than as
the instrumental dative) is also an indication that man is not
responsible for this order in creation, but it is given to him.
James uses the characteristic biblical division of the animal
kingdom into four classes: **of beast and bird, of creeping
thing and of sea creature** (Gen. i. 26, ix. 2; Deut. iv. 17; 1
Kgs iv. 33; Lev. xi defines the cleanness or uncleanness of the
four classes: the class of 'creeping things' includes small mam-
mals like the mouse and weasel; James's word for *sea
creature*, the adjective *enalios*, of the sea, is not found in the
LXX nor elsewhere in the NT).

The 'taming' of creation would involve not only the
domestication of certain animals but also man's power to hunt
wild animals. The universal dominion is qualified at some points
in the biblical tradition: the food laws presuppose the in-
accessibility of certain species; Job xxxviii. 39–xxxix. 12, 26–30
describes some creatures as expressly beyond man's control or
comprehension; and some versions of the story of the fall see the
rebellion of the beasts as a consequence of this (Apoc. Mos.
x–xii; Life of Adam and Eve xxxvii–xxxix). Here however it is
unequivocally asserted to point the contrast, that **no-one can** 8
tame the tongue (whether to 'domesticate' or to overpower it).
The logical inconsistency with v. 2b, which assumes that there
may be a man who can avoid sins of speech, shows that the
language here as in v. 2a is that of hyperbole, with an understood

153

exhortation to strive to do precisely what is said to be impossible. Hermas adapts the language and thought of James in his twelfth *Mandate*: in writing of 'the evil desire' he exhorts that 'thou . . . shalt bridle and direct it as thou wilt. For the evil desire is wild, and only tamed with difficulty' (*Mand.* xii. 1. 1 f.); and he later argues that since God has subjected all his creation to man, so that he is its master, man ought to be able to master the commandments (xii. 4. 2 f.).

The tongue is **a restless evil**, *akatastaton kakon*; an odd phrase for which some texts (C, *ψ*, *33*) read 'uncontrollable evil', *akatascheton kakon*. This fits better with the context, but is probably an emendation. The adjective *akatastatos* has already been seen to be part of James's vocabulary in i. 8, in reference to the double-minded man who prays and doubts; it is quite appropriate that it should be re-introduced here to describe the tongue, which will be seen in v. 9 as the instrument of doubleness, again in relation to address to God. The tongue may be described here as *restless* because it is the instrument of this inconsistency, or because it is seen as like an uncontrolled, 'restive', beast. Hermas, in *Mand.* ii, another section of his work showing knowledge of the epistle, describes 'evil slander' as 'a restless demon' (ii. 3; cf. on i. 5). Further, it is **full of deadly poison**; a description which assumes the obvious comparison between the tongues of men and of serpents (Pss lviii. 3 f., cxl. 3, quoted in Rom. iii. 13; for the tongue as death-dealing cf. also Ecclus xxviii. 18, 21).

9, 10   At this point, James at last provides a specific example of the evil working of the tongue; and typically for this author the sin described is one of inconsistency, doubleness: **with it we bless the Lord and Father, and with it also we curse men.** James does not pause to commend blessing or to condemn cursing *per se* (contrast 2 Enoch lii. 1–4, where the man who blesses God is blessed, and he who curses his neighbour is cursed), for it is their incongruity with which he is concerned (and which would presumably for him render the blessing valueless). The theme of the contradictory work of the tongue has many parallels in Greek and Jewish sources. It appears, for example, in Prov. xviii. 21; Ecclus v. 9 f., 13 (cf. xxviii. 12); and Test. Benj. vi. 5, 'the good mind has not two

154

tongues, of blessing and cursing'. Plato warned that a judge in a competition should not give his verdict carelessly, lest he swear falsely with the same mouth with which he invoked heaven on taking up his position (*Laws* 659a); Philo urged self-examination before oath-taking since 'it would be sacrilege to employ the mouth by which one pronounces the holiest of names, to utter any words of shame' (*De Dec.* 93). A similar story is told of the servant of R. Simeon b. Gamaliel who, sent into the market to buy first good and then bad food, brought back tongue in either case (*Lev. R.* 33); and of one Pittacus who, told by the king of Egypt to cut out the fairest and foulest meat of a sacrificial animal, cut out the tongue for both purposes (Plutarch, *De Garrul.* 8. cf. the story as told of one Bias in *De Aud.* 2).

James sharpens the incongruity by reminding his readers that men **are made 'in the likeness' of God**, and so both the blessing and the curse are in a way addressed to God. The blessing of God may reflect the familiar Jewish custom of glossing reference to him in the form, 'the Holy One, blessed be he' (cf. Rom. i. 25, ix. 5; 2 Cor. xi. 31; 'the Blessed' is a circumlocution for God in Mk xiv. 61). Thanksgiving prayers, such as the Eighteen Benedictions, opened in the form, 'Blessed art thou . . .', and 1 Pet. i. 3 and Eph. i. 3 follow greetings with thanksgiving in this form: 'Blessed be the God and Father . . .'. The phrase **the Lord and Father** does not appear elsewhere in the bible, the nearest analogies being 1 Chron. xxix. 10; Is. lxiii. 16; Ecclus xxiii. 1, 4 and Matt. xi. 25, and the common form 'God and Father', found in i. 27, is read instead in a number of texts (K, L, most miniscules, the Vulgate and Coptic versions). The more difficult reading, which anyway has better textual support, is clearly to be preferred; it provides a further example of James's retaining the title *Lord* for God.

As *Father*, God is creator of man (cf. i. 18), and he created him in his own image. Appeal to the character of man as the image of God is found in Jewish ethical teaching from as early as Gen. ix. 6, and is taken up in 2 Enoch xliv. 1 f. R. Simeon b. Azzai judged reverence for the image in one's fellow men to be the most comprehensive principle in the Law (*Gen. R.* 24.

7, cited by Moore, *Judaism* I, p. 446 f. and II, p. 85). In the account of man's creation, Gen. i. 26 records God's intention as to make man 'in our image, after our likeness'; LXX, *en eikoni hēmōn, kath' homoiōsin hēmōn*. Gen. v. 27 and ix. 9 refer simply to man's creation 'in the image', *eikōn*, of God, and this is the word used in this connection by Ecclus (xvii. 3), Wisdom (ii. 23), and Paul (1 Cor. xi. 7; 2 Cor. iii. 18, iv. 4, of Christ as the image). James however adopts instead the word **likeness**, *homoiōsis*, a word rare in the LXX outside Gen. i. 26 and not found elsewhere in the NT. Possible explanations of his choice could come from what is seen to be a distinction between the two words. There could be a motive of reverence: *homoiōsis*, like the Hebrew *demuth* which it translates in Gen. i. 26 denotes a resemblance rather than an exact reproduction; man is like God, but not exactly like him (the cognate noun *homoiōma* is used to translate *demuth* in Ezekiel's vision, with this nuance clearly present, Ezek. i. vv. 5, 10, 26). Philo, commenting on the two words in Gen. i. 26, sees *eikōn* as relating to the mind of man, which is 'a god to him who carries it', but as images do not always correspond to their pattern, the author added the second term to show that 'an accurate cast' was intended (*De Opif.* 69–71). On this argument, *homoiōsis* would be used to indicate the faithfulness of the image in man. Irenaeus distinguished between man's *eikōn*, his fundamental nature as rational, and *homoiōsis* as his moral potential, which might therefore seem the more appropriate term in an ethical context (*Adv. Haer.* v. 16. 2). There is, however, no indication of any such distinction in James, nor is it likely that he avoids *eikōn* as having become a term for wisdom (Wisd. vii. 26) or for Christ (2 Cor. iii. 18). The probability is that he deliberately uses the more unusual of the two words in Gen. i. 26 to make a specific allusion to that passage (a technique he employs in i. 10 and v. 4), and so to add force to his argument. The man who uses his tongue to bless God and curse men is not only using it inconsistently, but is acting against the work of God in creating man by thus taking up a diametrically opposed attitude to God and to him whom scripture presents as in God's *likeness*.

1, 12   A final pair of metaphors make the point that the inconsistency shown in this double use of the tongue is 'unnatural'. **Surely a spring does not gush forth fresh and bitter 11 waters from the same opening?** The adjective *pikros*, bitter (as in v. 14), is often used of salt water (cf. *halukos* in v. 12); Hadidian therefore follows Mayor in seeing an allusion to the fresh and salt springs by the Dead Sea ('Palestinian Pictures in the Epistle of James', p. 228), but no specific reference seems intended, and indeed James's argument would hardly be assisted by pointing to a situation where these opposites in fact co-exist. (The same image of unnatural order is drawn on in 2 Esd. v. 9, where the mixture of salt and sweet waters is part of the cosmic upheavals preceding the End.) Similarly, **a 12 figtree cannot produce olives or a vine figs**. As with the images of vv. 3–5, some commentators remark on the incongruity of the images: blessing and cursing, fresh and salt water, are mixtures of good and bad; but olives and figs are both good. Jesus' argument, 'Do men gather grapes from thorns, or figs from thistles? Even so every good tree brings forth good fruit; but the corrupt tree brings forth evil fruit' (Matt. vii. 16 f., Lk. vi. 43 f.), would be more appropriate. Cantinat and Dibelius, however, demonstrate the popularity of such images of figtree and vine in Stoic teaching, as in Plutarch, 'We do not expect the vine to bear figs nor the olive grapes' (*De Tranquill. An.* 13); Seneca, 'Good does not spring from evil any more than figs grow from olive trees' (*Ep.* lxxxviii. 25; cf. also Epictetus, ii. 20. 18 f.; Marcus Aurelius, *Meditations*, viii. 46). This could then be a further example of James's familiarity with the popular language of Hellenistic philosophy, but the drawing of images from olive, figtree and vine is hardly surprising in the Mediterranean area. His own point is in fact quite clear: inconsistency in human speech should be as much out of the question as it is for one tree to produce a different fruit.

The final clause of v. 12, **no more can salt water produce fresh**, is unnecessary to this argument, and provides a rather lame conclusion to the section. It is also syntactically difficult, and hence there are many variants in the textual tradition. Dibelius suggests that it is a later gloss intended to bring the two images into close conformity: v. 11 spoke of the waters not coming out of the same place, but v.

12a of the trees not producing the same fruit, and so it is
further asserted that salt water cannot *produce* fresh. The
gloss could be the author's own, but he does not normally
handle his images in such a wooden fashion, and at this point
a corruption of his original text seems more likely.

10. THE WISDOM FROM ABOVE

iii. 13–18

**(13) Who among you is wise and understanding? Let
him demonstrate from his good mode of life that his
works are done with the humility of wisdom. (14) If you
have bitter jealously and selfish ambition in your
hearts, do not boast and lie against the truth. (15) This
is not the wisdom which comes down from above, but
is earthly, unspiritual, demon-like. (16) For where
there is jealousy and selfish ambition, there is instability and every sort of mean action. (17) But the wisdom
from above is in the first place pure, then peaceable,
equitable and persuadable, full of mercy and good
fruits, not making distinctions and without dissimulation. (18) And the 'fruit of righteousness' is sown in
peace for those who make peace.**

This next section also has a self-contained character, and
again reads like the development of a theme introduced in the
first chapter: the man who lacks wisdom should ask it of God
the giver (i. 5), and all such good gifts are from above (i. 17).
Now the character of that wisdom from above is described.
The transition from a discussion of the dangers of speech to a
discussion of the nature of wisdom is not an extraordinary
one, especially as the former section was reminiscent of
passages in the wisdom literature, e.g. Ecclus xxviii. 13–26,
but no precise connections are made. In particular, there is no
indication that the description of wisdom is addressed especially to the would-be teachers of iii. 1, who might have
thought of themselves as 'wise men' *par excellence.* According

to i. 5, it is open to anyone to ask for wisdom, and so here the 13
opening question of v. 13 is addressed to the readers in
general, to whoever, including no doubt the would-be
teachers, might think himself **wise and understanding**. The
adjective *epistēmōn*, understanding, is not found elsewhere in
the NT, but the combination of the two is familiar in the OT,
e.g. Deut. i. 13, iv. 6 (cf. also 1 Kgs iv. 29; Job xxviii. 28; Dan.
v. 12), and James's challenging question is reminiscent of
Paul's in 1 Cor. i. 20, quoting Is. xix. 12.

The challenge to make good a claim to wisdom is also
reminiscent of the challenging offer in ii. 18, 'I will show you
my faith from my works', but the invitation is not simply, as
might have been expected, to demonstrate wisdom from
works (contrast the recommendation of 1 Clem. xxxviii. 2 that
the wise should 'display his wisdom, not in words, but in
good works', and Matt. xi. 19, 'wisdom is justified from her
works'; no relation exists anyway between James and these
two passages). It is the **works** that are to be exhibited from
their setting in a man's **good mode of life**. The rôle of
wisdom in this demonstration is not immediately clear. The
phrase **with the humility of wisdom** might be attached to
the verb, so that the man would **demonstrate** his works with
appropriate, and wise, humility (cf. Ecclus iii. 17, LXX). It is
however more closely and readily attached to the noun *works*:
the demonstration of these works is of them as performed (the
verb is not present in the Greek) in the spirit of humility that
is 'of wisdom'. The argument will be that a man's whole
manner of life should demonstrate that his works are guided
by wisdom, and will therefore in effect demonstrate his
wisdom. (The noun *anastrophē*, here translated *mode of life*,
is especially characteristic of the vocabulary of 1 Peter, whose
author lays stress on the importance of the whole style of
Christian living as a testimony of their faith to outsiders: 1
Pet. i. 15, ii. 12, iii. 1 f., 16.) The assumption that humility is
characteristic of wisdom, and is a virtue, is clearly made in
other Christian literature (cf. the references to the humility of
Christ, Matt. xi. 29; 2 Cor. x. 1; Phil. ii. 8), but is often said to
be unfamiliar in the contemporary environment: 'There was
some place for humility in Hebrew thought, in Plato, and in

the Greek distaste for hybris; but the dominant morality of the day associated it with meanness and grovelling. It is linked with adjectives like ignoble, abject, servile, slavish, downcast and low. Epictetus names it first in a list of moral faults' (E. Osborn, *Ethical Patterns in Early Christian Thought*, Cambridge 1976, p. 32; cf. also Mitton).

14   This style of behaviour should exclude **bitter jealousy and selfish ambition**, *zēlos kai eritheia*. These two words are also found in Paul's lists of vices in 2 Cor. xii. 20; Gal. v. 20. The latter word is uncommon, confined to James and Paul in the NT (also Rom. ii. 8; Phil. i. 17, ii. 3), and its meaning is uncertain. Aristotle uses it of intriguing for political office; used generally it presumably denotes an unscrupulous determination to gain one's own ends (cf. AG). The verse opens with a conditional clause, *If you have . . .*, but logically the following prohibition would remain valid whether or not the condition were realised: boasting and lying would be condemned whether or not they arise from jealousy and ambition. The wording of the prohibition, **do not boast and lie against the truth**, is compressed and unclear. Some copyists obviously found the notion of lying against the truth tautologous, and separated the two verbs to give 'do not boast against the truth, and lie' (thus Sinaiticus). Ropes sees them as in a causal relationship, 'do not boast, and thus play false against the truth'. James's thought may be that **the truth** in this context consists in the fact that humility is characteristic of wisdom; jealousy and self-seeking will issue in boasting and lying which are both *against* that truth (cf. NEB).

Clearly James seeks to dissociate any claim to wisdom from a spirit of competition, and it might be argued that he does so because he is aware of a situation where rival claims are being made. There is an obvious comparison to be drawn with the opening chapters of 1 Corinthians, where Paul both attacks the contentiousness associated with the Corinthian 'parties' (i. 10–13, iii. 3 f.), and also seeks to provide a proper interpretation of Christian 'wisdom' (i. 18–ii. 15, iii. 18–21). Ropes thinks that the jealousy and ambition to which James refers is that of rival candidates for the position of teachers in the community, who vie with each other to be considered 'wise men'. This of course assumes a reference back to the warning of iii. 1, and a link between the two sections of the chapter. Alternatively it might be thought that James is opposing a different understanding of wisdom, of an intellectual and esoteric type current among a self-styled élite, against which he outlines the nature of wisdom in terms of practical virtues, open to all to practice. This reconstruction of the situation would rest on what are thought to be the implications of the adjectives in v. 15, and whether they indicate that over 15 against the **wisdom which comes down from above** there is another 'wisdom' which is **earthly, unspiritual, demon-like** (this last adjective, *daimoniōdes*, is very unusual, not found in the LXX or classical literature before James, nor elsewhere in the NT; its form suggests similarity rather than origin: wisdom that is 'like a demon's' rather than 'demon-inspired'). Philo contrasts an earthly and a heavenly wisdom in *Leg. Alleg.* i. 43, where God's planting the garden in Eden is taken to represent his provision of earthly wisdom for the aid of man's soul; but this is seen as a copy of the heavenly wisdom, not as opposed to it. Hermas, probably again adapting the language of James, contrasts true prophecy, inspired by the spirit of God and 'from above', with false prophecy which is 'earthly' (*Mand.* xi. 5 f.) and comes from the devil (xi. 17): here there are two rival forms of prophecy in mind. (In *Mand.* ix, a section in other respects dependent on the epistle, cf. on i. 6–8, Hermas contrasts faith which is 'from above' with *dipsuchia* which is 'an earthly spirit from the devil', *Mand.* ix. 11.)

The question of whether a deliberate contrast between two wisdoms, or two understandings of wisdom, is being made, centres on James's second adjective, *psuchikos*. This is occasionally used in classical literature in antithesis to *sōmatikos* of what pertains to the soul rather than to the body, but it comes to have a wide currency in gnosticism in antithesis to *pneumatikos*, there designating an inferior order of being and experience in contrast to that of the 'spiritual'. Those who do not partake of special knowledge and enlightenment remain at the level of the *psuchē*; that is, the merely human man living as part of the 'natural' world-order, sharing the life-force of the animals, responsive only to his senses and untouched by the divine spirit[1] (the Montanists, men of the Spirit, also described their catholic opponents as *psuchikoi* Tert. *Adv. Prax.* i. 6 f.). In the NT both Paul and Jude adopt the language for polemical purposes, turning what would seem to be the vocabulary of their opponents against them. Thus Jude describes the false teachers whom he wishes to attack (v. 3 f.) as *psuchikoi*, 'not having the spirit' (v. 19). Paul, dealing in Corinth with claims to a special spiritual understanding, describes this variously as a wisdom 'of this world' (1 Cor. i. 20), 'according to the flesh' (i. 26), 'of men' (ii. 5), 'of this age' (ii. 6), and as put forward 'in words which human wisdom teaches' (ii. 13); epithets which would add up to a comprehensive definition of what is meant by being *psuchikos*, and presumably to precisely what the group at Corinth claimed that they were not. Against this Paul describes his own preaching as of Christ 'the wisdom of God' (i. 23 f.), taught by the Spirit, and received by the *pneumatikos* but not the *psuchikos* man (ii. 13–15; he further adapts the language for his own argument in 1 Cor. xv. 44, 46).

James, then, uses in relation to his teaching on wisdom an adjective which would be taken to imply a contrast (hence the translation **unspiritual**, adopted also by RSV and GNB); and in his context there might seem to be a contrast between two forms of wisdom. However, in contrast to Paul and Jude, there is no other indication that he is opposing an alternative, and to him false, system of teaching. His opposition, in v. 14 and again in v. 16, is directed towards jealousy and selfishness

16 and their consequences in **instability and every sort of mean action**. It is not indicated that these arise from the rival claims of competing wisdoms, and indeed in iv. 1 f. such divisiveness is rather said to arise from the pursuit of individual desires. James is concerned to show his readers that any claim to wisdom is vitiated by such behaviour as he

[1] The gnostic use of the distinction between *psuchikos* and *pneumatikos*, and its possible derivation, is usefully discussed by B. A. Pearson in his monograph, *The Pneumatikos-Psychikos Terminology in 1 Corinthians*, Missoula, Montana 1973; Pearson implausibly attributes James's use of the term *psuchikos* to a literary dependence on Paul, p. 13 f.

describes: it becomes a 'non-wisdom' (cf. Ecclus xix. 22 f., LXX). His point is not that there is a different wisdom in opposition to the true one, but that a claim to true wisdom cannot be upheld in the context of an inconsistent style of life. In making this point James uses a term which he is aware has a pejorative force, and assumes to be familiar, but again uses it without its full connotations (cf. i. 18, iii. 6). Dibelius sees the three adjectives as rising to a crescendo, from 'earthly' to 'demonic', with *psuchikos* as the middle term meaning not merely 'natural' but 'sensual' (*sinnlich*; cf. NEB). They can also be seen as each carrying a negative force: wisdom claimed without appropriate works is *earthly*, i.e. 'non-heavenly', and *unspiritual*, i.e. merely human, whereas true wisdom is the gift of God; indeed it is *demon-like*, in being the sort of wisdom a demon might possess, as a demon's faith is in ii. 19 a sort of faith, but without the works in which faith is properly seen.

Positively, an outline of the real nature of wisdom shows 17 that it cannot be present in a jealous or selfish atmosphere. Nothing is said about an intellectual or doctrinal content for wisdom; James's wise men will not be the guardians of an esoteric tradition (cf. 2 Esd. xiv. 45 f.). Wisdom is understood in terms of moral virtue and practical goodness. It is **in the first place pure**, *hagnē*, a word rare in the LXX, used in the cultic sphere of the deity and everything belonging to him as being free from defilement (cf. 1 Jn iii. 3), but carrying also the sense of freedom from moral imperfection (Phil. iv. 8; 1 Pet. iii. 2). It is **then peaceable**, and thus incompatible with jealousy and selfish ambition. It is **equitable and persuadable**, *epieikēs* and *eupeithēs*, a pair of adjectives having a basic common meaning of gentleness or reasonableness, but the first being often associated with the exercise of justice and the second with the attitude of obedience. They may be seen as a complementary pair, two sides of a coin: wisdom is reasonable or gentle both in a dominant and a subordinate position. It is **full of mercy and good fruits**, as 'true religion' is seen in acts of kindness in i. 27, and faith comes alive in works of charity in ii. 15 f. Finally, there is another pair of alliterative adjectives, *adiakritos* and *anupokritos*, similar to the first pair in having a basic overlap and a nice distinction. The former is the more unusual word (only found here in the NT), and can mean 'not separated', but here its meaning may best be deduced from the cognate verb *diakrinomai* which James uses in i. 6 and ii. 4. Wisdom is without doubleness, **not making distinctions**, as it is also **without dissimulation**. James's description of wisdom is characteristic of his consistent attack on disunity, in man's character and in his approach to God and men. There is nothing here of the picture of wisdom as the child of God (Prov. viii. 30; cf. Ecclus i. 4, 9); the pre-existent agent of creation (Prov. viii. 22 ff.; Wisd. vii. 22, ix. 9); a pervasive spirit (Wisd. vii. 22–24); even of wisdom as embodied in the Torah (Ecclus xxiv. 23). It is difficult to think of James's wisdom as personified in the terms of the later Jewish wisdom literature (and maybe of the Johannine prologue); rather 'wisdom' is for him a form of expression for the sum-total of human, albeit God-given, virtues.

There are obvious affinities between James's description of wisdom and elements of similar descriptions in, for example, Prov. viii and Wisd. vii; as also with the description of the spirit of truth in contrast to the spirit of deceit in 1 QS iv. 3–11; Paul's list of the 'fruits of the spirit' in Gal. v. 22 f., his delineation of *agapē* in 1 Cor. xiii. 4–6, and of the 'elect of God' in Col. iii. 12 ff.; and with Hermas's account of the man who has the spirit from above, *Mand.* xi. 8. Particularly striking is the correspondence between parts of James's description and those of the Matthean beatitudes which have no parallel in Luke, which do not promise reversal of situations, but rather pronounce blessing on those of particular character: the merciful, the pure in heart, the peacemakers (Matt. v. 7–9); the blessing on the meek, *praeis*, too, would correspond to James's reference to wisdom's humility (*praütētes*) in v. 13. There is not, however, sufficient verbal identity to argue James's knowledge of or dependence on the Matthean passage. The probability is that the different authors, whether Jewish or Christian, share a common tradition of what constitutes moral goodness, and that they express it in their own terms. James puts his individual stamp on his list with his two alliterative and complementary pairs of adjectives, especially the second.

The final verse of the section appears to stand somewhat 18 apart from what precedes it. There is a link between the 'good fruits' of v. 17 and the 'fruit' of righteousness, and between the description of wisdom as peaceable and the reference here to the sowing and making of peace, but James now writes not of the fruit of wisdom but of **the fruit of righteousness**. Dibelius therefore sees the verse as a detached aphorism connected only by verbal links to the account of wisdom. It is however not surprising that James, seeking as he is to warn against jealousy, ambition and their consequences, should conclude his argument with a statement of the reward of peacemaking, rather than simply leaving 'peaceable' as one among the many qualities of wisdom. Jealousy and ambition are divisive; peacemaking is their antithesis. The *fruit of righteousness*, then, is the reward **for the peacemakers**. (The dative with a passive verb could be taken to denote its agent: the fruit is sown 'by the peacemakers'; but this would give little more than a repetition of the statement that the fruit is **sown in peace**, and the dative of advantage is thus to be preferred, as in iii. 7.) James's promise to the *peacemakers* inevitably recalls again Jesus' promise that they should be called 'sons of God' (Matt. v. 9); but the definition of the reward is quite different here.

Righteousness and peace are often associated in the OT (e.g. Pss lxxxv. 10 and lxxi. 7 (LXX); Is. xxxii. 17); while 'the fruit of righteousness', *karpos dikaiosunēs*, is a phrase familiar in the LXX, though usually without a precise equivalent in the Hebrew text (Prov. iii. 9, xi. 30; Amos vi. 12; cf. Phil. i. 11; 2 Cor. ix. 10; Hermas, *Sim.* ix. 19.2; a particularly close parallel to the language and ideas of James is found in Heb. xii. 11). The genitive can be read as one of possession or as epexegetic: the fruit is either that which belongs to or springs from righteousness, or is the fruit that consists in righteousness. The majority of commentators (including Hort, Chaine, Cantinat and Mitton) adopt the latter interpretation, and see *peace* as the condition from which righteousness will be produced, as fruit (by contrast with anger which, in i. 20, provides a situation in which righteousness cannot be effected). Ropes, by contrast, argues that the LXX parallels create a presumption in favour of the former sense: righteousness has itself a fruit which will be produced in the context of peace. The solution to this exegetical difficulty, and to the place of the verse in this section of the epistle, may be found in terms of OT allusion. In Prov. xi. 30 the 'fruit of righteousness' is described: it is 'a tree of life'. But in Prov. iii. 18 it is wisdom herself who is 'a tree of life'. It is not difficult to make the connection that the 'fruit of righteousness' is in fact wisdom. James's argument, assuming this connection, would then run as follows: there is no wisdom where there is divisiveness, for wisdom is peaceable (cf. Prov. iii. 7, 'her paths are peace'); it is the peacemakers, then, who possess wisdom, which is the *fruit of righteousness*. James draws on Prov. iii elsewhere in his epistle (iv. 6), and such an allusive use of the OT is characteristic of him (cf. on i. 10, iii. 9, v. 4). The promise of *the fruit of righteousness* will then be a coherent and satisfactory conclusion to this section, because it is implicitly a promise of the true wisdom from above.[1]

11. DESIRES AND DIVISIONS

iv. 1–10

(1) Where do wars and battles among you come from? Is it not there, from the pleasures warring in your members? (2) You desire and do not have: (so) you murder; and you are jealous and cannot obtain: (so)

[1] Although such allusive reference to the OT is characteristic of James, it may be that he is here reflecting an already familiar association of Prov. iii. 18 and xi. 30. In Heb. xii. 5 ff., the author encourages his readers to see their difficulties in terms of the divine chastening spoken of in Prov. iii. 11 f., the passage preceding the description of wisdom as 'a tree of life'; and he concludes in v. 11 that such chastening brings 'peaceable fruit', that is, 'the fruit of righteousness'. This sequence of thought and language could well be explained as drawing on a common connection of the language of Prov. iii with Prov. xi.

you battle and make war. You do not have because you do not ask; (3) you ask and do not receive because you ask wrongly, in order to spend on your pleasures. (4) Adulteresses! Do you not know that the friendship of the world is enmity to God? So whoever wants to be a friend of the world appoints himself an enemy of God. (5) Or do you think that scripture speaks to no effect? Does the spirit which he made to dwell in us long enviously? (6) But he gives more grace, which is why it says: 'God resists the proud, but gives grace to the humble'. (7) So submit to God; but resist the devil and he will flee from you. (8) Draw near to God, and he will draw near to you. Clean your hands, sinners, and purify your hearts, double-minded men. (9) Make yourselves wretched and mourn and weep; let your laughter be turned to mourning and your joy to dejection. (10) Be humble before the Lord and he will exalt you.

The passage here set out as a new section of the epistle contains a number of self-contained ideas which however inter-relate, and may be subsumed under the general theme of the disastrous effects of the pursuit of human pleasures, and the need for thoroughgoing repentance. (The command to resist the devil in v. 7b does not fit very obviously into this theme but its presence may be explained as part of an established pattern.) Stylistically, the harsh forms of address, 'adulteresses' (v. 4) and 'sinners . . . double-minded men' (v. 8), contrasts with the return to addressing 'brethren' in v. 11. Within the section the style changes from the argumentative and explanatory tone of vv. 1–6 to the imperative of vv. 7–10, and a division might well be made at that point, save that the language of the quotation in v. 6 is taken up in the exhortation of v. 7. There is no structural link with the preceding section, unless the echo of *zēlos*, jealousy, in iii. 14, 16, in *zēloute*, 'you are jealous' in iv. 2, is deliberate, but the transition from the subject of peace to the subject of war is an understandable one.

The first argument, that the source of violent dispute lies in the pursuit of pleasures, is presented in vv. 1–2b in a chiastic

167

structure, with the opening nouns echoed in reverse order by their cognate verbs: '... wars and battles ... you battle and
1 make war'. It is unnecessary to take **pleasure**, *hēdonē*, here as equivalent to 'desire', *epithumia*, as Dibelius does, comparing i. 14; it is obviously desire for an object that leads to striving for it, but it is the object desired that is the focus of the striving, and James in v. 3 considers the nature of this object in relation to the satisfaction or frustration of desire. Desire and its object each presumes the other, and the object here is *hēdonē*, a word used often, though not always, of sensual pleasure, and frequently with overtones of unworthy or evil enjoyment, as here and in Lk. viii. 14; Tit. iii. 3. Pleasures, and the pursuit of them, create a division **in your members.** Some commentators, including Ropes and Blackman, take this as referring to the 'members' of the community (seen under the familiar image of a body, cf. the 'fable of Menenius Agrippa', Livy, ii. 32. 9–12, and in relation to Paul's characterisation of the Church as the 'body of Christ', Rom. xii. 4 f; 1 Cor. xii. 12–26; 1 Clem. xlvi. 7, where the factions at Corinth 'rend asunder the members of Christ'). On this interpretation, the violence would spring from the competing pursuits of different individuals. It is, however, easier to understand the division as within the individual, himself in his own body torn by differing desires, and this would be consistent with James's recurrent theme of the divided man (cf. i. 6–8, ii. 4, ii. 14–17, iii. 9 f.).

This picture of man as a 'battlefield', subject to internal conflict, has parallels in the New Testament: Peter writes of 'fleshly lusts which war against the soul' (1 Pet. ii. 11), and Paul of the warfare of the two 'laws', of God and of sin, in his 'members', (Rom. vii. 21–23), and of the opposition of flesh and spirit (Gal. v. 17). The imagery of warfare is found in all four, but the identification of the antagonists differs, and no direct relationship is likely. Both the idea and the imagery are found also in Qumran, where the two spirits, of truth and falsehood, which govern all human affairs also struggle within the heart of man (1 QS iii. 17 ff., iv. 23; cf. also the location of different desires in different organs in Test. Sim. iii. 3). The idea of desire as the ultimate source of all human conflict is also a familiar one in contemporary Hellenistic literature; Ropes describes it as 'a commonplace of popular moralizing'. Plato had identified 'the sole cause of wars and revolutions' as 'nothing other than the body and its desires' (*Phaedo*, 66c) Philo sees *epithumia* as the cause of all famous wars of history and legend (*De Dec.* 151–53) and Lucian makes it responsible also for conspiracies and murders (*Cynicus* 15); while Cicero sees *cupiditates* as the source of hatred, quarrels, strife, sedition and wars (*De Fin.* i. 13. 43–44). James, then, combines two ideas, neither of which is original to himself: pleasure, and the desire for it, create division in man, and from this internal division comes external strife.

In particular, as v. 2 continues, strife arises from the frustration of desire: **you desire and do not have**. The exegesis of v. 2 involves three inter-related questions: the punctuation of this verse; the nature of the language of conflict and whether it is to be literally, generally or figuratively understood; and the possibility of textual corruption. Central to all three is the interpretation of the statement **you murder**. The UBS text and RV translation adopt the punctuation suggested by the position of the Greek conjunctions, and give a sequence of three propositions: 'You desire and do not have; you murder and are jealous and cannot obtain; you battle and make war.' This has the effect of making murder part of the preliminary stage of frustrated desire which leads to strife, and also creates a bathetic sequence of murder and jealousy in the second proposition. An alternative punctuation is adopted by WH, the RSV and NEB translations, and the majority of commentators, and gives two parallel statements of cause and effect: **you desire and do not have: (so) you murder; and you are jealous and cannot obtain: (so) you battle and make war**. No conjunction is expressed between cause and effect in either case, but such a staccato construction is paralleled in vv. 6, 13. On the other hand, the two statements would be joined by *kai* rather than being left to stand side by side; but this may be intended to make them distinct, in view of the abrupt construction of each. 'Murder' then becomes, more comprehensibly, a consequence of frustrated desire, rather than an element in that experience.

THE EPISTLE OF JAMES

The question then arises as to whether this statement, *You murder*, should be taken literally, and as reflecting a known situation in James's community. The objections to this are obvious: that it is unthinkable that murders should be taking place in a Christian community living under the law of love (Sidebottom compares Irenaeus's statement that Christians have abandoned wars and fightings because of their 'law of liberty', *Adv. Haer.* iv. 34. 4); and that James could hardly write in the consolatory and encouraging tones of i. 2 f. and v. 7 f. to a community so seriously at fault. In answer to the first, comparisons are sometimes made with other passages in the NT where murder might seem to be contemplated in a Christian community: 1 Pet. iv. 15; Acts xxiii. 12, if 'the Jews' there include Christian Jews, as from xxi. 20 ff. it might be they would; Jas v. 6 itself. Reicke suggests that the situation is one where fanatical Christians have by disruptive activity exposed others to persecution and martyrdom, and compares 1 Clem. v–vi where Christians recently martyred are seen as victims of others' *zēlos*. For this to be described without explanation as 'murder' seems, however, improbable. Some commentators (Cantinat, and apparently Mitton) suggest that 'murder' should be taken figuratively, as meaning 'anger' (cf. Matt. v. 21 f.) or 'hatred' (as 1 Jn iii. 15). The terms for **wars and battles** (*polemoi kai machai*) are commonly used in non-military contexts for personal quarrels, disputes and factions; this is not so much a figurative use, but represents a more general meaning of the words (so, e.g. the existence of rival factions in Corinth is described in 1 Clem. xlvi. 5 as a *polemos*, and disputes about the law in Tit. iii. 9 as *machai*). However, there is no evidence that 'murder' would be commonly understood in such a non-specific sense. The extension of its meaning is clearly stated in the Matthean and Johannine passages, and it is unlikely that even a Christian author who has absorbed much of the teaching of Jesus, as James has, would simply assume it (if the author of 1 Jn is dependent on that teaching, he still finds it necessary to tell Christian readers that hatred is to be seen as murder, he does not simply use 'murder' to mean 'hatred').

A more drastic solution to the problem is the suggestion

that the original text read not *phoneuete*, 'you murder', but *phthoneite*, 'you envy'. That these verbs could easily be confused in copying and textual corruption thereby arise is shown by the variant readings of the cognate nouns in 1 Pet. ii. 1, where the majority of texts read *phthonous* but B reads *phonous* (a further example may be found in Gal. v. 21, if the longer text, *phthonoi phonoi*, is thought to be original, the shorter *phthonoi* alone being due to an omission in the careless copying of similar-sounding words). This emendation would have advantages other than merely removing the difficult reference to murder: the punctuation suggested by the position of the conjunctions would be adopted with the second of the three statements now containing a natural pair of verbs: 'you are envious and jealous and cannot obtain'; and a link would be created with the idea of envy in the succeeding v. 5. The conjecture, which has no MSS support, that *phthoneite* was the original reading of Jas iv. 2 goes back to Erasmus's second edition of the Greek Testament (1519). The reading was adopted by Luther and is reflected in the modern English translations of Moffat and Phillips. Of the commentators Mayor inclines to accept it and both Chaine and Dibelius do so. It is undoubtedly the case that during the period of textual transmission before that for which we have manuscript evidence, a number of variations from the original text of the NT documents were established, but their identification can be a matter of guesswork only, and it is undesirable to adopt a reading for which, in the nature of the case, there can be no positive evidence. It must be preferable to make sense of the text as it stands.

In doing so, two points should be borne in mind. First, the object of James's attack is not war, battles and murder, but the desire for and pursuit of pleasure which he sees to be the source of them. Secondly, in making this point, he is reiterating a theme familiar in contemporary moral teaching, as illustrated above. Two interpretations of the text may be proposed in the light of this. James could be seen to address his readers not as members of a particular group but as human society in general. He is not attacking a specific argument, as in ii. 21–25, nor envisaging a possible situation arising in the community setting, as in ii. 2 ff., but draws the readers' attention to the experience of the world at large. 'Where do wars and battles (of every sort) among you, i.e. mankind, come from? ... It is when men pursue their desires and are frustrated that they, you, murder, war etc. Therefore beware of this desire for pleasure!' The familiar scene is dramatised and sharpened by direct address. The warning is of course relevant to the readers, but its relevance is not due to particular events in the life of their community, and no reconstruction of that life can be based upon it. A second interpretation is perhaps more straightforward. The theme of desire as the cause of conflict is a familiar one, and James, wishing to impress upon his readers the serious and inevitable consequences of this emotion writes of its consequences as if they were already present. Thus what is really a warning that 'If you desire, you will murder; if you are jealous you will fight' (cf. *Did.* iii. 2) is expressed as 'You desire ... you murder; you are jealous ... you battle'. The present tense and the indicative clauses are used for didactic effect (the paraphrases of both the NEB, 'you are bent on murder', and JB, 'you are prepared to kill', catch the sense, but weaken the force), and again the explanation lies in the intention of the author and not in the circumstances of the readers.[1]

It has been made clear that the desire that carries these consequences is frustrated desire, and this leads James to a new idea: that the reason for this frustration lies in the neglect or failure of prayer. **You do not have because you do not ask**; an accusation immediately followed by a second which appears to contradict the first, but is clearly intended

3 instead to qualify it: **you ask and do not receive because you ask wrongly** may be glossed, 'and even if you do ask;

[1] The comment of Kelly on 1 Pet. iv. 15, another apparent reference to the possibility of murder in a Christian community, is similar: 'He (the writer) is not naming these sins because he seriously supposes people are likely to commit them . .. his object in citing them then is simply to underline ... the world of difference between paying a penalty when you are guilty of a misdemeanour and paying a penalty which you deserve ... The more heinous the example of the former he selects, the more effective his argument'.

you still do not receive ...'. The argument proceeds, as
before, by the juxtaposing of absolute, unqualified statements.
Jesus' promise that prayer will be answered (Matt. vii. 7; Lk.
xi. 9, cf. on Jas i. 5) was unconditional, based upon a confidence in God as Father, but the experience of apparently unanswered prayer poses a problem for which James here
supplies a second explanation. In no case is the 'failure' of
prayer to be attributed to God; the fault lies with the man
who prays. In i. 6–8, prayer will go unanswered if it is the
prayer of a man who doubts (whether about the capacity of
God to answer, or about whether the object is really desired);
here prayer is unanswered because it is for the wrong object
(ii. 16 may be also added to the picture: there the 'prayer' fails
because it is not accompanied by appropriate action). This
explanation serves also to correct a possible misunderstanding of the preceding statement: 'You do not have because you
do not ask' does not mean that any request that is made will
be granted. Wisdom is a proper object (i. 5); the satisfaction
of pleasure is not. To **spend on your pleasures** is to waste
or squander whatever might be requested; the same verb
dapanaō, is used of the prodigal son in Lk. xv. 14. The
promise that prayer will be answered is implicitly qualified in
a similar way in 1 Jn: it is the requests of those who keep the
commandments which will be answered (iii. 21 f.), as also
requests made according to God's will (v. 14 f.). For Hermas's
treatment of the question of unanswered prayer in *Mand*. ix,
cf. on i. 6.

The next idea, that opposition between God and the world 4
is such that **the friendship of the world is enmity to God**,
is again quite self-contained, but can be connected logically
with what has preceded it. The act of prayer implies a
relationship to God of trust and loyalty, but prayer made in
the pursuit of pleasure expresses an attitude to the world with
which that relationship is irreconcilable. In i. 27 true religion
before God involved an avoidance of the world: here the opposition of the two is unambiguously stated. There is here
some further indication of the connotations of 'the world' for
James: in ii. 5 it related to human judgments as distinct from
God's; here it is associated with human pleasure-seeking. It is

not obvious that the pleasures associated with 'the world' are specifically those of pagan society, cf. 1 Pet. iv. 2 f., or that there is an understood contrast between 'this world' with its values and 'the world to come' cf. 1 Cor. vii. 31–33. 'The world' for James denotes in general the values of human society as against those of God, and hence the man who pursues pleasure aligns himself with the world and compromises or actually denies his relationship with God, he **appoints himself an enemy of God** (cf. 1 Jn ii. 15 f.); such people are therefore stigmatised as **adulteresses.** This pejorative address derives from the familiar biblical image of the relation between God and his people as one of marriage, on the basis of which the prophets frequently portray unfaithful Israel as an adulterous wife (Is. liv. 5 f.; Jere. iii. 6–14, 20; Ezek. xvi, xxiii; Hos. ii; cf. Mk viii. 38; Matt. xii. 39, xvi. 4). The marriage image passes into Christian use for the relation between Christ and the Church (2 Cor. xi. 2; Eph. v. 23–32; Rev. xix. 7, xxi. 9). The metaphor is usually used of the community *vis-à-vis* God or Christ, but its transference to individuals is not extraordinary, and may be paralleled in Ps. lxxiii. 27, cf. possibly 1 Cor. vi. 15. The variant reading 'adulterers and adulteresses' has early support in a large number of Greek MSS, but it is to be explained as owing to scribes taking the address literally (as indeed Hort does, thinking that the figurative meaning would be too abruptly introduced) and considering that men as well as women should be castigated for the sin of adultery. Possibly the 'pleasures' of vv. 1, 3 were understood specifically as sexual indulgence. (In fact James has no teaching directed specifically to women, but the passages where he uses *anēr* rather than *anthrōpos*, i. 8, i. 12, iii. 2, do not seem to require a reference exclusively to men!)

5   The next verse presents a number of difficulties. It appears to be intended to reinforce the foregoing argument by an appeal to scriptural authority: **Or do you think that scripture speaks to no effect?** Yet, notoriously, the following sentence does not correspond to any passage in the OT. Its meaning, too, is uncertain in three respects: it may be read as a statement or as a question; 'the spirit' (*to pneuma*) may be the subject or object of the main verb; and this 'spirit' in-

dwelling men may be understood as the spirit given at creation (Gen. ii. 7, vi. 3 LXX, cf. Job xxvii. 3, xxxii. 8; 1 QH iv.
31), whether seen as good or evil, or as the special endowment
of the Holy Spirit (cf. Test. Sim. iv. 4; 1 QH xii. 11 f.). These
ambiguities cannot, of course, be solved by appeal to the
original context of the 'quotation' when that cannot be identified. A comparison of some major English translations of the
NT provides some illustration of the variety of possible interpretations. RSV understands the sentence as a statement
about God's attitude to the human spirit: 'He yearns jealously
over the spirit which he has made to dwell in us' (cf. also
Hort, Ropes, Dibelius, Cantinat and Blackman). As 'God' is
clearly the subject of the subordinate clause, as the one who
causes the spirit's indwelling, and also of the quotation in v. 6,
it is plausible to see him as the subject of the main verb here.
The connection with the argument of v. 4 would also be clear:
the warning that a love of the world involves an alienation
from God is reinforced by a reminder of the divine jealousy.
JB reads the sentence as a statement about the Holy Spirit:
'the spirit which he sent to live in us wants us for himself
alone' (cf. Mayor), which would make a similar connection
with the argument of v. 4. AV and NEB take *to pneuma* as
subject and read a statement about the evil propensities of the
human spirit which 'lusteth to envy' (AV) or 'turns towards
envious desires' (NEB; Mitton is sympathetic to this interpretation). The train of thought would then be that the
human spirit will of its nature incline to envy and the pursuit
of pleasure and the friendship of the world, putting itself at
enmity with God; but he, according to the quotation of v. 6,
responds to this with grace and the possibility of reconcilia-
tion. Finally, RV reads the sentence as a question about the
human spirit: 'Doth the spirit which he made to dwell in us
long unto envying?', leaving it uncertain whether the question
expects an affirmative or a negative answer (Sidebottom, who
also understands it as a question, answers this with the NEB
interpretation: the human spirit is indeed by nature envious
but God's help is available).

The relation of the sentence to 'scripture' is also variously
understood. The attempt to link the question about scripture

with the quotation of Prov. iii. 34 in v. 6, with the sentence in
v. 5 seen as an aside, is normally rejected, since Prov. iii. 34
would then be supplied with a double introduction. The main
solutions are either to see the sentence as making a general
reference to the scriptural idea of the divine jealousy as found
for instance in Ex. xx. 5 or xxxiv. 14, together with that of the
endowment of man with God's spirit in Gen. ii. 7, vi. 3 (so
Mayor, Blackman and Cantinat; Hort raises the possibility of
a Greek paraphrase of the OT, of a targum type; Ropes
speaks of a 'poetical rendering' of the idea of Ex. xx. 5); or to
see it as a quotation of an otherwise unknown source, considered as 'scriptural', cf. the quotations of 1 Cor. ii. 9; 1
Clem. xxii. 3; 2 Clem. xi. 2 (so Dibelius, who however rejects
Spitta's suggestion that the source is the lost book of *Eldad
and Modad* quoted in Hermas, *Vis.* ii. 3. 4; and Sidebottom,
who is more sympathetic to this idea). Reicke identifies the
sentence as like i. 17 an imperfectly quantified hexameter and
describes it as an 'epigram'.

In attempting a solution to the problem of the interpretation of this verse, the following points may be taken into account. First, if the sentence is seen to refer to the Holy Spirit,
it would be the only such reference in the epistle. Hermas uses
phrases comparable to **the spirit which he made to dwell
in us,**[1] and he has probably derived them from the epistle. In
Mand. v. 1. 2 the indwelling spirit is called 'the Holy Spirit'
(cf. *Sim.* v. 6. 5), and in *Mand.* iii. 1 'the spirit which God
made to dwell in this flesh' appears also to be referred to as
'the Lord who dwells in you'; yet this spirit can be oppressed
and even crushed out by an evil spirit manifesting itself in
anger (*Mand.* v. 1. 2–4; cf. x. 2), and it is itself described in
terms of truth (*Mand.* iii. 1) and purity (v. 1.2). The probability
is that Hermas means by this spirit the God-given 'good self'

---

[1] The causative verb katō*ikisen,* 'he made to dwell' is read in a number of
MSS, including p 74, ℵ, A and B. The intransitive *katōikēsen,* 'he dwells'
is read by others including K, P, most miniscules, and versions including
the old Latin, Syriac and Coptic. The verb *katoikizō* is found nowhere else
in the NT, in contrast with the familiar *katoikeō* and the probability is
therefore that the second reading represents a scribal replacement of an
unfamiliar verb with a well-known one. Hermas uses both verbs.

of man, rather than the divine Spirit. Hermas may not be a
reliable interpreter of James; certainly his dualistic picture of
the two spirits has no basis in the epistle; but his application
of James's phrase may be an indication of the way it was
originally understood. It is certainly more probable that
James writes of the spirit imparted to man at creation; his
only other reference to *pneuma* is to the spirit which vivifies
the body (ii. 26).

Secondly, the hypothesis of a lost source for the 'quotation'
cannot by its nature be disproved, and certainly in the earliest
period of Christianity more books were thought to be 'scripture' than have emerged as our biblical canon. However,
James's other quotations are all from the LXX (ii. 8, ii. 11, ii.
23, iv. 6), which creates a strong probability that that would
be the point of reference here. His habitual use of the LXX
raises a third point. Certainly the idea of the divine 'jealousy',
the love of God for Israel that demands an absolute loyalty in
return, is a familiar one in the OT (to Ex. xx. 5 and xxxiv. 14
may be added Deut. iv. 24; Josh. xxiv. 19; Is. xxvi. 11; Ezek.
xvi. 42; Zech. i. 14 *et al.*), but for God to be said to **long enviously** (*pros phthonon epipothei*) would be very surprising.
In the LXX the verb *zēloō*, with its cognate noun and adjective and the compound verb *parazēloō*, is virtually a technical
term for the divine jealousy (as exemplified in all the
references given above), as is the Hebrew root *qnr* which it
generally translates. Certainly the verb and noun are also used
of men, with human 'jealousy' seen both in a good light (e.g.
the zeal for God of Phineas, Num. xv. 11, and Elijah, 1 Kgs
xix. 10) and a bad (as, indeed, in Jas iv. 2), but they are clearly
used by the translators to carry a special sense in application
to God, and this is reflected, for instance, in 2 Cor. xi 2. By
contrast, despite its similar range of meanings in regard to
human longings, the verb *epipotheō* is never used to translate
qnr, and is never applied to God (except perhaps in the eagle
image of Deut. xxxii. 11), and the noun *phthonos*, which does
not appear in the translation Greek of the LXX, is always
used of a base human or devilish emotion (Wisd. ii. 24, vi. 23;
1 Macc. viii. 16; 3 Macc. vi. 7) and so figures in the NT lists
of vices (e.g. Rom. i. 29; Tit. iii. 3; 1 Pet. ii. 1). A writer of

James's familiarity with the LXX is highly unlikely to write of God's jealousy in a way that neglects the usual terms and adopts language unprecedented and unsuitable in this context. (The same conclusion cannot, obviously, be drawn about an unknown source which he may be quoting, but if it was thought to be either a Jewish or a Christian document written in Greek, some similar sensitivity to biblical usage might be expected of it.) So far as the meaning of the sentence goes, then, it is probably to be taken as a statement or a question about the envious longing of the human spirit.

The connection of this statement or question with 'scripture' remains to be accounted for. On the occasions where James quotes the OT, his quotation is clearly introduced as 'according to the scripture' (ii. 8); 'the scripture which says ...' (ii. 23); 'which is why it says ...' (iv. 6); and, with somewhat different effect, 'he who says ... says also ...' (ii. 11). Here a question is asked about scripture, do the readers think that it *speaks to no effect?*, but no link is made with the following sentence so that it is clearly identified as the 'scripture' in question. James of course makes reference to the OT in a way other than direct quotation, that is by allusion, with the connection being established through the use of a distinctive word or phrase (so in i. 10, iii. 9, iii. 18, v. 4). Here he is using the verb *epipotheo* with the human spirit as its subject. The verb is unusual in the LXX, appearing in all eleven times. Of these, it is used in the psalms three times of the human spirit, which longs for God (xli. 2); for the courts of the Lord (lxxxiii. 3); and for the judgments of the Lord (cxviii. 20, cf. the longing of the psalmist for the Lord's commandments, v. 131, and his salvation, v. 174, where the verb is also used). An allusion to any of these would produce a coherent argument proceeding by rhetorical questions: man is torn by frustrated desires, aligning himself with the world against God. Does scripture mean nothing? Is this (according to scripture) the way the human spirit's longing is directed, by envy? The implicit answer, once the allusion is caught, is: surely not! According to scripture, the object of the spirit's desire is God, and the things of God; and scripture says, too, that God gives grace to those who come humbly to him (vv. 6 f.).

There are two major difficulties with this interpretation. First, in all three psalm passages, the human spirit is termed *psuchē*, not *pneuma*, as here. This is not insuperable. The terms are virtually interchangeable in application to man in the LXX (e.g. Wisd. xv. 11), but for James *psuchē* may have unfavourable connotations which show themselves in the pejorative terms *psuchikos* (iii. 15) and *dipsuchos* (i. 8, iv. 8; but not in i. 21 or v. 20). Moreover, James underlines the enormity of man's being on the world's side against God by referring also to God's creative gift of the spirit to man, *the spirit which he made to dwell in us*, and in Gen. vi. 3 *pneuma* is used of this indwelling spirit. Secondly, it is not clear precisely which of the psalms would be the subject of the allusion. In Ps xli. 2 the verb is used in the same form as in James, and the desire of the spirit is directly for God. However, if Ps. lxxxiii. 3, where again the verb is in the same form, were the point of the allusion, and the whole context of the psalm were in mind, its assurance in v. 12 that God gives 'grace and glory' would explain James's transition to the thought of v. 6 (and James's unusual description of God as 'the lawgiver', iv. 12, would find precedence in Ps. lxxxiii. 7). On the other hand, v. 20 of Ps. cxviii is followed in v. 21 by the statement that God 'has rebuked the proud', which could be the transitional link to James's quotation of Prov. iii. 34. Maybe the allusion is not to any one of the psalms exclusively, but is intended to make from their overall impression the point suggested above: the desire of the human spirit is, according to scripture, for God and the things of God. This interpretation of the verse cannot be said to be absolutely convincing, but it would provide a solution to its problems that is congruous with the drift of the argument in context and with James's practice in appealing to the OT.[1]

The appeal to scripture in v. 6 is, by contrast, quite 6 straightforward. Prov. iii. 34 is cited in its LXX version (not an exact translation of the Hebrew text, in which God is described as the one who 'scorns the scorners') with only one

---

[1] This argument is also presented in an article by Sophie S. Laws, 'Does Scripture speak in vain? A reconsideration of James iv. 5', *NTS* 20, 1973–74, pp. 210–215.

difference, the expression of the subject *God* for the main verb. The Hebrew text lacks an expressed subject; the LXX as we have it reads *Kurios*, 'Lord'. All the other early Christian citations of the verse (1 Pet. v. 5; 1 Clem. xxx. 2; Ignat. *Eph.* v. 2) agree with James in quoting it with 'God' as subject: possibly the tetragrammaton was written in their text and variously expressed in quotation, with *Kurios* subsequently being standardised in the MSS. The connection between the scriptural text and the proposition it is intended to support, that God **gives greater grace**, and the previous verse, is unclear. The comparative adjective would seem to indicate a contrast. If the subject of v. 5 were seen to be the divine jealousy, the point might be that God's gracious giving is even more a mark of his character than his threatening jealousy (cf. ii. 13, perhaps). If the reference there was seen to be the inherently evil desires of the human spirit, the argument would run that God's grace is stronger than this human tendency, so that it may be overcome. Alternatively, the contrast could come from the argument of v. 4: the gift of God is greater than any gifts of the world; how nonsensical it would be then for the human spirit to seek the 'friendship of the world' in envious longing! However, the strict comparative sense of *meizon* was often lost (its disappearance is demonstrated in the forming from it of a new comparative adjective *meizoteros* of 3 Jn 4), nor does the conjunction *de* joining vv. 5 and 6 necessarily indicate a contrast between them. On the interpretation of v. 5 given above, v. 6 would take the thought a stage further: the spirit should naturally turn its desire to God, and God's response to it is one of expansive graciousness or benevolence. The expression of this gracious attitude will be deduced from vv. 8, 10: God draws near to man in a mutual approach, and exalts the penitent.

The quotation is introduced for its statement that God *gives grace*, which reinforces the author's assertion. It would be natural then to take up from it the specific claim that it is **to the humble** that this gift is given; as James appears to do in the exhortation and promise of v. 10, 'be humble before the

7 Lord and he will exalt you'. The immediate sequel to the quotation is, however, an exhortation to **submit to God**

(using the imperative *hupotagēte* rather than the *tapeinōthēte*
of v. 10 which echoes the *tapeinois* of the quotation), and to
resist the devil. A verbal link is established by the repetition
in the latter clause of the verb *anthistēmi*, used of God's
resistance to the proud in Prov. iii. 34, but the exhortation to
resist the devil introduces a new idea which intrudes (as do
the calls to repentance of vv. 8b–9) into what would be the
natural order of the section. The three-fold sequence, of
quotation of Prov. iii. 34, exhortation to submit to God, and
to resist the devil, is however exactly paralleled in 1 Pet. v.
5–9, though its application and expression differs from
James's in a number of respects. Peter introduces the quotation to reinforce an exhortation to good order in the community, the submission of younger to older members. Both
submission to God and resistance to the devil are given an eschatological reference not apparent in James: God will exalt
the humble 'in the time' (*en kairōi*, 1 Pet. v. 6, cf. i. 5, iv. 17),
and their resistance to the devil is made in a situation of
suffering, which is being 'completed' by the Church in the
world (cf. Rev. vi. 9–11). The exhortation to submit to God is
made in the imperative *tapeinōthēte*, echoing the language of
the quotation immediately (and deliberately, since Peter
habitually uses the verb *hupotassō* in counselling submission,
ii. 13, 18, iii. 1, 5, v. 5); and the devil is vividly described as 'a
roaring lion' seeking his prey (imagery probably derived from
the 'passion psalm', xxii. 13).

On the other hand, Peter lacks James's promise that if the
devil is resisted, **he will flee from you**. This phrase, like that
of ii. 19b, probably played a part in the language of magic:
MM cites the command of a Christian amulet to a spirit to
'flee' (under θεύγω); and in Tobit the reaction of the demon
to a magical concoction of fish offal is also (not surprisingly)
flight (Tob. vi. 7 f. S, 16 f., viii. 2 f. BA). The promise that the
devil, unclean spirits or Beliar will 'flee from' the righteous
man is also frequently given in the Testaments (Sim. iii. 5,
Naph. viii. 4, Benj. v. 2, Iss. vii. 7, Dan v. 1; in Dan vi. 2 the
phrase itself is not used, but an exhortation to beware of
Satan is followed by a call to draw near to God, cf. Jas iv. 8),
and in Hermas *Mand.* xii instruction is given as to how the

flight of the evil desire (xii. 2. 4) or of the devil (xii. 4. 7, 5. 2)
may be effected (as Hermas is dependent on James in other
parts of this *Mandate*, cf. on iii. 8, it is probable that here
too the language of the epistle is being adapted).

This third element in the three-fold sequence is also
paralleled in the command of Eph. vi. 10–17 to withstand the
devil, standing fast in the armour of God. Ephesians here uses
the term *ho diabolos*, as in Jas iv. 7; 1 Pet. v. 8: a departure
whether by Paul or his disciple from the usual Pauline
preference of the transliteration *Satanas*, which may itself indicate dependence on an established formula. It is the
existence of this third, partial, parallel which, together with
the differences between them noted above, makes it unlikely
that either James or Peter is dependent upon the other, and
probable that they, and Ephesians, each draw on a common
pattern of ethical teaching. Either James or Peter could be
argued to represent the earlier form of the pattern: Peter's
elaboration of the devil motif with OT imagery, and his community interest, could be said to be later developments: but so
equally could James's association of the language of humility
with the idea of repentance (see below, on iv. 10), and hence
his loss of the natural language-link with the quotation, which
Peter retains, and also the absence of Peter's eschatological
reference. Resistance to the devil is encouraged, not by the
hope of an imminent salvation (1 Pet. v. 10), but by the present possibility of routing him, maybe through exorcism.
They are better seen as varying forms, rather than as
progressive stages, of the development of a common pattern
of teaching; though the close similarity of their presentation
may argue that there is some link between the communities
where this development is taking place (cf. Introduction, p.
20).

It is, finally, worth noting that the common pattern of
James iv. 6 f. and 1 Pet. v. 5 f. provides just one example of
the use made of Prov. iii in Christian ethical instruction. The
chapter seems to have been early established as a valuable
source: v. 4 is reflected in Rom. xii. 17 and v. 7 in Rom. xii.
16; v. 9 may be reflected in Heb. xii. 11, and vv. 11 f. are
quoted in Heb. xii. 5 ff.; v. 12 is quoted in 1 Clem. lvi. 4; v. 18

may underlie Heb. xii. 11 and Jas iii. 18; Gal. vi. 10 and Jas iv. 14, 17 may draw on vv. 27 f.; Polycarp quotes v. 28, Ep. x. 2; and v. 34 is also quoted in 1 Clem. xxx. 2 and Ignat. *Eph.* v. 2, as referred to above. The interruption of the natural sequence of the section by the exhortation of v. 7b therefore becomes understandable. James's quotation of Prov. iii. 34 in the interests of his argument recalls its place in a familiar pattern of instruction which is then 'attracted in'. A further intervention between the quotation in v. 6 and the reiteration of its language in v. 10 comes in the call to repentance of vv. 8–9, though such a summons is congruous with the accusation and warning of vv. 1–4. Verse 8a has the same balance of exhortation and 8 promise as 7b, but there the element of promise was probably added by James; Peter and Ephesians reinforcing the call to resist the devil with a further call to 'stand firm' (1 Pet. v. 12, Eph. vi. 13 f.). The whole verse is characterised by language which has cultic connotations, but is here used without reference to a cultic context (cf. on i. 27). To **draw near to God** was the function of the priest, on his people's behalf (Ex. xix. 22; Ezek. xliv. 13; cf. Heb. iv. 16, vii. 19), though this access is also experienced through prayer (Ps. cxlv. 18; contrast Is. xxix. 13), and pure living (Wisd. vi. 19), and made possible by divine choice (Deut. iv. 7). Here the context makes it plain that the approach is made in repentance and amendment of life, and that it meets a reciprocal response: **he will draw near to you** (cf. 2 Chron. xv. 2, 4; Zech. i. 3; Mal. iii. 7; and Hermas's quotation of *Eldad and Modad*: 'the Lord is near to them that turn to him', *Vis.* ii. 3. 4). There is no hint that the nearness of God is thought of here, as in Jas v. 8, in eschatological terms, as a nearness in time; it is rather an ever-present accessibility.

The call to **clean your hands ... and purify your hearts** might also evoke ideas of ritual purification (the verb *hagnizō*, purify, in particular is most often used in that context, e.g. Jn xi. 55; Acts xxi. 24, but cf. also 1 Pet. i. 22; 1 Jn iii. 3), but the language of cleansing is familiarly used with the metaphorical sense of moral innocence, in deed and thought (Ps. xxiv. 4 is a particularly close parallel, cf. also Ps. lxxiii. 13; Job xvii. 9, xxii.

30; Is. i. 16; Ecclus xxxviii. 10; Matt. v. 8 and Pilate's acting out
of the imagery in Matt. xxvii. 24. Hermas's call to 'cleanse your
heart from double-mindedness', *Mand.* ix. 7, is again probably
derived from James in view of the other drawings on the epistle
in that *Mandate*, cf. Introduction p. 22). The two-fold call is addressed to **sinners** and **double-minded men**; the *dipsuchoi*
could thus be singled out as a particularly heinous class of
sinners, but more probably, since the two clauses are parallel (or,
if *hands* and *hearts* be seen to relate to deeds and words, complementary), the terms are seen as synonymous. The *double-
minded* are the archetypal *sinners*; for James doubleness is of the
essence of human sin, seen in the divisive desires of the individual (iv. 1) and the 'adulterous' attempts to combine prayer
to God and a quest for the friendship of the world (iv. 3 f.).

9   The language of the following verse is also strikingly
reminiscent of the OT, the summons to **make yourselves
wretched and mourn and weep** evoking such passages as
Jere. iv. 8; Joel ii. 12 f., and to **let your laughter be turned
to mourning and your joy to dejection** recalling Amos viii.
10. No particular passage is drawn on, but the overall effect is
of a call to radical repentance deliberately given in prophetic
style. It is surprising that a verse with so familiar a ring
should contain as many as four words not found elsewhere in
the NT (*talaipōreō, gelos, metatrepō* and *katēpheia*; of which
the last is not found in the LXX either), but all are known in
other literature and none is therefore of James's coining. It is
sometimes suggested that the first imperative should be read
as a call to acts of mortification or abstinence (cf. Joel's
fasting), since the verb *talaipōreō* from which it is derived
may mean 'to afflict', but more probably it is part of a
cumulative call to sorrow and **make yourselves wretched**
for those sins for which purification is necessary (cf. Paul's
description of himself as *talaipōros* in Rom. vii. 24). There is
a striking coincidence between James's summons to the *dipsuchoi*, followed by the call to *be wretched*, and the
pronouncement 'wretched are the double-minded' (*talaipōroi
hoi dipsuchoi*) which opens the unidentified quotation
variously described as 'scripture' (1 Clem. xxiii. 3 f.) and 'the
prophetic word' (2 Clem. xi. 2 f.). So striking is the similarity of

language that Seitz has seen in this apocryphon the source of
James's *dipsuchia* language ('The relationship of the
Shepherd of Hermas to the Epistle of James'). This is improbable, since in the 'quotation' the doubt of the *dipsuchoi* is
concerned with the coming of the kingdom of God and
answered in a parable of the vine, a concern and an image that
have no place in the contexts of either Jas i. 8 or iv. 8. This
dissimilarity of interest makes it equally unlikely that the
'quotation' is dependent on James. Words of the *talaipōros*
group are not so strikingly unusual that two authors might
not use them independently, but *dipsuchia* and its cognates
are not known in any document prior to James, and the common vocabulary of James and the 'quotation' may be due to
their sharing in the idiom of a particular area (see Introduction, p. 25, and on i. 8; Hermas also couples the adjectives
dipsuchos and *talaipōros* in *Sim.* i. 3, cf. *Vis.* iii. 7. 1).

There are echoes of this verse in the later call to the rich to
weep, but the words are used there to different effect. In v. 1
the rich are called to weep in face of the afflictions
(*talaipōriai*) which are to come upon them, and the language
is that of threat, not of exhortation (cf. the 'woes' of Lk. vi.
24 ff.). In iv. 9 the summons to sorrow is seen in the light of the
foregoing summons to purification, as a call to repentance.
Hence in v. 10, when at length the promise of God's grace to   10
the humble is taken up from the quotation of v. 6, those who
are **humble before the Lord** are characterised not as the
poor (cf. i. 9 f.; Lk. i. 51–53) nor as the oppressed (cf. 1 Pet. v.
6, 10, where the submission to God seems to involve an
acceptance of the necessity of suffering), but as the penitent.
It is those who are humble *before God* in repentance whom **he
will exalt** (as with i. 9 f., there may be here an echo of the
gospel aphorism, cf. its application to the parable of the
pharisee and the publican, Lk. xviii. 14). This interpretation
of the promise of God to the humble is of interest in assessing
James's attitude to rich and poor: humility here is a matter
not of a social but of a moral and spiritual condition.

12. ON PASSING JUDGMENT

iv. 11–12

(11) Do not speak against one another, brothers. He who speaks against his brother or passes judgment on his brother speaks against the law and passes judgment on the law; and if you pass judgment on the law, you are not a doer of the law but a judge. **(12) There is one who is lawgiver and judge, he who is able to save and to destroy; and who are you to judge your neighbour?**

From a general call to reformation and repentance of sins, which are not specified but presumably are those involved in the pursuit of desires and the consequent disorders of vv. 1–4, James moves to prohibit a particular activity. The form of address also changes, from the pejorative to the personal, from the rhetorical stigmatising of 'adulteresses' to a reasoned argument with *brothers*. Dibelius would include these verses with the admonitions of vv. 7–9, but the change in address, the inclusion of argument, and the form of prohibition rather than imperative suggests that they should be treated as a new and self-contained section of the epistle.

11 The translation of the prohibition as a command to the readers not to **speak against one another** represents the general meaning of the verb *katalaleō*. This does not appear to have carried the specific meaning of *false* speaking against another, i.e. slander, in classical Greek, though it later, with its cognate noun and adjective, acquires this meaning when included in lists of vices with other sins of falsehood (e.g. Rom. i. 30; 1 Pet. ii. 1; 1 Clem. xxxv. 5; Barn. xx. 2; Hermas, who devotes half of his second *Mandate* to *katalalia*, understands it as slander; cf. also Pss xlix. 20, c. 5). However, it can also mean speaking against someone in harsh criticism, accusation or condemnation (Num. xii. 8, xxi. 7; Ps. lxxvii. 19; 2 Cor. xii. 20 classes it with vices of jealousy and faction and 1 Pet. ii. 12, iii. 16 refers to accusations that must in fact be proved false). James's meaning should also be derived from the context, and the association with passing judgment

186

suggests that he is thinking of criticism or accusation made against others. It is difficult to see how the law could be slandered; easy to see that it might be implicitly criticised. The connection of this prohibition with the previous section could be that verbal attack, whether by true or false accusation, are particular examples of the 'wars and battles' of vv. 1–2 (so Ropes). Hermas may be interpreting James in this way when he comments that 'the restless demon' *katalalia* is 'at home among factions' (*Mand.* ii. 3; this *Mandate* takes up the language of the epistle at other points, cf. on i. 5, iii. 8). Alternatively it may be understood in relation to the call of vv. 8 f.: the summons to self-examination and accusation is not to be made a pretext for criticising others and condemning others (the principle would be that of Matt. vii. 1–5, Lk. vi. 37, 41 f., but James's development of his argument in relation to the law is independent of the gospel tradition).

The man who sets himself over against his brother, criticising and judging him thereby also **speaks against the law and passes judgment on the law**. The definite article is not used with *nomos* in this section, but it is quite clear from the transition from judging the brother to judging the *neighbour* in v. 12 that a reference to 'the royal law' of Lev. xix. 18 is intended, and that this critical and condemnatory attitude is seen, like discrimination between persons in ii. 8 f., as an example of what that law is intended to exclude. To set oneself over against another in this way is to break the law of love, and this in turn must be seen as implicitly taking up a critical attitude towards the law itself, for not to keep it is to judge it to be invalid or unnecessary. The transgressor thus puts himself into the position of being **not a doer of the law but a judge**. The phrase *poiētēs nomou* would in classical Greek denote a law maker rather than one who obeys the law, cf. on i. 22. James may be conscious of this other meaning, when he describes God as the 'lawmaker' in v. 12: God and man are 'doers of the law' in different ways, and man must not take on himself the rôle that is God's; only God is above the law.

As in the argument of ii. 10 f., James is not content simply to define man's status *vis-à-vis* the law itself, but directs

12 attention to the personal authority behind it: **there is one who is lawgiver and judge**. That God is *judge* is a biblical commonplace (e.g. Gen. xviii. 25; Ps. lxxxii. 1, 8; cf. Rom. iii. 6; Heb. xii. 23); that he is the *law-giver* is a basic assumption of the Pentateuch and expressed in the Sinai tradition. (Even if, as argued on ii. 8, Lev. xix. 18 is cited with the known authority of Jesus behind it, his authority cannot be that of the ultimate law-giver.) The noun *nomothetēs* used to express this is used in the LXX only in Ps. ix. 21, though God is described in a participial phrase as *ho nomothetōn* in Ps. lxxxiii. 7 (Philo and Josephus apply these terms to the function of Moses: *De Vita Mos.* ii. 9; *Cont. Ap.* i. 284 f.; *Ant.* i. 19). The order of the sentence, lit. *one there is*, serves to stress again the oneness of God (cf. ii. 19); here he is *one* as having the sole title to the functions of law-giver and judge, and thus uniting them. (A comparable stress is found in the assertion of the goodness of God alone in Mk x. 18; and in R. Ishmael b. Jose's argument that God alone can judge alone, *Aboth* iv. 8.)

As the sole judge, God is also able to carry out his verdict, **to save and to destroy**. James here echoes the OT description of God as one who 'kills and makes alive' (Deut. xxxii. 39; 1 Sam. ii. 6–7; 2 Kgs v. 7), though his own expression of this lacks precedent in the LXX. Matthew refers obliquely to God as the one 'able to destroy soul and body in Gehenna' (Matt. x. 28, cf. Lk. xii. 4 f.), but James shows no link with the Matthean context where, anyway, the other side of the balance is not presented. Hermas may be seen again to take up the phrase from James in *Mand.* xii. 6. 3, repeating it in *Sim.* ix. 23. 4. James here describes the permanent prerogative of God, without relating it to an expected act of judgment in the future, as in v. 9. In the face of this prerogative and power, only a rhetorical question remains to be asked about presumptuous human judging: **who are you to judge your neighbour?** (the infinitive expresses in English idiom the force of the Greek participial phrase *ho krinōn*). Paul asks a similar question in Rom. xiv. 4, returning a similar answer, 'to his own Lord he stands or falls'..

13. AN EXAMPLE OF ARROGANCE
iv. 13–17

(13) Come now, you who say, 'Today or tomorrow we shall go to this or that city and spend a year there and trade and profit'. (14) You do not know the course of the morrow. What is your life? You are a mist, appearing for a little while and then disappearing. (15) Instead you should say, 'If the Lord wills, we shall both live and do this or that'. (16) But now you are boasting in your arrogance: all such boasting is evil. (17) Therefore for the man who knows how to do good and does not do it, it is sin for him.

The merchants who here come under James's attack are often seen as providing for him an example of those who seek the friendship of the world (iv. 4; so e.g. Chaine, Cantinat and Dibelius), but, though there may be an element of this, the section more probably connects with the immediately preceding verses in presenting a second instance of human arrogance. A distrust for traders or merchants is frequently expressed in the OT: Prov. xx. 23 and Mic. vi. 11 denounce the use of dishonest measures, and Amos viii. 4 f. those who can hardly wait for holy days to pass before recommencing their trade; Ben Sira is deeply pessimistic about the possibility of a merchant's avoiding sin (Ecclus xxvi. 29–xxvii. 2), and Ezekiel condemns the mercantile city of Tyre (Ezek. xxvii), as the author of Revelation later does that of Rome (Rev. xviii. 11–19). Here the merchants are specifically condemned for their presumption in laying plans without reference to God, as are the 'rich fools' of Ecclus xi. 14–19 and Lk. xii. 16–21.

This passage raises again the question of the relation between James's targets for criticism, and the composition or situation of the community he addresses. The traders envisaged here are not the small-scale business dealers of the local markets (where presumably the slave Hermas had conducted his shady business deals, *Vis.* ii. 3. 1, *Mand.* iii. 5), but men who make ambitious plans involving movement between

13

cities and looking some way ahead into the future. They are persons who belong to the mercantile world of the great cities of which Rome was of course the chief, and such cities as Alexandria, Antioch, Ephesus and even Jerusalem are also important centres; and who carry out trade between them (perhaps the *negotiatores* of the Roman Empire, who were often also bankers, landowners and workshop employers). It may be that the verb James uses to denote their **trade**, *emporeuomai*, carries nuances of the distinction between the *emporoi*, the wholesale travelling traders, and the *kapēloi*, the local retailers. It seems highly unlikely that persons of this status and influence would at this period have been attracted into a Christian community in such numbers as to constitute a group within it which is the object of special criticism. James has, moreover, reverted from the argumentative style he employs to 'brethren' (iv. 11 f., cf. ii. 5 ff.) to a rhetorical address: **Come now!** Presumably James's readers will be familiar with the people he apostrophises, as citizens of their world they may observe their activities and draw appropriate conclusions from them. (It is sometimes argued that since James seems to expect the merchants to know better than to behave as they do, they must be members of the Christian community, but the pious formula James commends to them is not a specifically Christian one, and the ability of outsiders to recognise and indeed to do what is right is admitted by Paul, Rom. ii. 14 f., xiii. 3 f., and in 1 Pet., ii. 12, iii. 13.)

14 All this large-scale planning stands, however, under the threat of the uncertainty of **the morrow**. The theme is a universal one, traceable back as far as the teaching of Amen-em-opet 18: 'Do not spend the night fearful of the morrow. At daybreak what is the morrow like? Man does not know what the morrow is like' (*ANET* p. 423). It is a reflection producing different responses: a similar end to boasting in Prov. xxvii. 1; a readiness to perform acts of charity (Prov. iii. 17 f. LXX; contrast the 'epicurean' quest for pleasure in face of the transitoriness of life in Wisd. ii. 1–9); the resignation of the Stoic, because 'no one has any right to draw for himself upon the future' (Seneca, *Ep.* ci. 5); the freedom from anxiety of Amen-em-opet and Matt. vi. 34 (Ropes and Dibelius cite further examples from Philo, *Leg. Alleg.* iii. 80; Pseudo-Phocylides, 116 f.,

and Plutarch, *Cons. ad Apoll.* 11). The ultimate uncertainty is of the time of death, as for the 'rich fools', the king of Ecclus x. 10, and the father who saves for his son's wedding feast when that son will die an infant, in the conversation between R. Simeon b. Halafta and the Angel of Death (*Deut. R.* 9). Uncertainty, transitoriness, is a perpetual feature of human existence: James shows no signs of translating it into eschatological terms (contrast 1 Cor. vii. 31); human life is **a mist, appearing for a little while and then disappearing.** This imagery, too, has parallels, in Hos. xiii. 3; Wisd. ii. 4, cf. v. 12–13; 2 Esd. iv. 24, vii. 61; and 1 Clem. xvii. 6, in the quotation of a saying ascribed to Moses, on which Lightfoot comments that this image is 'a Stoic commonplace'. (The image of smoke in Pss xxxvii. 20, lxviii. 2, cii. 3 and Is. li. 6 has connotations rather of judgment and destruction than of the sheerly ephemeral quality of life.)

Although the general sense is perfectly clear the original text of the verse is uncertain. B reads the first half of the verse as a single statement, 'You do not know what your life is like on the morrow', and this is followed by UBS. Most MSS, however, read a singular or plural article with *tēs aurion*, giving a statement, 'You do not know the course of the morrow' (so e.g. ℵ , K, ψ and versions including the old Latin and Vulgate, Armenian and some Syriac) or 'You do not know the affairs of the morrow' (so A, P, miniscules including 33 and other Syriac MSS); followed by a question, 'What is your life?' The translation above adopts the second alternative, as being the best attested, with the change to a plural article being a likely improvement upon it: the plural 'affairs' emphasises the variety of unknown possibilities. The meaning is not materially affected in any event, though Ropes feels that the first alternative would direct attention specifically to the course of the merchants' lives, rather than to the transitoriness of life in general. In the second half of the verse there are variant readings of the verb as a second person plural, 'You are a mist', (B, some miniscules and Syriac MSS) or third person singular, in either present or future tense, 'It (i.e. your life) is a mist' (L and a few other Greek MSS, the Vulgate and Coptic versions) or 'will be a mist' (A and the old Latin). Here a desire to conform the verb to the nearest preceding noun, and the familiarity of the image of

191

life as a mist would explain a change from the original second to third person readings, especially as *estē, estin* and *estai* would be easily confused. The decision here is a simpler one, but again the sense of the verse is unchanged.

15   In face of this uncertainty in life, the proper response is to commit all plans to the will of God: **Instead you should say,** (lit. 'instead of saying'; the construction looks back to the opening of v. 13, '. . . you who say . . . instead of saying . . .') **'If the Lord wills'.** It is striking that the formula which James commends to his merchants, and thereby presumably to his readers as well, is one which has no biblical precedent. The idea of the supremacy of the divine will is of course maintained in such passages as Prov. xix. 21, but SB can give no Jewish parallel to this expression of it before the eleventh-century *Alphabet of Ben Sira*. By contrast, it is part of Graeco-Roman idiom from Socrates's commending of it to Alcibiades (Plato, *Alc.* i. 135d) to the Latin tag *deo volente*; and cf. Minucius Felix, *Octavius* xviii. 11. Mayor, Ropes and Dibelius cite numerous parallels in Greek and Latin literature, and it is clear that the formula played a 'touch wood' role in popular superstition. James's commendation of a pious phrase of undeniably heathen origins may be a further indication of his own place in the Hellenistic world, though parallels to its baptism into Christian use are supplied by Paul in 1 Cor. iv. 19, xvi. 7 and the authors of Acts, xviii. 21, and Heb., vi. 3. If the merchants are indeed outside his community, it is possible that James is imaginatively thinking himself into their position: even in their own terms, they can give expression to a proper attitude towards their plans for the future (a technique of argument similar to that employed by Paul in Athens, according to Acts xvii. 28 f.). If God wills, then, **'we shall both live and do this or that'.** This clause can be punctuated so as to give a double condition, 'If the Lord wills, and (if) we live, . . .' but it is more probable that James would maintain that everything, including the contingency of life and death, is conditional solely upon the will of God.

16   As it is, James concludes to his supposed merchants, **you boast in your arrogance** (the phrase is adverbial: they 'boast arrogantly'), and **all such boasting is evil.** James

shows some interest in legitimate and illegitimate boasting: the poor may boast, i. 9, and mercy boasts in the face of judgment, ii. 13; but the boasting of the tongue, because of its effects, iii. 5, and of human presumption, because of what it ignores, are to be deplored. The merchants are not attacked for their pursuit of gain, nor for the wealth they already possess (which if they are the 'international men' suggested, would be considerable). It is not because they travel to *trade and profit* that they are in the wrong (it is simply assumed that that is what they travel for), but because they plan to do so without reference to God. As with v. 10, the interest is in a spiritual attitude, not in material or social conditions. In this, James stands closer to the treatment of the 'rich fool' in Ecclesiasticus, where 'poverty and riches are alike from the Lord' (xi. 14) than to that in Luke, where the concluding verse serves to point the parable against wealth as well as against arrogance: 'So is he that layeth up treasure for himself, and is not rich towards God' (Lk. xii. 21). In this respect too, the section contrasts sharply with v. 1–6, which is introduced in the same style, but where the rich are attacked *qua* rich, and therefore, so it seems, as oppressors. (Similarly, it is life that is transitory here, not just the rich men, cf. i. 11.)

Despite the conjunction **therefore**, the connection of the 17 last statement in the chapter, **for the man who knows how to do good and does not do it, it is sin for him**, with the situation under discussion is unclear. James might be expected to interest himself in sins of omission (cf. i. 22, ii. 26), but his merchants have not been charged with such sins, save with the omission to commit their plans to God's will. James's appeal to so popular a formula for this might be intended to suggest that they indeed know that they should do so and yet do not. James might indeed say to a man using that pious formula, 'You do well' (*kalōs poieis*), as he does to the man professing belief that God is one (ii. 19), but the use of the noun in the phrase *to do good* (*kalon poiein*) indicates that it is rather deeds of goodness that are here in mind. The saying sounds like a proverb, and is quoted by Origen in *De Princ.* i. 3. 6, concluding his exposition of Jn xv. 22 with what he calls 'that other saying' (there is no indication that he is

quoting James here). Yet even if this is so, it is not necessary
to treat the verse as an isolated saying intervening between
two sections of similar character; the explanation of its
presence may lie, as with iii. 18, in James's knowledge of the
OT. He has drawn one conclusion from the transitoriness of
life: that in face of this human arrogance is excluded (as in
Prov. xxvii. 1), and commitment to God's will demanded; he
is no doubt aware of other conclusions that might be drawn.
Prov. iii. 27–28 admonishes the reader not to put off till the
morrow the good he is able to do in the present, and in the
LXX this is reinforced by the added reflection 'You do not
know what the morrow will bring forth'. Prov. iii has already
been drawn on in this chapter, in v. 6, and probably also in iii.
18, and was, as has been said, popular in Christian ethical
teaching. It is not quoted here but it seems quite possible that
what we have is an afterthought or additional reflection by
James, based upon his knowledge of that passage. James's
therefore relates to the uncertainty of the morrow: in the light
of this, and of the scriptural command relating to it,
omissions now will be counted as sins.

14. THE COMING OF THE END

v. 1–11

**(1) Come now, you rich men, weep and wail because of
your coming miseries. (2) Your wealth is rotten and
your garments are moth-eaten, (3) your gold and silver
are rusted, and their rust will be a testimony against
you, and will eat your flesh like fire. You have stored up
treasure during the last days. (4) See, the payment of
the workers who harvested your lands, which was
withheld by you, calls out; and the cries of the reapers
have entered 'the ears of the Lord of Sabaoth'. (5) You
have lived on the earth in luxury and self-indulgence,
you have fattened up your hearts in the day of
slaughter. (6) You have condemned, you have
murdered, the righteous man; he does not resist you.**

(7) So then, be patient, brothers, until the coming of the Lord. See how the farmer waits for the precious fruit of the earth, being patient with it until it receives the early and the late (rain). (8) So you also be patient, strengthen your hearts, for the coming of the Lord is near. (9) Do not keep complaining about each other, brothers, lest you be judged; see, the judge is standing at the doors. (10) Take for an example of patience under hardship, brothers, the prophets who spoke in the name of the Lord. (11) Remember, we call those who endure blessed; you have heard of Job's endurance, and you have seen the end the Lord brought to it, for the Lord is full of compassion and merciful.

The opening of vv. 1–6 is identical with that of the previous section, and again the address is rhetorical, the author's words being for the benefit of his readers, who will draw appropriate deductions from them, rather than written in any expectation of attention from those apostrophised. However, there are striking contrasts in content between the two sections. First, the merchants are told that their arrogance is evil (iv. 16), and its folly is exposed through reflection on the general transitoriness of human life (iv. 14), but the rich men addressed here are threatened, even before their offence is described, with judgment (v. 3) and with a disaster that is both inevitable and peculiarly theirs (*your miseries*, v. 1). Secondly, in the reference to the popular catchphrase of iv. 15 there may be a suggestion that the merchants know better than to behave as they do, perhaps even a recommendation to them, whereas in v. 1 the rich are called to weep and wail; the language of iv. 9 ironically taken up where there is clearly no place given for repentance. Thirdly, the merchants were not criticised for their wealth, but for their presumptuous making of plans, but here the attack is on the rich *qua* rich: on the indulgent lives their riches enable them to live (v. 5); on their abuse of their position of power as paymasters (v. 4); and on their wealth as itself essentially worthless (v. 3). Finally, whereas the terms in which the criticism of the merchants was made had either no Old Testament background, in the use of the pious formula, or no specifically Old Testament background, in the appeal to human transitoriness, the attack on the rich and consequent exhortation to the readers not only appeals to Old Testament exemplars (vv. 10 f.), but is made in language which is prophetic in tone and appears to be consciously archaised or 'biblicised' (especially vv. 4, 7): the author does not always write in this style; his decision to do so at this point must be deliberate.

It is this feature of the section that makes it very questionable whether deductions may be drawn from it about the situation of James and of his readers. If the passage were read as reflecting actual experience, the conclusion would be drawn that James represents an agricultural community; that he speaks for or to the agricultural poor oppressed, sometimes even to death, by powerful landowners (as with the merchants, the picture is of wealth on a large scale: the **lands**, *chōrai*, on which the workmen have laboured are not just a few fields, but estates); and the setting would, from the climatic reference of v. 7, be Palestine or Syria. However, a recognition of the traditional character of James's language makes it doubtful that its details can be so literally interpreted. It could, of course, be argued (as apparently by Chaine and Cantinat) that the correspondence of James's accusations with accusations levelled in the Old Testament simply shows the persistence of such crimes, but it is more probable that James has chosen to use these terms to add particular force to his general argument. It would be preposterous, though, to suggest that James has introduced into his epistle an Old Testament *pastiche* that bears no relation to his readers' situation. In ii. 6 he appeals directly to their experience, 'Do not the rich oppress you and drag you into the courts?'; yet the vignette of ii. 2 f. indicates that they were ready, indeed eager, to welcome wealthy visitors to their meetings. The attitude of the readers *vis-à-vis* the rich members of their society was obviously not clear-cut, and James's tirade can be seen to relate to two aspects of it. Inasmuch as they experience hardship from the exercise of power by men of wealth, he assures them of the imminent downfall of such per-

196

sons in divine retribution. Inasmuch as they are ambitious to
have men of wealth among them, he recalls the sins with
which wealth is associated, and points to the real
worthlessness of riches. His adoption of the language of the
Old Testament emphasises both these points. By repeating
accusations familiar in scripture, he presents the rich as the
traditional enemies of God and of his innocent people:
therefore their judgment must be sure; and therefore too they
should be mistrusted. James did not, in ii. 1–9, positively for-
bid his readers to receive rich visitors to their meetings, but
the character of his invective here shows that, to say the least,
he would not encourage them to do so.

The invective is unqualified. James does not address 'the
rich who oppress', or 'the rich who indulge themselves',
leaving room for a possibility that there might be rich men
who, like Ben Sira's, are 'furnished with ability, living
peaceably in their habitations' (Ecclus xliv. 6). Any possible
qualification of his hostility to the rich would have to be
deduced from the fact that in i. 9 and ii. 5 he has no corresponding idealisation of poverty as such. Here, though, the 1
rich men are threatened and denounced simply as *rich men*
and therefore, so it seems, also unrighteous (cf. i. 10 f.). The
passage is comparable to similar unqualified threats in the
Lukan 'woes' (Lk. vi. 24 ff.) and in the 'admonitions' of 1
Enoch (e.g. xciv. 6–11, xcvi. 4–8, xcvii. 3–10). The rich are
called to **wail**. The onomatopoeic *ololuzō* is found only here
in the NT; in classical Greek it is used for cries of prayer or
thanksgiving, but in the LXX for cries of violent grief. It is
frequently found in prophetic tirades against foreign nations,
threat oracles clearly uttered for the benefit of the prophet's
Israelite audience rather than for the nations addressed (thus
Isaiah against Babylon, xiii. 6, Philistia, xiv. 31, and Moab,
xv. 2 f., xvi. 7; Zech. xi. 2 against Lebanon; cf. also Amos viii.
3, the howlings of Israel upon whom the end has come). Their
weeping and wailing is a recognition of the **coming miseries**. The use of the noun *talaipōria* recalls that of the verb
talaipōreō in iv. 9, but to ironic effect: there the
wretchedness, with weeping, is self-imposed as an expression
of repentance in the hope of divine forgiveness; here the

weeping of the rich can only be an expression of their horror at the disaster to be inflicted upon them (cf. Jere. iv. 8; Joel i. 5, 11; see further on v. 3c).

2–3a James's first attack is on the substance of the rich men's wealth, as itself essentially valueless; **your wealth is rotten and your garments are moth-eaten, your gold and silver is rusted.** Some commentators (e.g. Mayor, Dibelius and Cantinat) treat the perfect tenses used in these clauses as prophetic: the destruction of their riches is part of the coming misery to be inflicted upon the rich men, and so certain as to be described as present fact; but the author changes to future tenses in v. 3b, in describing the future rôle of these riches. He is more probably here concerned to insist upon the present worthlessness of material possessions, so far as man's spiritual hope is concerned: the same argument as in Matt. vi. 20–22; Lk. xii. 33 f. Mayor sees the three clauses as comprehending the three kinds of wealth, food, fabric and metals, that which 'rots' being corn and other food-stuffs, but this is to interpret the language too precisely. A general proposition, that all riches are corruptible, is expanded in relation to the common outward manifestation of wealth in clothing and personal ornament, as the visitor of ii. 2 declares himself a rich man by his gold ring and splendid clothing. Windisch deduces that James must be himself a poor man, unused to silver or gold, since these do not become **rusted** (though silver, of course, will tarnish, and both may lose their lustre if stored away). This is again to take the figure of speech too rigidly, and thereby to miss its dramatic effect: gold and silver might as well be base metals for all the worth they really are for their possessors. For the same image of gold and silver as eaten away by rust cf. Ep. Jere. vv. 11 f., 24 (which also envisages the moth-eating of splendid clothing); and Ecclus xxix. 10.

Not only are their riches seen to be worthless to the rich men, they will also be turned against them, as instruments of
3b both their conviction and their punishment: **their rust will be a testimony against you.** The phrase *eis marturion* is ambiguous, the question of whether the testimony serves to enlighten or to convict those to whom it is given must be deduced from the context. Thus the leper's sacrifice in Mk i.

44 gives information about the fact of his cure, whereas the disciples' shaking of the dust off their feet in Mk vi. 11 is a declaration against those cities which have not received them (Mk xiii. 9 remains ambiguous: the trial of Christians could serve as a means of declaring the gospel, as in Matt. xxiv. 14, or could be a sign of judgment upon their accusers). So here the corruption of their wealth could serve as a sign to the rich, presenting them with evidence of their folly, but such is the note of threat in the context of the passage that it is more likely that the corruption is seen as evidence against them (1 Enoch xcvi. 4, 7 similarly threatens the rich with future testimony against them, 'for a memorial of (your) evil deeds'). Dibelius interprets this evidence on analogy with Ecclus xxix. 10: the rust on the rich men's silver shows that it has not been employed in almsgiving; but this is to introduce a new idea, for the accusation of inhumanity is not explicitly levelled against the rich until v. 4, and then not in terms of withholding charity. The details of the evidence cannot be precisely defined; the threat is simply that the rich will stand before the judgment as men of worthless possessions; and that these will bring their own retribution, and **eat your flesh like fire**. Rust destroys by eating away at the substance to which it clings: fire similarly destroys by consuming, and the transition to this new image is understandable. A further nuance of threat may be added since the judgment of God is spoken of as a devouring fire in, e.g., Is. xxx. 27, 30; Jere. v. 14; Ezek. xv. 7 and Amos i. 12, 14. It is the judgment of God upon their worthless possessions that will really destroy the rich. Alternatively it may be justifiable to read in the allusion to fire the threat of Gehenna, the place of burning to which those condemned at the last judgment are consigned (1 Enoch liv. 1 f.; Mk ix. 47 f. and Matt. xiii. 42; cf. also Jude 7; Judith xvi. 17 for a threat very similar in its terms to James's; and on iii. 6).

The reference to fire might, however, seem abruptly appended to the series of three congruous verbs describing corruption, *rotten . . . moth-eaten . . . rusted*. To read the verse in this way is also to leave the main verb of 3c without a 3c direct object; a construction Ropes judges to be 'impossible'.

He therefore takes the phrase *hōs pur* with *ethēsaurisate*, a
reading also adopted by JB: 'it was a burning fire that you
stored up as your treasure' (so also the Syriac version; and cf.
the fool who treasures up fire in the LXX of Prov. xxvi. 27).
The thought would be that of Rom. ii. 5, of the storing up of
punishment for the time when it will be meted out (one
Vulgate MS indeed brings the 'wrath' of Romans into the text
of James); in contrast to the building up of a treasury of merit
for reward as in Mk x. 21; Lk. xii. 33; cf. Ecclus xxix. 12;
Tobit iv. 9. However, *thēsaurizō* is found without an object
in Lk. xii. 21; the transition to the image of fire from that of
rust has been shown above to be both logical and suggestive;
and 3c is best read as a brief, pregnant sentence: **you have
stored up treasure during the last days.** It is consistent
with their reading of the phrase *hōs pur* that Ropes and JB
understand *en eschatais hēmerais* as '*for* the last days': the
last days are the days of judgment; and the behaviour of the
rich is such that a weight of punishment will await them
when that time comes. This is to strain the meaning of the
preposition *en*, as is also Mitton's suggestion that the phrase
has a proleptic sense: the rich are laying up a store of punishment (implicitly understood) 'to be available in' the last days.
The phrase relates rather to the present than to the future
situation of the rich, and the period in which they now live is
thus characterised as **the last days.**

This understanding of their own time as that in which the
present age is drawing to its close, finally to be concluded by
the intervention of God in judgment, is found in other Christian writers. The difficulties experienced by the Churches
from the presence of false prophets and other teachers is seen
as a feature of their living 'in the last days' by the authors of 2
Tim., iii. 1; 2 Pet., iii. 1; and the *Didache*, xvi. 3; cf. also
Jude 18; 1 Jn ii. 18. For the author of Hebrews, it was 'at
the end of these days' that God spoke in his Son (i. 2, cf. ix. 26
and 1 Pet. i. 20), and a further, final coming is expected (Heb.
ix. 28, xii. 26 f.); Peter in Acts ii. 16 f. sees Joel's prophecy
as of 'the last days', before the day of the Lord, and as fulfilled
at Pentecost; Paul describes himself and his readers as those
'on whom the ends of the ages have come' (1 Cor. x. 11, cf. vii.

31). This, then, is the time in which the rich are laying up treasure. Dibelius understands the statement literally, and as a first accusation against them: that they are hoarding silver and gold ignorant (whether wilfully or no) of the nature of the times; it could be understood figuratively: their behaviour serves to amass a 'treasure' of punishment now very soon to be delivered. Most probably the tone is ironic, containing both ideas, and both statement and threat: the rich, even at the end of the present age, continue to amass material wealth, but what treasure it is that they are really laying up for themselves will soon be revealed. Their *miseries* are still to come; these should not, then, be understood as the 'messianic woes', the sufferings at the end of the present age that presage and usher in the age to come (which sufferings are anyway of universal scope, involving both believer and unbeliever, cf. Mk xiii. 6–23; 1 Pet. iv. 17), but as the sufferings that for the sinner follow judgment (as Rev. xxi. 8).

Thus far the denunciation has not contained an explicit accusation, but in v. 4 James levels against the rich a specific charge: **the payment of the workers who harvested your lands** has been **kept back by you.** (The majority of texts read a stronger accusation, that the wages 'were stolen', *apesterēmenos*, rather than just 'withheld', *aphusterēmenos*, but this is probably a case where a more familiar verb has been substituted for an unusual one. It would anyway be assumed that the wages were withheld with intent to defraud.) The importance of paying the day-labourer at the end of his day's work is emphasised by the laws of Lev. xix. 13; Deut. xxiv. 15; the instructions of Tobit iv. 14; and in *Test. Job* xii. 4 and Ps.-Phoc. 19. The vineyard-owner of Matt. xx. 8 follows the proper course, but Jeremiah and Malachi inveigh against the employers of their day who omit to do so (Jere. xxii. 13; Mal. iii. 5), and Ben Sira warns of the guilt that follows this (Ecclus xxxiv. 22). Jeremias describes the situation of day-labourers in Jerusalem in the first century, where they were numerous by comparison with slaves: their earnings were pathetically small and it could be 'very serious if a day-labourer found no work', and so *a fortiori* if the wages for work were unpaid (*Jerusalem in the time of*

Jesus, p. 111). James's singling out of this offence would be an indication of his situation if it were thought that he was accusing known rich persons of a known crime. It is, however, more probable that he reiterates a typical accusation against the rich as a class, and one that shows them to be in contravention of the law of God.

This effect is heightened by the two-fold **cries**, of **the reapers** and figuratively of the wages themselves, for withholding the day-workers' wages is one of those sins which in the OT 'cry to heaven' (Deut. xxiv. 15; cf. the blood of Abel, Gen. iv. 10; Heb. xii. 24; and the sin of Sodom, Gen. xviii. 20, xix. 13), because considered as particularly heinous and demanding of God's retribution. The literary character of James's reference is seen in his statement that these cries reach the ears of **the Lord of Sabaoth**, for this title is found nowhere else in the NT save Rom. ix. 29, and then only in quotation. The LXX translators with the exception of the translators of Isaiah and, sometimes, 1 Samuel, prefer to translate it as *kurios tōn dunameōn*, (e.g. Ps. lix. 5) or as *pantokratōr*, ruler of all, (e.g. 2 Sam. v. 10), and the title also fell into disuse in Hebrew and Aramaic-speaking Judaism, appearing only once in the Mishnah. Yahweh was 'Lord of hosts' as commander of the armies of Israel (1 Sam. xvii. 45), or, more frequently, of the host of heaven, the stars and angels (Ps. ciii. 21), but James was probably unaware of the meaning of the expression he uses. His adoption of it is a deliberate 'biblicising': the use of a term familiar only from the reading of the scripture, so that his own invective is given that association. The familiarity would come particularly from the reading of Isaiah, where the title appears four times in chapter v alone (vv. 7, 9, 16 and 24); a chapter containing a similarly sustained invective against the rich for their inhumanity in depriving the poor of the means, and even the place, to live (vv. 8–10); for their luxurious living (vv. 11 f., 22); and for their perversion of justice (v. 23). That this chapter is indeed in James's mind may be argued from the fact that the phrase **the ears of the Lord of Sabaoth** appears only there in the LXX (v. 9; Ps. xviii. 7 provides a less precise comparison), and it is characteristic of James to use a striking and unusual phrase to point an OT allusion (cf. i. 10, iii. 9). It may, in addition, be not too fanciful to see in the cry of the withheld wages (*krazei*) a reminiscence of the cry (*kraugē*) heard by the Lord from his vineyard in Is. v. 7. The total effect of the accusation, framed as it is, is to present the rich as a class traditionally under the condemnation of God's law and of his prophet and liable to his judgment.

From their inhumanity to others, James turns to attack the 5 rich for indulgence of themselves; the hardship they have inflicted on others is sharply contrasted with the softness of their own living: **you have lived ... in luxury and self-indulgence** (the verbs *truphaō* and *spatalaō* are virtually interchangeable, though the latter tends to be used with a more pejorative sense). The contrast is comparable to that between Luke's rich man and Lazarus (Lk. xvi. 19–21), though the rich man is not there accused of causing the beggar's suffering, only, implicitly, of ignoring it. The detail that they have so lived **on the earth** may carry the added nuance that such a life cannot last, being the life of this world and not of the world to come, as in the 'then—now' contrast of Lk. xvi. 25. The rich have **fattened up** their **hearts**: a sentence which, like that about their 'treasuring' in v. 3c, contains both statement and threat. They have fattened themselves up no doubt literally by 'fairing sumptuously every day', but to fatten the heart in Is. vi. 10 (quoted in Matt. xiii. 15; Acts xxviii. 27; cf. Rom. xi. 8; Jn xii. 40) is to make oneself, or to be made, ignorant, uncomprehending, and so beyond the scope of forgiveness.

As also with 3c the statement and threat are related to an understanding of the nature of the time, for the rich are so acting **in the day of slaughter**. However, whereas *the last days* is a familiar eschatological term, whether it is taken to denote the closing period of the present age or the final point of judgment itself, the connotations of the *day of slaughter* are not so clear. In 1 Enoch xciv. 8 f., the rich who 'have not remembered the Most High in the days of your riches' are 'ready for the day of slaughter' which is identified as 'the day of darkness and the day of the great judgment' (cf. xcviii. 10), but xvi. 1 refers to the 'days of the slaughter' of the giants, from which point the evils of the

present age begin. It is unlikely that *the day of slaughter* was a
familiar technical term for the day of judgment, even if it has
that meaning in 1 Enoch xciv. The phrase is part of an image of
the slaughter of cattle in Jere. xii. 3, cf. 1. 27; Ps. xliv. 22; Prov.
vii. 22. The term 'slaughter' is also part of the language of warfare, as in Is. xxxiv. 2; Ezek. xxi. 15; and probably Jere. xxv. 34;
and Blackman finds here a metaphor from the celebration
following a battle: the rich behave like feasting victors. On a
different line, *the day of slaughter* may be understood as a
dramatic reference to the sufferings of the poor: defrauded of
their wages, they are left to starve, in v. 4; in v. 6 they are condemned to death, yet the rich feast on unmoved (so Dibelius, and
apparently JB). Most probably verb and temporal clause go
together to provide an image of the rich as cattle, continuing to
be fattened up even into the very day of their killing (so NEB;
some texts insert the comparative particle *hōs*, making the
phrase clearly metaphorical: '*as* in the day of slaughter'). The
image again implies a threat, and the parallel structure of vv. 3c
and 5b suggests in the latter the eschatological reference of the
former: the day with which the rich are in reality threatened is
that of judgment and consequent condemnation.

6   Finally, James levels a third accusation against the rich,
again traditional, that they have abused their power in the
perversion of justice: **you have condemned, you have
murdered, the righteous man.** That those in positions of
authority, who were generally also (whether or not this is
specified) men of wealth, used their power unjustly and to the
disadvantage of innocent people weaker than they, is a
frequent complaint of the prophets: Amos v. 11 f., viii. 4; Is.
iii. 10 (LXX), 14 f., v. 23; Mic. ii. 1 f.; cf. 1 Enoch xcvi. 8.
That sinners can go so far as to compass the death of the
righteous is also a theme found especially in the wisdom
literature: e.g. Prov. i. 10 ff.; Ps. xxxvii. 14, 32; Wisd. ii. 20.
This last passage is particularly close to James: 'Let us condemn (*katadikasōmen*) him (the righteous man, *ho dikaios* of
v. 18) to a shameful death' corresponding to the accusation
here, *katedikasate . . . ton dikaion*, but the words in common
are not particularly unusual ones and in default of any other
evidence that James knew Wisdom it is unnecessary to

suggest literary dependence. In the light of these comparisons, James's accusation should be understood in general terms. The *righteous man* is not a known individual, but a representative figure. His *murder* need not be specified as due to starvation following the withholding of wages (cf. Ecclus xxxiv. 21 f.), or even, despite the reference to *condemnation*, to judicial murder (though both these ideas may be included), but as an indication of the length to which oppression may be carried (cf. the reference to murder in iv. 2). It would, of course, be open to the readers to associate with this accusation their own experience as reflected in ii. 6, but the point to be taken would then be that they stand in a long tradition of the oppression of God's righteous people by men of power (cf. also Matt. xxiii. 35); this is the light in which they should see the rich, and in which also they may hope for vindication against them.

Some commentators have followed Oecumenius, Cassiodorus and Bede in finding here a specific reference to the unjust condemnation and execution of Jesus, surely for a Christian writer the supreme example of such an event, and so seen James's invective as directed specifically against the Jewish rulers in Palestine (so, most recently, A. Feuillet, 'Le sens du mot Parousie dans l'Evangile de Matthieu', pp. 274–6, cf. Introduction, p. 13). 'The righteous one' is found as a christological title in a number of early Christian documents, particularly those with some anti-Jewish interest. The LXX version of Is. iii. 10, 'Let us bind the righteous man, for he is troublesome to us', reflected in Wisd. ii. 12, is explicitly applied to Christ in Barn. vi. 7; by Justin in *Dialogue* xvii. 1, cxxxiii. 1, cxxxvi. 1 f.; by Melito, *Homily* 72; and in the *Dialogue of Papsicus and Philo* lxix. 4 ff. Is. liii. 11, from which in the LXX the noun 'servant' has dropped out, so that 'the just one' appears substantively, is similarly applied in 1 Clem. xvi. 12 and again by Justin in *Dialogue* xiii. 7. The title appears with a quotation of Is. lvii. 1 in *Dialogue* cx. 6, and independent of OT quotation in *Dialogue* xvi. 4, cxix. 3; and may also be read in the *Odes of Solomon* xlii. 2. Precedent for it is found in the NT in such passages as Acts iii. 14, vii. 52, xxii. 14; 1 Pet. iii. 18 and 1 Jn ii. 1; and possibly also in the

THE EPISTLE OF JAMES

characterisation of Jesus as 'righteous' in 1 Jn i. 9, ii. 29, iii. 7; Lk. xxiii. 47; Matt. xxvii. 24. It is unlikely that it can be traced back to a Jewish messianic title (though 1 Enoch xxxviii. 2, liii. 6 are possible examples), and may well have developed in Christian use precisely through seeing Jesus as an epitome of the righteous, suffering people of God.[1] It would not, then, be surprising to find in an early Christian document a reference to the death of Jesus under the title 'the righteous one', but it is improbable that there is such a reference in James, and that responsibility for the death of Jesus should be just one of the charges levelled against the rich without being singled out as obviously the supreme or culminating crime (cf. on v. 11). Even Mayor, who inclines to find here a reference to the cross, admits that 'the righteous man' is primarily a generic term, whose reference is not exhausted in one individual. (Even less probable is it that there is a reminder here of the death of James called 'the Just', see Introduction, p. 38 f., though Greeven in editing Dibelius pleads that the pseudonymous ascription of the epistle might allow for the taking of such a veiled allusion, ET p. 240 n. 58.)

The final sentence of James's invective *ouk antitassetai humin*, is problematical, since it may be read as a statement or as a rhetorical question, and the subject of the verb, being unexpressed, is debatable. Those who understand the sentence as a question may take it as about the rôle of the righteous. If v. 6 were thought to reflect Wisd. ii. 20, and the wider context of that verse was in mind, this question might be about the accusatory rôle of the righteous, 'does he not resist you?' in the sense that 'he upbraideth us with sins against the law' (Wisd. ii. 12), and that is why he is to be put out of the way. The question might alternatively be a threatening one about the future rôle of the righteous at judgment: 'does he not resist you?', in testifying against the rich at that time (so Ropes, comparing 1 Enoch xci. 12, xcviii.

[1] For the history of *ho dikaios* as a christological title, see Foakes Jackson and Lake, *Beginnings of Christianity*, I. p. 4; R. N. Longenecker, *The Christology of Early Jewish Christianity*, London 1970, pp. 46 f.; L. W. Barnard, 'St Stephen and early Alexandrian Christianity' in *Studies in the Apostolic Fathers and their Background*, Oxford 1966, p. 68 f.

12, where the righteous in fact carry out the sentence upon their former oppressors). The question might instead be seen to be about the rôle of God in the judgment; will not God, who 'resists the proud' in iv. 6, Prov. iii. 34, pronounce his verdict against them? (So, apparently, Hort, who prints *antatassetai* in the capitals that indicate an OT quotation). If 'the righteous' were identified with Christ, the same question might be asked about him: will not he (the Righteous One) stand against them in judgment? (cf. Matt. xxv. 31 f.; so Feuillet). The last three suggestions require the present tense of the verb to be taken as referring to the future, but when James wishes to make such a reference, in v. 3b., he alters his tenses accordingly. When the sentence is read as a statement it describes the righteous one as either helpless before the oppressive power of the rich (so Blackman and Dibelius); or as meekly accepting the sufferings visited upon him, on the analogy of Is. liii. 7 f.; Matt. v. 39; 1 Pet. ii. 20 (so Cantinat; if 'the righteous' were identified with Jesus, the analogy would be with 1 Pet. ii. 23); or as innocent, not 'resisting' the rich by acts which have provoked their hostility (so Chaine). Ropes regards any such statement as an anticlimactic ending to the flow of accusation and threat, but the sentence is certainly more easily read as a statement than as a question along any of the lines indicated above. The statement is too brief for the nuances of accepted suffering or non-provocation to be certainly present in it, but a simple statement of powerlessness need not be seen to be lacking in force: the abuse of power by its possessors is seen most clearly in the oppression of those completely at their mercy, either through dependence (like the day-workers of v. 4), or impotence.

The statement, echoing as it does a traditional theme, would certainly be seen to be in place by a community which had some experience of oppressive power and of abuse which no doubt underlined their inferior position (ii. 6 f.). Accordingly, James now turns to address them directly, with encouragement. In the change from a rhetorical address to the personal address to *brothers* (a transition which effectively excludes the rich from the title of brethren, compare i. 9 f.), and in the change of tone from imperatives used for denun-

ciatory effect to those used to encourage and constructively to
warn, vv. 7–11 contrast sharply with vv. 1–6. The two
paragraphs are connected, however, by the eschatological
reference of each, and, syntactically, by the conjunction *oun*,
7, 8 **so then**, in v. 7. This does not indicate that a conclusion
should be drawn specifically from v. 6, but rather that a
deduction should be made from the passage as a whole. The
threat to the rich is an indication that there will be an end to
oppression, and that the readers should therefore **be patient**;
the verb *makrothumeō* denotes a patient waiting rather than
an active endurance of suffering, for which (although the
verbs are to some extent synonymous) *hupomoneō* would be
the usual expression.

The term to their patience will be supplied by **the coming**
parousia **of the Lord**. There is some difficulty in deciding
when in this chapter *Lord* is used as the title of God or of
Christ. In vv. 10 and 11, in the appeal to OT exemplars, the
reference must be to God, but *parousia* in the NT
characteristically denotes the return of Christ. It has indeed
almost the status of a technical term, being found in this connection in NT documents from the earliest to the latest: 1
Thess. ii. 19, iii. 13, iv. 15, v. 23; 2 Thess. ii. 1 (in ii. 8, 9 it is
used in deliberate contrast of the coming of Antichrist); 1
Cor. xv. 23; Matt. xxiv. 3, 27, 37 and 39; 1 Jn ii. 28 and 2 Pet.
i. 16, iii. 4; iii. 12 refers to the *parousia* 'of the day of God'.
(Ignatius seems to be the first Christian author to apply the
term to the incarnation, *Philad* ix. 2; while Justin is the first
to contrast Christ's two *parousiai, Dialogue* xlix. 8.) The
original meaning of the word is 'presence' (cf. 2 Cor. x. 10),
but it takes on the meaning of *'coming, advent* as the first
stage in presence' (AG), and in the papyri is used of a state
visit (see MM). It is rare in the LXX, used of the arrival of an
individual (Judith x. 18) or of an army (2 Macc. viii. 12, xv.
21; 3 Macc. iii. 17), but not of a coming of God. Josephus indeed uses it of such a coming, but in theophanies of the past
(*Ant.* iii. 80, 202, ix. 55). There is no certain evidence that the
eschatological coming of God in the Day of the Lord was
referred to by this term in pre-Christian, Greek-speaking
Judaism; Cantinat who interprets v. 8 in that sense, cites

Test. Ab. xiii; Test. Judah xxii. 2; 2 Baruch lv. 6 (cf. xxx. 1, of the Messiah), but all these are subject to uncertainties of date, text, or possible Christian influence. Blackman, who like Cantinat, is impressed by the meaning of *kurios* in the context of vv. 10 and 11, comments that 'an interpretation of the phrase in purely Jewish terms ... cannot be entirely ruled out', and this is so, but the strong probability must be that in a Christian document the phrase *parousia tou kuriou* would be understood as denoting the return of Christ, however else that title might be used in the surrounding context.

This coming of Christ is described in v. 8 as **near** (*ēngiken*, the perfect tense of the verb *engizō*): a fact implicit in that the rich are living 'in the last days', but now clearly stated. A confidence, variously expressed, that the eschaton is near, is found in other parts of the New Testament: Jesus is recorded as preaching that 'the kingdom of God is near' (Mk i. 15, again using *ēngiken*, with parallel in Matt. iv. 17; though see C. H. Dodd, *The Parables of the Kingdom*, revised edn London 1961, pp. 36 f. for the argument that Jesus' original teaching was that the kingdom had come); as had John the Baptist (Matt. iii. 2); and as commissioning others to preach the same (Matt. x. 7; Lk. x. 9, 11). Mk xiii. 39 is understood in Lk. xxi. 31 as similarly declaring the nearness of the kingdom, cf. Lk. xxi. 28; that 'the day' is near is affirmed in Rom. xiii. 12, figuratively (and in v. 11 'salvation is nearer'), and in Heb. x. 25; in Phil. iv. 5 'the Lord is near'; as is 'the time' in Rev. i. 3, xxii. 10; and 'the end of all things' in 1 Pet. iv. 7. (In all these examples the verb *engizō* or adjective *engus* is used; comparison may also be made with Paul's apparent expectation that he and at least some of his readers would be alive at the Lord's coming, 1 Thess. iv. 15–17; 1 Cor. xv. 51 f.) A declaration of the nearness of the End seems often to be associated with the experience, or expectation, of suffering, and therefore with the assurance that this will not have to be long endured: so in Mk xiii. 29, Lk. xxi. 31 the declaration follows a description of widespread disaster, including the persecution of Christians (Mk xiii. 9–13, Lk. xxi. 12–19). In 1 Pet. iv. 12 ff. the readers are warned of a coming 'fiery trial' when they may have to suffer *hōs Christianos*, with judgment

beginning 'at the house of God', but iv. 7 assumes that the
end is at hand; in Rev. vi. 9–11 the martyrs must wait for
their full number to be made up, but in xxii. 10 the time is at
hand, and the Lord assures the seer that he is coming 'quickly' (xxii. 20); less obviously, in Heb. x. 32 ff. the readers are
reminded of their early trouble, and that they have need of endurance; they have 'not yet resisted unto blood' (xii. 4), but
may perhaps be called upon to do so, and the day is drawing
near (x. 25).

James's reiterated call to patience until the Lord comes,
and his encouragement to **strengthen your hearts**, might
seem to fit into this pattern, but if he similarly envisaged his
readers as suffering under attack from outside, his parable of
the farmer would be a singularly inept illustration. *The
farmer* is in no sense persecuted by the rotation of the seasons
and the variation of the climate; he simply waits for these to
take their necessary and familiar course (there is no hint at
this point of an extraordinary interruption such as Elijah's
drought!). The hardships he may suffer in the process are
those of everyday life. It seems probable that James is here
adapting a familiar theme to different circumstances. His
readers are not called upon to endure the acute suffering of a
direct attack upon them, but this does not mean that they
need abandon the hope of the Lord's coming of which such
suffering was thought to be an indication. They are involved
in the perennial difficulties of ordinary, daily human life, and
in this situation, too, confidence that the Lord is coming soon
may be kept alive (cf. on i. 2–4, 27, and Intro. p. 28 f.).
James's choice of illustration is consistent with his use of the
verb *makrothumeō* in addressing his readers. Presumably,
therefore, the oppression which they experience from the rich
should be seen not in terms of an extraordinary outburst of
persecution, but of the continual pressure exercised by the
powerful upon those in an inferior social and economic situation. To reiterate a traditional hope in changed circumstances
is not to render that hope merely a conventional expression;
nor should James's counsel to perseverance through the continuing trials of everyday life be taken as an admission that
the *parousia* is delayed. There is no indication that they must

strengthen their hearts because they have to wait longer than expected: (as Mitton; contrast 2 Pet. iii. 3–10, where the author tacitly admits what he attacks others for saying, that the Lord is coming less immediately than originally thought); James's affirmation that the coming of the Lord is near contains no hint of how its nearness may be calculated (so also A. L. Moore, *The Parousia in the New Testament*, Leiden 1966, pp. 149–51).

James's farmer patiently waits for his crops to receive **the early and the late (rain)**. He could be a tenant farmer, working the land allotted to him, or a permanent employee like the vinedresser of Lk. xiii. 6–8. The parable is often thought to be an indication of the geographical situation of James and his readers, for the two significant rainfalls are a characteristic phenomenon of the climate of Palestine and Southern Syria, the *early* rain falling in late October or early November, to prepare the hard ground for sowing and to enable seeds to germinate, the *late* rain falling in April and May and determining the size of the harvest by assisting the fruit to ripen and mature. The importance in Palestine of these two rainfalls is reflected in the tractate *Taanith* in the Mishnah, sections i. 1–7 defining the dates for prayer for the two rainfalls (quoting Joel ii. 23 in i. 2), and iii. 1–3 ruling when the *shofar* should be blown because drought threatens. By contrast, the peculiarity of the expression to later copyists is reflected in the variety of the textual tradition at this point. The majority of Greek MSS, including A, K, L, P, ψ, and the Syriac versions, read *hueton*, rain, but in texts of both the Alexandrian and Western traditions no noun is present, e.g. 𝔭 74, B, the old Latin and Vulgate, and some Coptic MSS; and yet others, notably א , read *karpon*, fruit, instead (the sense would then be that the farmer waits until he receives the earlier and later harvests, of barley and wheat, rather than that he waits until the fruit has itself received the rains). UBS adopts the second and shortest reading, arguing that the alternative nouns would have been supplied to clarify its ambiguity: *hueton* from its familiarity in the LXX (the phrase appears in Deut. xi. 14; Jere. v. 24; Hos. vi. 3; Joel ii. 23; Zech. x. 1) or, additionally and in the case of the Syriac MSS, from

actual knowledge of the phenomena; *karpon* is a guess by
Egyptian scribes unfamiliar with the climatic conditions, but
echoing the use of the two adjectives in some classical
literature in relation to early and late crops (the only biblical
precedent would be the reference in Jere. xxiv. 2; Hos. ix. 10
to 'early' figs). Alternatively, *hueton* might have been in the
original text, as in all the LXX passages cited, and have been
omitted or replaced because of its seeming oddity to the
copyists. In either event, it is to the double rainfall that James
refers. The question is whether this reference derives from actual experience or represents a literary allusion. The former is
supported, among others, by Hadidian ('Palestinian Pictures
in the Epistle of James', p. 228) and Ropes (*ad loc.*, and p. 38 f.),
who argues that a literary allusion would be out of keeping
with the direct appeal of the verses, (the readers could hardly
be asked to 'observe' something not in their own experience),
and that the absence of the phrase from the writings of the
Apostolic Fathers and early Apologists shows that it had no
currency in Christian religious vocabulary, and would
therefore be unfamiliar to readers outside a particular
geographical area. However, the 'biblicist' language of vv.
1–6, and the appeal to OT exemplars in vv. 10 f., supports the
notion of a literary reference. Familiarity with the phrase
would come from a knowledge of a LXX, and Dibelius notes
in addition that Deut. xi. 14 is part of the Shema, and hence,
too, the expression would be familiar in a liturgical context to
anyone with some contact with the synagogue.[1]

The example of a farmer, waiting patiently for his harvest
in the circumstances of ordinary life, would of itself illustrate
James's instruction. His presentation of this example in
language consciously scriptural gives it extra dimension: first,
by again setting his instruction to his readers, and their
experience, in relation to tradition; and secondly, because *the
early and the late rain* is always in the OT explicitly the gift

---

[1] For the retention of reference to 'the former and the latter rain' in a
liturgical context where it would be wholly unfamiliar in actual
experience, cf. John Keble's rogationtide hymn, *Hymns Ancient and
Modern*, revised edn London 1950, no. 144 v. 3; and the thanksgiving for
rain in *The Book of Common Prayer*.

of God, and in Hos. vi. 3, indeed, an image of the coming of God, the farmer's waiting is seen to be even more closely analogous to their own. He waits upon God the giver of rain, and they may wait upon the coming of the Lord.

Between James's parable with its application, and his 9 exemplars of vv. 10 f., appears a warning against mutual recrimination: **do not keep complaining about each other, brothers.** Its introduction seems to intrude into the illustrative material, and Dibelius suggests that it is an independent saying, attracted into the context by the similarity of its eschatological sanction to that of v. 8: the coming of the Lord is near; *the judge is standing at the doors.* It is not, however, a saying inappropriate in the context, for James seeks to encourage and strengthen his community in its everyday trials, and one of the perennial sources of weakness to a community is internal bickering and fault-finding (cf. the extreme case of 1 Cor. vi. 1–8; the author of Hebrews also adds to his encouragement to personal firmness a warning against the weakening of community fellowship, in the light of the approaching 'day', x. 23, 25). A reiteration of the admonition of iv. 11 would not be out of place in this context. As in iv. 11 f., the readers are reminded to take account of a **judge**; and again the passage presents a problem of identification. In Mk xiii. 29, Matt. xxiv. 33 it is not specified who, or what, is **at the doors**; the parallel in Lk. xxi. 31 reads 'the kingdom of God is near'. In Rev. iii. 20, where the language seems liturgical rather than eschatological (if such a distinction is appropriate) the one who *stands at the door* is the exalted Lord of the opening vision. Although Christ may be presented in the NT, as in Matt. xxv. 31 f., as judging, the phrase *the judge at the doors* would not seem to have the established christological connection that *parousia* has, and in view of James's insistence in iv. 12 that there is one judge, and one alone, it is probable that his reminder here is of the coming judgment of God. (There is, of course, no scope for a definition of the relation between the coming of Christ and the judgment of God; all that can be said is that both are elements of James's eschatological expectation.)

After providing a parable illustrating patience, James refers

10 his readers to a known **example of patience under hardship** (*lit.* 'of hardship and of patience'; the phrase is understood as a hendiadys), in the experience of **the prophets.** The NT itself provides evidence of a growing tradition that a prophet will be also a martyr (Matt. v. 12, Lk. vi. 22 f.; Lk. xi. 49, viii. 33; Matt. xxiii. 39–41, 34 f.; Acts vii. 52; 1 Thess ii. 15), an idea not characteristic of the OT, where, although Jeremiah is clearly a suffering figure, the only prophet to meet a violent death is Zechariah the son of Jehoiada (2 Chron. xxxvi. 16). Legends grew up of the manner of the prophets' deaths; the *Ascension of Isaiah* contains an account of his being sawn apart[1] (reflected, perhaps, in Heb. xi. 37), and cf. M. R. James, *The Lost Apocrypha of the Old Testament*, London 1920, pp. 68 f., 75, for references to the martyrdoms of Ezekiel and Zechariah. If it was in this sort of suffering that the prophets were presented as examples to James's readers, the situation of the latter might be thought to be one of more acute crisis than has been suggested. However, James does not indicate that his reference is specifically to the manner of the prophets' deaths, and his term *kakopatheia* is a general one for *hardship* and misfortune in various forms, not just for acute suffering. (AG supports the alternative meaning 'perseverance' for *kakopatheia* here, arguing that this is the preferred meaning in later texts and inscriptions: the prophets would then be examples of 'perseverance and patience', with even less indication of the circumstances in which such qualities were exercised.) James glosses his appeal to the prophets with the reminder that they **spoke in the name of the Lord,** understanding their own words to have the authority of God's, and so prefacing them with the characteristic 'thus saith the Lord' (e.g. Amos i. 3; Is. i. 2; Jere. ii. 4 f.; cf. Acts xxi. 11; Rev. ii. 1), and this suggests that he is thinking of the whole course of the prophetic mission, with its continual difficulties, struggles against opposition and rejection, and in the case of Jeremiah, temptations to despair and give up (Jere. xx. 7–9). It is in the course of their lives, rather than in their deaths, that the prophets serve as an *example of patience.*

[1] Found in Charles, *Apocrypha and Pseudepigrapha II,* as Martyrdom of Isaiah, chapter v.

Further, James reminds his readers of the high regard in which perseverance is familiarly held: **we call those who 11 endure blessed.** At this point, James employs the verb *hupomoneō* with its stronger connotations of the endurance of actual suffering, but in doing so he is probably reproducing traditional language, perhaps even quoting a current macarism, cf. on i. 12. As in i. 12 James seemed to take advantage of an ambiguous word, *peirasmos*, to present endurance in terms of the inner experience of temptation rather than that of external testing and trial, so his chosen example of *hupomonē* will indicate the circumstances in which he thinks of its exercise: **Job** was not a man under attack from others, but one who experienced, albeit in an acute from, the ordinary human affliction of poverty, bereavement and ill-health. Job does not figure elsewhere in the NT, though Job v. 13 is cited in 1 Cor. iii. 19, but he serves in 1 Clement as an example of a righteous man humble enough to admit his sin (1 Clem. xvii. 3, citing Job i. 1, xiv. 4 f.), and as one who expresses a hope of resurrection (1 Clem. xxvi. 3, Job xix. 26); and figures also in 2 Clement in an argument about individual responsibility (vi. 8, drawing on Ezekiel's reference to Job, Ezek. xiv. 14, 18). *Test. Abraham* xv (A) describes him as a 'marvellous man'; and *Sotah* v. 5 records a Rabbinic discussion of the quality of his piety: of whether he served God from fear or from love. He is not, therefore, an obscure figure to select for an exemplar.

The Job of the canonical book would not seem remarkable for his endurance, either of God or man, and indeed the word *hupomonē*, rare anyway in the LXX, only appears in the book of Job at xiv. 19, and then not in relation specifically to Job himself. Strikingly, however, *hupomonē* is, with *eleēmosunē*, the key word in the *Testament of Job*, the theme, introduced at i. 8 f., which this re-telling by Job of his story is designed to illustrate.[1] The correspondence between the two documents is relevant also

---

[1] There are some other, less remarkable, similarities between the epistle and the *Testament*, but the uncertainty of the latter's date makes any theory of interdependence highly problematical, cf. Intro. p. 12. Most probably they both represent a way in which the story of Job has come to be told, more or less independently of the book that bears his name.

to the question of whether Job provides for James an example additional to that of the prophets, or whether he is singled out as providing a particular demonstration of what has been said about prophets in general. That Job could be classed among the prophets may be argued from Ben Sira's comment on Ezekiel, that he 'also made mention of Job among the prophets' (Ecclus xlix. 9, Hebrew text, though Charles, *Apocrypha and Pseudepigrapha* I, p. 505 n. 9 shows that the text is doubtful); and Charles compares with this the opinion of some Rabbis that Job was one of the prophets of the gentiles (citing *Seder Olam Rabba* xxi). However, if Job was familiarly taken as a type of *hupomonē*, it is more likely that we have here two examples of endurance, first the prophets, then Job, rather than one example presented first in general and then in particular terms. Finally, it is worth noting that Job was generally understood to be a gentile: in the Rabbinic reference above he is a gentile prophet; in the LXX he is described as *theosebēs*, from the land of *Ausitis* (Job i. 1); in the *Testament* his conversion from idolatry is described, culminating in his destruction of his father's idol: he fits well, then, with James's other exemplars, Abraham, the 'father of proselytes' and Rahab the typical proselyte (ii. 21, 25); perhaps also Elijah (v. 17), who in Lk. iv. 25 ff. is a prophet sent to the gentile world.

The readers have, then, **heard** the story of Job, and **seen the end the Lord brought to it** (lit. 'the end of the Lord'; *to telos kuriou*; that is, the restoration of Job by God, as described in Job xlii. 10–17). Some commentators understand *telos* as meaning 'purpose' (so Mitton, and cf. RSV and JB): the readers will then be invited to see the purpose underlying Job's experience, and therefore to find one in their own, as indicated in the chain of probation of i. 2 f.; but this is a less usual meaning of the word and to find attention directed to 'what the Lord did in the end' is more appropriate in a context where James is encouraging his readers to hope for a future intervention of God as the end of their period of endurance. The analogy is not, of course, exact, since *the end the Lord brought* to the experience of Job was a return to his former happiness, albeit on a larger scale, whereas what the readers look for is an event essentially new in kind. What they

perceive, though, in the ending of the story of Job, and what
gives them their own hope, is that **the Lord is full of compassion and merciful** (*polusplanchnos . . . kai oiktirmōn*).
James echoes here such passages as Ex. xxxiv. 6; Pss ciii. 8,
cxi. 4. The adjective *oiktirmōn* is frequently used in the LXX,
and almost always of God. James's first adjective is equivalent
to the equally familiar *polueleos*, but has itself no currency
before the epistle. The adjective is found in Hermas, *Mand.*
iv. 3. 5, *Sim.* v. 7. 4, as is the cognate noun *polusplanchnia*, in
Mand. ix. 2, *Vis.* i. 2. 2, ii. 2. 8, iv. 2. 3, cf. also Justin,
Dialogue lv. 3; it could be of James's coining, but may be easily explained as deriving from the use in both classical and
biblical Greek of *splanchnia*, lit. 'bowels', for emotion, especially pity (e.g. Lk. i. 78; Col. iii. 12).

James's appeal to the prophets and to Job as examples of
patient endurance of hardship and suffering has struck many
as extraordinary since the example of Jesus would seem the
obvious one in this respect for a Christian author, as indeed it
does to Peter (1 Pet. ii. 21–23, cf. also the author of Hebrews,
for whom in chapter xi the OT provides many examples of
faith, but for whom Jesus is 'the pioneer and perfecter' of
faith, xii. 2). There have been attempts to read in such a
reference in James, taking *telos* to mean 'death', as in Wisd.
iii. 19, and relying on the change of verb in the verse: the
readers have *heard* of Job, a figure of the past: they have *seen*
what happened to the Lord Jesus, in recent history. (Both
Augustine and Bede found in this passage a reference to the
example of Jesus' passion.) This interpretation is not convincing. The objection is not that it would demand taking *Lord*
as used in two different ways in the same sentence, first of
Christ and then of God, for this is not impossible (cf. on v. 8);
nor, as Mayor and Chaine object, that to refer to the death of
Jesus without his resurrection would not make the encouraging point that James intends, for any Christian reader
would take for granted that the resurrection of Jesus followed
his death. Rather, to read clauses b and c of v. 11 as of the endurance of Job and its sequel is to have a complete and self-
contained example for James's argument, and the two verbs
serve the same purpose of reminding the readers of a well-

known story. To read clause b of Job's patience only without its reward (even though no doubt knowledge of that could be taken for granted), and c as a reference to the suffering of Jesus made briefly, obliquely, and without its being singled out as in any way distinct from or more compelling than the others (cf. on v. 6) is a complication of the text that produces, in fact, a less satisfactory reading of it. To ask why James should use the example of Job rather than that of Jesus is to presume that he has made a real choice. It might indeed be that, as Chaine suggests, James was more interested in the glory and the return of Christ than in his suffering; or even that the example of Jesus, being one of the endurance of direct attack and of extreme suffering, would be less than appropriate for James's purpose; but the simple explanation is surely that James appeals to Job because he was a proverbial man of endurance. What we have evidence for is not a rejection of the example of Jesus, but a use of the example of Job; and that in itself is perfectly understandable.

15. LIFE IN THE PRESENT—RELIGIOUS CONVERSATION

v. 12–20

(12) Most importantly, my brothers, do not use oaths, not by the heaven nor by the earth nor any other form of oath; but let your 'yes' mean yes, and your 'no' no, lest you fall under judgment. (13) Is anyone among you in difficulties? Let him pray. Is anyone feeling cheerful? Let him sing praise. (14) Is anyone among you sick? Let him call the elders of the Church, and let them pray over him, anointing him with oil in the name of the Lord. (15) And the prayer of faith will save the sick man, and the Lord will raise him up; and if he should have committed any sins, it will be forgiven him. (16) Confess your sins to one another, then, and pray for one another, that you may be healed. The active prayer of a righteous man is very powerful. (17) Elijah was a

man just like us, and he prayed and prayed that it should not rain, and no rain fell on the earth for three years and six months. (18) And he prayed again, and the heaven gave rain and the earth produced its fruit. (19) My brothers, if anyone among you should stray from the truth and someone turn him back, (20) let him know that the man who turns back a sinner from his way of error will save his soul from death and will 'cover a multitude of sins'.

In the previous section, James was concerned to encourage his readers to patience and perseverance in the trials of daily life, in confident hope of the coming of the Lord and of judgment upon those who might be held to be, in some measure, responsible for their difficulties. However, life is also lived before God in the present, and in the final section of his epistle James turns to instructions about the proper conduct of daily life. The unity of the section has been disputed (cf. the analyses of Dibelius and Cantinat), but a train of thought, if not always a tightly logical one, may be discerned running through it. James takes up the theme briefly treated in i. 26 f., but deals here with more conventionally or obviously 'religious' activities, and, predictably for this author, in particular with religious utterance: prayer, praise, confession, and the use of oaths which, because they enrol the god as witness to his speech, might be thought a proper form of expression for a 'religious man'. On the contrary, though, James begins with an absolute prohibition of oaths.

His prohibition is prefaced with the phrase *pro pantōn*, lit. 12 'before everything (else)', which causes some difficulty in interpretation. Strictly applied, it would seem to indicate that the command thus introduced is the conclusion of a series of commands, but singled out as the most important of all. It is difficult to see how a prohibition of oaths would form such a conclusion to the imperatives of vv. 7 ff.; after James has laid such stress on patience, it would be odd for him to introduce a wholly new idea with the comment that it is much the most important! Ropes and Cantinat interpret the comparison as with v. 9: in time of hardship it is important not to lay blame upon others, or to make complaints against them, but even more vital to avoid an impatient or irreverent calling upon God. The strictly comparative sense of the phrase is not always to be pressed, however: it may perform an intensifying function, identifying something as particularly important in its own right, and not necessarily in comparison with other ideas. Thus some scholars see the prohibition as an isolated saying, included because it is a 'hobby-horse' of James, or because oath-making was especially prevalent among his readers, so that they particularly need to be warned against it (Mitton). Dibelius thinks that the saying was attracted into the context by a similar reference to judgment in v. 9. Such an isolation of the prohibition is unnecessary, since its substance harmonises well with what follows it: there are wrong, and right, ways of addressing or calling upon God. It seems best to read the phrase *pro pantōn* as introducing rather than concluding a section; the author moves on to a new line of thought with a transitional and emphatic '**most importantly** ...'. To read the prohibition in this way would be to solve another, minor difficulty: that despite the fact that he is giving direct instruction to his readers in vv. 13 ff., the author would not otherwise use the personal address, *brothers*, until v. 19. (A similar function may be seen to be performed by *pro pantōn* in 1 Pet. iv. 8: the exhortation to mutual love would read oddly as 'more important' than watching and praying at the nearness of the end, but is easily understood as introducing with emphasis the instructions to various forms of mutual service in vv. 9–11.)

James's opposition to oaths reflects a widespread reserve about them, as also about vows (promises of dedication to God). The decalogue includes the commandment not to take the name of the Lord in vain (Deut. v. 11, cf. Lev. xix. 12), although the Law requires oaths in some circumstances (Ex. xxii. 10 f., cf. 1 Kgs viii. 31 f.). Oaths must be made by the name of God and by no other god (Deut. vi. 13, cf. Jere. xii. 16). Notable figures such as Elijah are seen to make oaths (1 Kgs xvii. 1), and even God swears, by himself (Gen. xxii. 16, cf. Heb. vi. 13; Philo, *Leg. Alleg.* iii. 203 ff., *De Sacr.* 91–94, explains that this statement is merely a concession to the frailty of human imagination, for all God's words are oaths). Against this background, a complete interdiction would be difficult in Judaism, but there is evidence of a desire to limit oath-taking. It might be seen to be undesirable for a number of reasons: a low standard of truthfulness is indicated where the need is felt of resort to an oath; the name of God might be profaned by use in trivial matters, or by being invoked as witness to a lie; a man might, by binding himself with oath or vow, expose himself to disastrous consequences (of which Jephthah is the prime example, Jud. xi. 30–39, while the fate of the forty Jews of Acts xxiii. 12 ff. is unknown); there might be a temptation, in dealing with pagans, to adopt heathen formulae. Ben Sira warns against being 'accustomed to the naming of the Holy One', and of the danger of false swearing (Ecclus xxiii. 9–11). Both Josephus and Philo portray the Essenes as forbidding oaths (*BJ* ii. 135; *Ant.* xv. 371; *Quod Omn. Prob.* 84), though Josephus refers also to their 'tremendous oaths' on initiation into the community (*BJ* ii. 139, 142). He also describes them as in their avoidance of oaths following 'a way of life taught to the Greeks by Pythagoras' (*Ant. loc. cit.*), and Diogenes Laertius indeed records of Pythagoras that he taught his disciples 'not to call the gods to witness, man's duty being rather to strive to make his own word carry conviction' (*Lives of the Philosophers* viii. 22, the 'rather' makes the statement less than an absolute prohibition; cf. Epictetus, *Enchr.* xxxiii. 5, 'Avoid an oath, altogether if you can, and if not, then as much as possible under the circumstances'; Dibelius has a long note on the possibility of Pythagorean influence on Epictetus here). Although Josephus's account of the Essenes may be affected by his desire to present them as Jewish philosophers, it is congruous with the evidence of the Damascus Document, that oaths were administered on entry to their community (CD xv. 5 ff.) but were afterwards strictly limited in form (CD xv. 1 ff., not by any variation on the name of God, abbreviations of *Elohim* or *Adonai*, but by 'a binding oath by the curses of the covenant') and in circumstances (CD ix. 9 f., they must only be made in the presence of judges). Philo for his own part urges the avoidance of oaths in the interest of maintaining a high standard of truth-telling in all speech (*De Dec.* 84 ff.), but also suggests oath formulae which avoid the name of God and thus profanity, so safeguarding the third commandment (*De Spec. Leg.* ii. 2 ff.; such substitutes include swearing by one's parents, as images of creative power, or by the parts of the cosmos, as evidence of that power, rather than by the Creator himself). The Rabbis, controlled no doubt by scriptural precedent, are less obviously discouraging of oaths. *Nedarim* 20a counsels, like Ben Sira, 'Accustom not thyself to vows, for sooner or later thou wilt swear false oaths', but W. D. Davies comments that there was a 'regretful acceptance' of the practice (*The Setting of the Sermon on the Mount,* Cambridge 1964, p. 240 f.). Tractate *Shebuoth* of the Mishnah regulates the use of oaths, and like Philo treats of weakened formulae, though addressing rather the problem of the consequences of oaths than that of profanity: oaths by heaven and by earth are judged not binding by contrast with oaths by *Yah, El,* any substitute for the divine name or any attribute of God (*Sheb.* iv. 1).

Granted this widespread distrust of oaths in contemporary Hellenistic and Jewish thought, James's unqualified prohibition still finds its closest parallel in the teaching of Matt. v. 33–37, the closest point of contact, indeed, between the epistle and any other part of the NT. There are, however, certain important differences between the two passages. First, in giving examples of oaths, James uses the accusative case for the things sworn by, and Matthew *en* plus the dative case; James's is the correct Greek form while Matthew reflects Semitic idiom (cf. e.g. Jere. xii. 16). Secondly, Matthew provides more examples of oath formulae, adding 'by Jerusalem' and 'by my head' to James's **by heaven** and **by earth**. That this may reflect the evangelist's own interest in the topic is arguable from his return to it in Matt. xxiii. 16–22, a passage peculiar to this gospel; there is there an attack specifically in Jewish terms on 'avoidable' formulae, and Matthew may be conscious that the forms he quotes in vv. 34–36 would similarily be thought of as not binding. Hence, thirdly, he supplies a theological *rationalé* for the prohibition, absent from James: neither heaven, earth nor Jerusalem can be spoken of without reference to God; and man may not swear by himself, being powerless even over himself. Fourthly, in supplying an alternative to oaths, Matthew uses the imperative *estō*, 'let it be'; James *ētō*: and here Matthew's form is classical, James's colloquial. Fifthly, in the framing of this alternative, James includes the definite article: in speech it should be a question of *to nai nai* and *to ou ou*; Matthew has no article: speech should be *nai nai, ou ou*. This apparently slight difference in fact alters the content of the two alternatives. James counsels truth-telling, speaking in such a way that **'yes'** should **mean yes** and **'no'**, **no**, and thus no oath should be necessary; Matthew advocates plain speech, simple 'yes, yes' or 'no, no' without the elaboration of oaths. Finally, James concludes with a warning of judgment; Matthew with a ruling that 'anything more than this is evil'.

This amount of difference between the two in so brief a passage makes a literary dependence of either on the other unlikely, and it is probable that they therefore represent independent crystallisations into literary form of the same oral tradition. It might be argued that James represents an earlier, more original, form of that tradition than Matthew, since his version of the prohibition is, with its fewer examples, a simpler one, and his alternative, as an exhortation to truth-telling, gives a general precept by contrast with Matthew's 'casuistic' substitution of one mode of speech for another in, maybe, a Jewish-Christian community concerned with the framing of laws. It is, indeed, James's form of the alternative that is quoted, as the citation of a dominical saying, by Justin (I *Apol.* xvi. 5); Clement of Alexandria (*Strom.* v. 99. 1, vii. 67. 5) and in the *Clementine Homilies* (iii. 55. 1, xix. 2. 4); all quotations by authors who show no other sign of knowing the epistle, and who are therefore also drawing upon an oral tradition of the saying. On the other hand, if the instruction goes back to Jesus, it would originally have been given in a Jewish context and very probably with just such a polemical thrust as Matthew presents; James's presentation could be a simplification of the tradition as it passed outside the area of purely Jewish concerns, and his form of the alternative might reflect the accommodation of it to the popular theme of truth-telling as illustrated above (his own idiom is used by Paul in 2 Cor. i.

17; though Matthew's also finds parallels in 2 Enoch xlix. 1 and *Sanhedrin* 36a, where it is ruled that a repeated 'yes' or 'no' has in fact the value of an oath; cf. W. C. Allen, *The Gospel According to St Matthew*, 3rd edn Edinburgh 1912, *ad loc.*). Arguments for priority can be put forward on either side, and it is safer to conclude simply that Matthew and James represent alternative forms of the same tradition than to try to establish their relative antiquity.

One final major difference, however, remains to be noted. Matthew, of course, cites the tradition as the teaching of Jesus; James includes it without ascription in the course of his instructions (the suggestion that his introductory *pro panton* singles it out as of especial importance because dominical is unconvincing). It might therefore be argued that Matthew has taken a current saying from the general stock of ethical teaching and attributed it to Jesus. However, it is clear from Rom. xiii. 7, 8 ff.; 1 Pet. iii. 9, that words of Jesus were absorbed by Christian preachers into their teaching without differentiation, as well as being retained expressly as 'sayings of the Lord' (cf. Acts xx. 35; 1 Cor. vii. 10–12). As the unqualified prohibition of oaths seems to have no precedent before the Christian tradition, and as it would be an extraordinary stand to take in the Jewish context, given the OT background, it seems most probable that it derives from Jesus himself. James's lack of ascription is certainly no argument that it does not; though, equally, there can be no certainty that he himself knew that it did.

Oaths, then, must be avoided, **lest you fall under judgment**, cf. the warning of iv. 12, v. 9. The warning is given in general terms, and need not be specified, as by Mayor, as a threat of judgment for breach of the third commandment. (One variant reading, found in P, takes the point of James's admonition to truth-telling, and reads instead of *hupo krisin, under judgment*, a warning against falling *epi hupokrisin*, 'into hypocrisy'.) But if oaths are unacceptable, there are other forms of address to God that are, in differing circumstances,

13 right and proper. **Is anyone among you in difficulties?** (*kakopathei*, a general term, cf. *kakopatheia*, in v. 10). **Let him pray**; presumably for relief or deliverance. **Is anyone feeling cheerful? Let him sing praise** (*psalleto*; the verb in

classical literature referred to the playing of a stringed instrument, and is used of David's playing in 1 Kgs xvi. 23; in the LXX it is also used of singing to such an accompaniment, Pss vii. 17, ix. 11, xcviii. 4 f.; and in the NT of singing alone, 1 Cor. xiv. 15; Eph. v. 19). The sentiment of James is that of the author of the Psalms of Solomon: 'good is a psalm sung to God from a glad heart' (iii. 2); God should be addressed with thanksgiving in time of joy as well as with petition in time of grief. Contrasting conditions or moods of daily life are thus sketched in general terms, and James continues with detailed instructions for a specific situation, that of sickness.

The proper response of the **sick** man to his situation is to **14, 15** call to himself **the elders of the Church**. This is one phrase which gives a specifically Christian colouring to the epistle, since *ekklēsia* became at a very early stage the chosen self-designation of the Christian community, whether considered as an individual local unit (e.g. the house church of Philem. 2) or as the whole body of believers (e.g. Matt. xvi. 18; Col. i. 18; Paul's habitual opening address 'to the *ekklēsia* in . . .' may be understood in either way; as an address to a particular local community in its own right as an *ekklēsia*, or to it considered as a manifestation at one particular place of the total *ekklēsia*). By contrast, it does not seem to have had any real currency as a self-designation of Jewish communities, for whom *sunagōgē* would be the normal term (see on ii. 2). Outside the gospels, of which Matthew is the only one to use the term, it is found in all the NT documents except the Petrine epistles, 2 Tim. and Titus, 1 and 2 Jn, and Jude. Although it was a word current in secular Greek for an assembly (cf. Acts xix. 39), the probable background of its Christian use is to be found in its rôle in the LXX, where it generally translates *qāhāl*, a term used primarily for the assembly of Israel. Schmidt considers that James 'does not refer to a particular congregation, but to the Christian community as a whole, to which the Epistle is addressed' (art. *ἐκκλησία*, *TDNT* Vol. III, p. 5), but the immediate context of instruction to the individual in a particular crisis strongly suggests a local reference. It is to the leaders of this immediate community that a sick man would send, not to the highest authorities in

the whole Christian body. The organisation of local communities under the leadership of *elders* is paralleled in Acts in
reference to Jerusalem (xv. 2, 4, xxi. 18), Ephesus (xx. 17), Antioch, Lystra and Derbe (xi. 30, xiv. 23); in the Pastoral
epistles (1 Tim. v. 1, 17, 20; Tit. i. 5); and in the self-
designation of the authors of 2 and 3 Jn and 1 Pet. (v. 1).
Polycarp described the duties of elders (Ep. v. 1), and Clement
commands that they be shown respect (1 Clem. i. 3, xxi. 6,
though the reference here may be to older members of the
Church rather than to leaders). Despite the account in Acts of
his appointing elders, there is, however, no reference to such
leaders in Paul's letters. It is probable that this form of
leadership was adopted on the synagogue model (cf. Lk. vii. 3)
by Christian communities having at least some initial contract
with Judaism, whether as themselves Jewish Christians, or as
drawn from the gentile adherents to the synagogues of the
diaspora (cf. Introduction, p. 37 f.).

The elders when they come will **pray over him,
anointing him with oil** (the aorist participle *aleipsantes*
denotes an accompanying rather than a preliminary action).
The primary action, clearly, is the prayer. Prayer in time of
sickness might be thought of as having either of two functions. It might be prayer as intercession, a request for God to
heal (e.g. Ecclus xxxviii. 9: the advice seems to be to ask God
first, and then let in the physician as the mediator of his
healing gift; cf. *Baba Bathra* 116a, which advises a sick person to ask a wise man, presumably a Rabbi, to intercede for
him, without that man being considered his healer); alternatively, the prayer might be thought itself to effect the
healing, like that of Hanina b. Dosa, who is recorded as
knowing from the fluency of his prayer whether the patient
would recover or not (*Berakoth* v. 5; see G. Vermes, *Jesus the
Jew*, London 1973, pp. 72–78, for an account of Jewish
charismatic healers of the NT period). James seems to think
of the prayer of the elders as having this latter function, since
he explains that **the prayer of faith** (i.e. a prayer that is
made in faith and without doubt, cf. i. 6 ff.) **will save the
sick man.** However, the effectiveness of the prayer would ultimately be seen as an act of divine or heavenly power, hence

the further assurance that **the Lord will raise him up** (cf. the literal, and demonstrative, raising of the sick in Mk i. 31, ix. 27; Acts iii. 7, ix. 41).

The function of the **anointing** is left undefined. Oil was certainly widely used in the ancient world for medicinal purposes: e.g. for soothing and cleansing wounds (Is. i. 6; Lk. x. 34); for warming a sick person's body (Herod's, in Josephus, *Ant.* xvii. 172); for toning the muscles (Philo, *De Somn.* ii. 58; Seneca, *Ep.* ciii. 5, after sea-sickness); for paralysis (Galen, *De med. temp.* ii. 10 ff.); even for toothache (Pliny, *Nat. Hist.* xxiii. 79).[1] It would, however, be wrong to distinguish between the 'medical' and the 'religious' elements of James's picture. A distinction between remedies based on superstition and remedies based on science would have been foreign even to the practitioners of Greek medicine; and the Essenes would see the potency of their prescriptions as derived as much from the antiquity of their rubrics as from the inherent properties of their herbs (see Vermes, *op. cit.* pp. 61–63. Josephus, *BJ* ii. 136 and Jubilees x. 10–13). Because anointing with oil was widely associated with the relief of suffering (though, according to Josephus, *BJ* ii. 123, the Essenes were averse to it), it is an appropriate action to be performed where such relief is being sought, and sought through prayer. It would be misleading, however, to describe this anointing as either a 'symbolic action' expressing the intention of the prayer, or as a 'folk-medicine' accompaniment to it (Dibelius). The anointing is performed *in the name of the Lord*, and is thus part of the single event of spiritual healing, the request for which is the religious response to sickness.

The phrase **in the name of the Lord** contains a number of ambiguities. First, there is again the problem of the identity of *the Lord*, whether this is a reference to God or to Jesus; secondly the question of whether anointing *in the name* refers to an invocation of the person named, or a claim to act with

[1] In the Apocalypse of Moses ix (Life of Adam and Eve xxxvi), Adam hopes that God may send oil from the tree of life to heal the pain of his chastisement. This does not necessarily indicate a magical or miraculous value attached to oil as such, but is rather an adaptation in the terms of the myth of the notion of the use of oil in healing generally.

his authority; and thirdly whether this use of *the name* is part of the prayer, or is a different form of utterance. On the first question, granted that the setting is the life of a Christian community, the likelihood is that the Lord is the Lord Jesus Christ, since the practice of Christian healing in his name is reflected in Acts (iii. 6, iv. 30, xvi. 18) and the synoptic gospels (Mk xvi. 17; Matt. vii. 22; Lk. x. 17), and it would appear that so familiar was this that the form was adopted by other healers (Mk ix. 38; Acts xix. 13). Certainly in v. 10 *the name of the Lord* is that of God, who is also *the Lord* of v. 11, but in v. 14 as in vv. 7, 8, there is most probably a conventional, almost technical, expression whose interpretation is not controlled by its context. (Daube draws attention to the variant reading of B which omits the phrase *tou kuriou*, and comments that healing 'in the name' would be a more obviously Jewish way of referring to healing in the name of God, *The New Testament and Rabbinic Judaism*, p. 236; but this reading is unlikely to be original.)

A number of the healings in the name of Jesus referred to above are exorcisms, and Dibelius regards the scene in James as also that of an exorcising of the demon responsible for the disease, the name of Jesus being invoked in the citing or summoning of his master that is part of the exorcist's technique in addressing his adversary. This is an unwarranted elaboration of the picture. James clearly knows enough of exorcist language (cf. ii. 19, iv. 7) to have given his instructions in those terms if he had wished to do so. In the Markan tradition healing narratives told in terms of confrontation with the demon are in a number of respects different from those told without such a conflict, and one major difference is that physical contact with the patient plays no part in exorcisms. The physical contact through anointing in James's account indicates that this is a healing where demonic possession is not thought to be involved (cf. Mk vi. 13, the only other passage in the NT where anointing plays a part in Christian healing, and where the anointing of the sick and the exorcising of demons are clearly separate activities). Anointing *in the name* does not, therefore, refer to an exorcist's invocation as distinct from prayer. The phrase should probably be understood in terms of authority: on the analogy with the prophets of v. 10 who spoke

under Yahweh's commission and indeed in words which may be
called his, the healer acts under the command of Jesus and in an
exercise of his power. James is providing an interpretation of
how the healing is achieved, or the grounds on which it may be
expected, rather than an account of the form of words to be used
at anointing. It should be stressed again that the prayer and
anointing are not to be seen as separate but as parts of the same
action; the prayer would no doubt include a request to Jesus that
the healing power which he has given may be exercised.

Though James does not apparently here associate sickness
with demonic activity, he retains something of the long-
established connection between sickness and sin. That
sickness will be the result of sin is threatened in the curses of
Deut. xxviii. 21 f., 27 f., assumed in Ps. xxxviii. 1–8 and the
thanksgiving of Hezekiah, Is. xxxviii. 17; Ben Sira thinks of
repentance as a prophylactic (Ecclus xviii. 19 ff.) and warns
the sinner that he will find himself in the hands of the physician (Ecclus xxxviii. 15). The same connection is maintained
in the Testaments (Reub. i. 7, Zeb. v. 2 ff., Gad. v. 9 f.); in the
Prayer of Nabonidus from Qumran, see Vermes, *op. cit.* p. 67;
in *Nedarim* 41a: 'No sick person is cured of his disease until
all his sins are forgiven him'; and appears to be assumed by
Jesus in Jn v. 14, though rejected by him in Jn ix. 2 f. James
thinks of a possible, but not inevitable, association rather than
a direct cause and effect relationship: **if he should have
committed any sins**, then the restoration will be spiritual as
well as physical, and **it will be forgiven him**. There is no
suggestion of an additional form of response to the situation
where sin as well as sickness must be dealt with: forgiveness
is conveyed in the same single act of prayer and anointing.

James is clearly in all this describing something other than
the simple visiting of the sick which is a frequently
recommended act of charity (e.g. Ecclus vii. 35; Matt. xxv.
36; *Nedarim* 40a, 'He who visits the sick lengthens his life,
and he who refrains shortens it'; Polycarp, Ep. vi. 1, one of
the duties of elders). The visit of *the elders* is of a formal
character, with the expectation of healing attached to it.
James does not give the impression of instituting a new practice, rather of describing a response to the situation of

sickness that should be as obvious as praying in time of hardship or singing when cheerful (the optimism of his recommendation would presumably be conditioned by his account of 'unanswered' prayer in i. 6–8: if healing were not given, it would be because there was doubt in the prayer). Yet despite the assumed familiarity of the practice, it differs from the known analogies of both Jewish and Christian spiritual healings. There is no mention of the laying on of hands which could be a feature of Jewish healing (Daube, *op. cit.* pp. 228 f. and 234–6; 1 QGn Apoc. xx. 25–30; and cf. Mk v. 23, vii. 32 for popular expectation of Jesus) and which is a frequent element in the healings of Jesus and his followers (Mk vi. 5, viii. 23, 25, xvi. 18; Lk. iv. 40, xiii. 13; Acts ix. 12, 17). Indeed, so common is this action in healing, and so surprising its omission here, that Origen reads it into his quotation of James's instruction: '. . . call the elders, and let them lay their hands on him anointing him with oil . . . .' (*Hom. in Lev.* ii. 4, Latin translation). Then, the actions described are specifically those of *the elders*, the established leaders of the community. Vermes demonstrates the distinction in Judaism between the charismatic healers and Rabbinic authorities (Hanina b. Dosa healed the sons of R. Johanan b. Zakkai and R. Gamaliel, but is never quoted as an authority on the Law and is not himself a Rabbi; Jesus, a charismatic healer who also interprets the Law, may be the exception to this general rule), and in the tension between the two traditions the charismatic is squeezed out rather than taken over by the Rabbinic (*op. cit.* pp. 80–82). In the synoptic gospels and in Acts a commission to heal is given not only to the Twelve (if, indeed, they could be called 'established leaders'), but also to the seventy in Lk. x. 17, and to the individual disciple Ananias in Acts ix. 17. Paul, too, sees healers and administrators (*kubernēseis*) in the Church as exercising distinct gifts (1 Cor. xii. 28).

A precise line of development to James's practice from precedents in either Judaism or the mission of Jesus and other early Christian communities cannot be traced; James represents a community which has inherited both a charismatic character and an organised structure and leadership, and the hope of charismatic experience is

associated with the exercise of that leadership. An elder may
be expected also to be a healer (there is no suggestion that he
is an elder *because* he is a healer). James's picture is often contrasted with Paul's, that of a widespread and varied exercise
of charismata within the whole community (Rom. xii. 6 ff.; 1
Cor. xii. 4–11), and seen as a late development and as an
'institutionalising' of charisma. However, if James's community was from its beginnings an organised one with a
structure of leadership derived from prior association with the
synagogue, and if the initial reception of Christianity included
an adoption of charismatic hopes, then these hopes may well
have been from the beginning related to that structure. A
group accustomed to leadership and now encouraged to hope
for manifestations of the Spirit of God in, for instance,
healings, would be very likely to focus these hopes upon their
leaders. The scope of charismatic hope, and experience, may
be more limited than is Paul's, but this will not necessarily
imply there has been a retreat from his position (cf. Introduction, p. 35 f.).

The subsequent history of the rite of anointing in Christian
healing is chronicled by the older commentators, especially
Mayor and Ropes. This passage in the epistle was appealed
to in particular by the Roman Catholic Church as giving
scriptural warrant for the sacrament of extreme unction, the
anointing of a sick man in danger of death with a view to his
absolution and restoration; the health of soul and body.
Chaine (whose commentary was published with *Imprimatur*
in 1927) identifies James's elders as priests and finds the
gravity of the sickness indicated by the use of the verb
astheneō in v. 14 (cf. its use of sickness resulting in death in Jn
iv. 46, xi. 1–6; Acts ix. 37), and the apparent inability of the
sick man to leave his bed since the priests must be summoned
to him (surprisingly, he does not appeal to the use of the verbs
sōzō and *kamnō* in the phrase *save the sick man* in v. 15; the
former might be taken to indicate salvation in a life or death
situation, and the latter may be used of hopeless sickness, *hoi
kamnontes* even being a term for 'the dead'). By contrast Cantinat (commentary published in 1973, also with *Imprimatur*)
denies that the language indicates grave or mortal sickness.

This nuance is, in fact, neither demanded nor excluded; James's language may refer to any sickness from which healing is desired, and it is in physical healing that he is primarily interested, the hope of absolution, as commented above, being only associated in some cases.

From this description of the specific response appropriate in case of sickness, James reverts to general advice and obser-
16a vations. The sequence is not a strictly logical one. If v. 16 were seen to be dealing also, in broader terms, with the hope of physical healing, it could not be read as a generalisation from the instructions of v. 15. The admonition to **confess your sins** does not derive from a description of such a confession by the sick man of v. 15, and the exhortation to mutual activity by believers, who are to confess to and pray for **one another** contains no reference to the elders who are the chief actors in the preceding verse. Both the confession and the prayer here counselled are specifically mutual acts: the verse cannot be read as a further instruction to the sick to confess those sins which may have caused their sickness (Blackman) to the elders who have come to the sick room to pray for them (Sidebottom). Indeed, James might seem to have incorporated a piece of instruction from a tradition different from his own, in which sickness and sin are necessarily related, so that confession is an essential preliminary to healing, and in which the hope of spiritual healing is associated with the activity of believers in general and not the leaders of the community in particular. Dibelius thinks that the instruction derives from an originally independent logion about confession and intercessory prayer, attracted to v. 15 by the catchword *hamartia*, sin, and imperfectly conformed to the context by James's addition of a concluding statement of intent, *that you may be healed.* A certain sequence of thought, rather than a purely formal linguistic connection may, however, be observed. The situation he has sketched suggests two ideas to James, which he goes on, albeit unsystematically and not particularly originally, to explore. First, the fact of sickness raises the possibility of sin, hence he turns to deal with the proper response to sin in general experience, both as admitted in oneself (v. 16a), and as observed unacknowledged in others (v. 19 f.). Secondly, the expectation of healing is related to the efficacy of prayer, an idea important to

him which he takes the opportunity further to illustrate in vv. 16b–18.

The prevalence of sin even among believers was acknowledged by James in iii. 2, and the solution there would seem to lie in individual self-discipline. Here the response is a communal one, a mutual conversation whose content is a humble admission of fault and a generous giving of support (in sharp contrast to the mutual complaint condemned in v. 9). A confession of sins might be thought to be properly addressed to God, who 'cleanseth from sins a soul when it maketh confession' (Pss Sol. ix. 12; cf. Num. v. 5 ff.; Ps. li. 3 f.; 1 Jn i. 8 f.; 1 Clem. li. 3, lii.; Hermas, *Vis.* iii. 1. 5), and confession to fellow-members of the community can hardly be intended to replace that. James's reference should not, however, be seen as limited either to an admission of fault to persons one has actually injured (cf. Matt. xviii. 15; Lk. xvii. 3 f.) or to the making of confession in public (cf. *Did.* iv. 14, xiv. 1). It is not anyway clear whether this reciprocal confession and prayer is part of the public worshipping life of the whole community, or the private activity of smaller groups within it. Nor is the purpose of the confession of sins addressed to fellow-members of the community defined. It may be thought that if the community is made aware of a member's besetting sins it will be able to help him in resisting them, or that confession is a preliminary to mutual prayer: the sins confessed becoming the subject of intercession. What is stated is the object of this mutual conversation as a whole: it is **that you may be healed**. Such healing should not be seen in the light of vv. 14–15 as specifically physical healing from sickness. James's description of the response to sickness suggested the idea of sin, but the response to this is a topic in its own right. As with v. 7, the conjunction *oun* used in v. 16 suggests a general deduction from the preceding paragraph, rather than a specific conclusion drawn from it; in the case of sickness, one may hope for forgiveness of sins, **so then** this may properly be sought in other circumstances. The healing now thought of is from sin and its consequences (which may or may not include physical suffering), and the verb *iaomai* is likewise used in this connection in Is. vi. 10 (quoted in Matt. xiii. 15; Jn xii.

40; Acts xxviii. 27); Is. liii. 5 (quoted in 1 Pet. ii. 24); Hermas, *Vis.* i. 1. 9, *Sim.* ix. 28. 5.

The prayer that is part of the response of the community to the experience of sin is probably thought of as intercessory, calling for God's forgiveness and restoration of the sinner, rather than as having an effective power of its own, as in v. 15. However, the power of prayer is in any event to be 16b emphasised: **The active prayer of a righteous man is very powerful.** This sentence could be read as a final, encouraging comment on the intercessory prayer of v. 16a, or as introducing a second line of thought: the efficacy of prayer, as demonstrated by Elijah, in vv. 17 f. Most texts punctuate v. 16 so as to give a major pause between the two halves, JB even presenting 16b as the opening of a new paragraph. Its function is most probably transitional, taking up the theme of prayer from the instructions of both vv. 14 f. and 16a, with a view to expounding it by illustration. That powerful prayer is predicated of *a righteous man* may not be taken to indicate that the righteous are an *élite* whose prayer is more effective than that of the ordinary believer. James stresses that even his exemplar Elijah is *just like us*, at least in that respect. His language echoes the scriptural assurance that God hears the prayer of the righteous (Ps. xxiv. 15, quoted in 1 Pet. iii. 12; Prov. xv. 29), and *the righteous man* is, as in v. 6, the faithful man of God, who trusts in him. The description of this prayer as *active* represents the participle *energoumenē*, which closes the verse, but whose function in it is unclear. It may be understood adjectivally, as here, (cf. JB, 'heart-felt prayer'), or as giving an adverbial clause: this prayer is powerful 'when it is put into effect' by God or by the Spirit (thus Mayor and Blackman, reading the participle as in the passive voice); or 'when it is exercised' (Ropes and RV reading the participle as middle in voice).

The various options make little difference to the overall sense, but it is characteristic that James should suggest that prayer is to be understood as something active. He is concerned to encourage confidence in the efficacy of prayer, but the man whose prayer is efficacious will be one for whom it is not just a matter of words, and certainly not of half-hearted or doubtful petition (cf.

i. 5 f., ii. 16, iv. 2 f., and Mk xi. 22–24 for comparable teaching on
the power of prayer when made in full conviction).

It is at first sight surprising to find **Elijah**, commonly 17, 18
thought of as the archetypal prophet, appealed to as the
exemplary man of prayer, and in particular that the appeal is
not to that story of his miracles in which he is specifically
described as praying and which might seem more appropriate
to the context of James: the revival of the son of the widow of
Zarephath (1 Kgs xvii. 17–24, esp. v. 20 f.). In the narrative of
Kings, his action at both the beginning and the end of the
drought appears rather as prophetic announcement than as
prayer (1 Kgs xvii. 1, xviii. 1, 41, 44; cf. Ecclus xlviii. 3, and
the prophecy of the 'two witnesses' of Rev. xi. 6), but his
standing before God in 1 Kgs xvii. 1 and, less plausibly, his
crouching posture in 1 Kgs xviii. 42, might be interpreted as
attitudes of prayer (cf. Lk. xviii. 11, 13; Neh. viii. 6). He
appears, however, in the catalogue of men of prayer in 2 Esd.
vii. 106–110, in relation both to the giving of rain and to the
revival of the widow's son (v. 109). The marvel of rain-
making, or withholding, as a result of prayer had a certain
place in popular imagination, such stories being told of Onias
the martyr (Josephus, *Ant.* xiv. 22); of Honi the circle-drawer
and his descendants, and Hanina b. Dosa (*Taanith* iii. 8;
Taanith 24b; see Vermes, *op. cit.* pp. 69 f., 72, 76): even later of
James himself (Epiph., *Haer.* lxxviii. 14)[1]; which may explain
why it is that James appeals to this part of Elijah's activity as
demonstrating the power of prayer.

James emphasises the energy of Elijah's prayer, an example
of the *active prayer* he wishes to encourage: **he prayed and
prayed.** The repetition of noun and verb, *proseuchēi
proseuxato* is sometimes seen as representing the Hebrew
idiom of the infinitive absolute (cf. Josh. xxiv. 10; Is. xxx. 19;
and also Lk. xxii. 15), though Dibelius and Cantinat quote
parallels from classical literature; in any event, its function is
to intensify the statement, hence RV's 'he prayed fervently' or
NEB's 'earnestly' (Ropes's suggestion, 'he prayed a prayer',

[1] This development of the tradition about 'James the Just' may come from a
knowledge of the epistle itself: from what would be deemed to be, in v. 16 ff.,
James's own description of the activity and powers of 'the righteous man'.

weakens the force of the example). He also emphasises the ordinary human character of Elijah: he was **a man just like us** (*homoiopathēs hēmin*; cf. Paul's protestation to the Lystra crowds, Acts xiv. 15). This is an extraordinary statement in contrast with the adulation of Elijah in Ecclus xlviii. 1–12, the presentation of him as the eschatological prophet in Mal. iv. 5 f. and subsequent Jewish expectation, and, indeed, his place in Christian tradition, in the figure of John the Baptist (e.g. Lk. i. 17; Matt. xi. 14, xvii. 10–13). James may not be ignorant of such ideas, or intending to exclude them; his statement is related to his intention in the context. If the example of Elijah is to serve to encourage his readers to similarly confident and energetic prayer, it must be clear that the efficacy of Elijah's prayer is not related to any superhuman gifts or qualities in the man (even prophetic charisma) but only to the fact that he prayed, and prayed with fervour. (A comparison may be drawn with the presentation of Solomon as an ordinary man in Wisd. vii. 1–7: his wisdom was not a superhuman quality in him, but a gift of God for which, by implication, any man may ask. For Cantinat, this consideration explains why James does not appeal to the example of Jesus' prayer, so strongly stressed in the Lukan tradition, e.g. Lk. iii. 21, ix. 28 f., xxii. 44, and by the author of Hebrews, v. 7.)

James's description of the drought as lasting for **three years and six months** does not derive directly from the OT, where the announcement that the drought is to be lifted is simply said to be made 'in the third year' (1 Kgs xviii. 1). The known midrashic interpretations of this reference calculate the duration of the drought as either fourteen or eighteen months (*Esther R.*14; *Lev. R.*19; see also G. H. Dalman, *Jesus–Jeshua*, ET London 1929, p. 52. The calculation of fourteen months would presumably suppose that the drought is pronounced at the end of the first year, a month before the 'early' rains were due to begin, the second year would then be without a rainy season at all, and the drought would end at the beginning of the third year, for its 'early' rains to follow. For eighteen months, the pronouncement would come after the 'late' rains of the first year, with the drought period taken to include the months of dryness that normally follow.) A

three and a half year period of drought is mentioned also in
Lk. iv. 25 (cf. also the duration of the witnesses' prophecy in
Rev. xi. 2 f.), and this correspondence might be taken to
reflect another midrashic calculation whereby the drought is
seen to be broken at the end of the third year, after three con-
secutive years without rain, to which may be added the usual
dry period of the preceding year (so Chaine and Cantinat).
However, it may well be that no background of elaborate
calculation should be supposed; rather, 'three and a half years'
was a stock phrase for 'a considerable period' (so Dalman),
which seemed to harmonise well enough with the note in
Kings. The number 'three and a half' plays a certain rôle in
apocalyptic symbolism, as half the perfect number, seven, and
therefore as a sinister number (e.g. Dan. vii. 25, xii. 7; Rev. xi.
2 f., xii. 6, 14, xiii. 5); if James and Luke are using a stock
phrase, it is one which might appropriately suggest a time of
misfortune or disaster. (Also in the Lukan account of his activity,
Elijah is presented as a prophet sent to the gentile world, iv. 26; if
one could think James might be aware of this idea, his appeal to
Elijah would harmonise with his use of other 'gentile' exemplars,
Abraham, Rahab and Job.)

After the period of drought, **the heaven gave rain**. James
echoes biblical idiom rather than directly quoting the Elijah
narrative (cf. 1 Kgs xviii. 1, as also in his statement that *no
rain fell on the earth*, cf. 1 Kgs xvii. 7). In the narrative of 1
Kings it is God who sends the rain (1Kgs xviii. 1, cf. 1 Sam.
xii. 17; Acts xiv. 17; and on v. 7 above); James's neat balance
of statements that *the heaven gave rain* and *the earth
produced its fruit* might suggest that Elijah's prayer had a
direct effect upon the natural order, but he would
presumably expect his readers to take it for granted that it
has this effect because God acts in answer to it. It is interesting that by thus using Elijah as an example of the man
of prayer, James has in fact implicitly altered the course of the
original story. As a prophet, Elijah declared the prior decision
of God communicated to him; when his activity is seen as
prayer, it is rather God who responds to his intercession.

In the closing verses of the epistle, James returns to the 19, 20
question of dealing with sin within the community. Apparent-

ly assuming that the duty of trying to reclaim a sinner will be
recognised, he encourages the fulfilment of this duty by
reminding his readers of its outcome. (For a similar recognition of this duty, cf. the Matthean version of the parable of
the lost sheep, Matt. xviii. 12–14; Gal. vi. 1 f.; 1 Thess. v. 14;
2 Thess. iii. 14 f.; Jude 22 f.; 2 Clem. xvii. 2; Hermas, *Mand.*
viii. 10; Ecclus xix. 13 f.; and in relation specifically to sins
committed against oneself, Matt. xviii. 15–17; Lk. xvii. 3 f.;
Test. Gad. vi. 3; 1 QS v. 25–vi. 1.) The nature of the error
from which the sinner is to be reclaimed is not defined; most
probably it is moral rather than doctrinal error, although
James is unlikely to distinguish between ethical **truth** and the
truth of the gospel as a whole (cf. i. 18, iii. 14). The metaphor
of the **way** is frequently employed in Jewish ethical teaching,
e.g. Ps. i. 6; Prov. iv. 14, and is developed in the 'Two Ways'
pattern of instruction in 1 QS iii. 13–iv. 26; *Did.* i–vi. 1;
Barn. xviii–xx; cf. Test. Asher i. 3 ff.; Hermas, *Mand.* vi
1; 1 Jn i. 6 f. A variant reading of v. 19 by Sinaiticus balances
the reference to **his way of error** (or, 'the error of his way',
ek planēs hodou autou) in v. 20 with one to a straying
specifically 'from the way of truth' (*apo hodou tēs aletheias,*
cf. Wisd. v. 6).

The reclamation of an errant member of the community
has far-reaching consequences: it achieves the salvation of a
20 **soul from death,** and forgiveness of sins (for the idiom
cover ... sins as meaning forgiveness, cf. Ps. xxxii. 1). Here,
however, James's language is ambiguous, and it is not clear to
whom these blessings are seen to accrue: to the converted
sinner or to the man who converts him. The attention of v. 19
is focused upon the act of the converter consequent on the
error of another, and it might seem logical that v. 20 should
assure him of his reward in terms of future salvation. That
merciful deeds deliver their doer from death is affirmed in
Tob. iv. 10, xii. 9, cf. Dan. xii. 3 and contrast Ezek. xxxiii. 9;
that they effect atonement for his sins is variously indicated in
Dan. iv. 27; Ecclus iii. 3, 30; *Did.* iv. 6, Barn. xix. 10; 2 Clem. xvi.
4. This interpretation is favoured by Mayor, who, however,
finally rejects it as offering a motive of reward inconsistent with
the Christian gospel; he therefore interprets the verse as

assuring the converter of the double blessing he has achieved for his fellow. That salvation from death is the consequence of conversion for the sinner seems most probable. James has himself affirmed the connection of sin with death in i. 15 (cf. Rom. v. 12); the 'Two Ways' of the *Didache* are the ways of life and of death, as the choices of Deut. xxx. 15–20 are ultimately between life and death. However, if the converted sinner is deemed to have been rescued from death as the consequence of his sins, he must be deemed already to have been forgiven: an announcement of his forgiveness following this announcement of his deliverance would be an odd sequence. It seems feasible, then, that James holds out an assurance of blessing both to the converted and to the converter; the act of conversion is of mutual benefit: the man who is turned from error is thereby delivered from death, and the man who reclaims him experiences himself forgiveness of his sins. It is, of course, assumed that the man who takes it upon himself to reclaim his fellow from error will be conscious of errors of his own for which he too stands in need of forgiveness. Such an interpretation might seem consistent with the picture of a mutual response to sin, and mutual benefit, in v. 16. That v. 20a refers to the converted and 20b to the converter is also concluded by Blackman, Dibelius, Ropes and, with reservations, Mitton.[1] Other commentators, however, point out that 20b is not James's own composition, but is a popular expression, and might therefore have a more general reference: to the sins of both converter and converted (Chaine); or to the community at large, affected by the presence of sin (Reicke, and cf. Sidebottom). This seems less probable; James presents to his readers a situation focused on two actors, albeit in their midst, and is likely to present its outcome also in specific reference to these two.

The ambiguity of the verse is reflected in two variant readings within it. First, the imperative with which it opens is variously read as in the third person singular, *ginōsketō*, **let him know** (so the majority of Greek MSS and versions), and

---

[1] Comparison may be made with the mutual benefit to reader and teacher in 1 Tim. iv. 16, and to counsellor and counselled in 2 Clem. xv. 1, xix. 1; *Epist. Apost.* xxxix. 10 ff., Hennecke-Schneemelcher I. p. 225, though there the situation seems to be one of personal injury, maybe of rich to poor.

in the second person plural *ginōskete*, know you (so, e.g., B and the Ethiopic version). The latter probably represents a desire to harmonise the imperative to the opening address to *my brothers*; less plausibly, it may have been felt that to address the converter directly would be to speak only of his reward, an impression some scribes may have wished to avoid. Secondly, the first assurance, that the converter of a sinner will save **his soul from death**, (*psuchēn autou ek thanatou*) is so read in, e.g., ℵ, A, 33, most of the old Latin and the Vulgate, the Syriac and Armenian versions and the Bohairic; but the pronoun is omitted by many Greek MSS, including K and ψ, and by the Sahidic version, while in p 74, B and some old Latin MSS it is transposed to give '... save a soul *from death itself*' (*ek thanatou autou*.) It seems more probable that the pronoun originally stood in the text and was variously omitted or re-positioned than that it was originally absent and variously introduced. To take the first alternative as the original reading of the verse is not, however, to solve the problem of its ambiguity at this point; since *autou* is frequently confused with the reflexive *heautou* (especially in its contracted form *hautou*), the reference might still be either to converter or to converted. (The reading *ek thanatou autou* would appear to be an escape from that ambiguity, though it is supported by Wikgren in a dissenting judgment from the UBS edition; see Metzger's *Textual Commentary on the Greek New Testament, ad loc.*)

The terms of the second assurance, that the converter **will cover a multitude of sins** corresponds to those of the exhortation to love in 1 Pet. iv. 8, because 'love covers a multitude of sins'. The correspondence in each of the phrase *plēthos hamartōn* suggests a closer relationship than a merely coincidental use of the biblical idiom 'cover sins'. Peter's statement appears to be a rendering of the Hebrew text of Prov. x. 12, 'love covers all sins', although not that of the LXX translation, where love (*philia* rather than Peter's *agapē*) is rather said to 'cover all those who do not love strife' (an accommodation of the second proposition of the verse to the first, 'hatred stirs up strife'). It is unlikely that either James or Peter is drawing upon the Hebrew text here, in contrast to the normal practice of both of using the LXX. The aphorism is quoted, in the form in which it appears in 1 Peter, by certain of the early Fathers, cf. 1 Clem. xlix. 5; 2 Clem. xvi. 4; Tert. *Scorp.* vi. 11; Clem. Alex. *Paed.* iii. 12. 91 and *Quis Div.* 38; Origen, *Hom. in Lev.* ii. 4; and in the *Didascalia*, ii. 3. 3. By the last three, the form is attributed to Jesus; Origen cites it in connection with Lk. vii. 47, and the words of Jesus about the sinful woman could in fact be understood as a citation or paraphrase of the OT aphorism. (Incidentally, all those who thus cite the saying understand the sins forgiven as those of the man who loves, which might give weight to interpreting James's assurance in relation to the converter, not the converted.) The probability is that the saying, originally derived from scripture, became proverbial in the Palestinian Church, as perhaps it was also in Jewish teaching, and so passed into Greek-speaking Christianity without the medium of the LXX. James has adapted it to his context, relating forgiveness to the work of conversion, and using the verb in the future tense (this does not necessarily imply a reference to the future judgment when sins will be forgiven, but only a consequential relationship between conversion and forgiveness). He does not appear to ascribe to it scriptural authority, since he neither introduces it as a quotation nor employs his technique of allusion by use of a striking LXX phrase, or dominical authority. It is also uncertain if, by thus adapting an aphorism whose original subject is love, he intends conversion to be interpreted as a work of love, since this principle of Christian action plays no part in his argument after his citation of the 'royal law' in ii. 8.

James concludes, then, with a picture of a Christian community whose members take responsibility for their errant brothers, to their mutual benefit, as they regularly act together for their common deliverance from sin and its consequences (v. 16). He accepts that this need exists, and that sin remains a fact of Christian life. Yet he is optimistic; he does not consider the contingency of failure to convert a brother (contrast Matt. xviii. 17; Ezek. xxxiii. 9), or the possibility of sin so grave that reclamation may not be attempted (cf. Heb. vi. 4–6; 1 Jn v. 16b; possibly also 1 Cor.

v. 2–5). It is, however, with reclamation of the errant member only that he is concerned, and thus with the maintenance of the existing community. There is no reference to the conversion and incorporation of outsiders, though some of the language used could have been given such a reference (the verb *epistreptō, turn*, is so used in Acts xiv. 15; 1 Thess. i. 9; and the reference to the saving of Rahab's soul, Josh. ii. 13, was understood in terms of her membership of Israel when she was seen as the archetypal proselyte; cf. on ii. 25). The community is not an enclosed, exclusive body, since visitors may be welcomed, sometimes too enthusiastically (ii. 2 f.), and the author's own writing shows an openness to the language and ideas of the wider environment; but there is no evidence of an enthusiasm to extend its bounds and to take its gospel out into the world.

Some scribes sought to mitigate the abruptness of James's conclusion with the addition of a final *Amen*, or of a doxology (cf. 2 Pet. iii. 18; Jude 24 f.). Certainly there are none of those final greetings and messages that characterise a personal letter of the Pauline type. Yet, especially in this last section, the author has seemed to envisage and address an actual community in the course of its daily life (whether or not he thought of it as typical of all Christian communities so that his advice would have a general reference), and his work thus has an immediacy which sets it apart also from the category of an essay in conventional wisdom or a would-be philosophical tract.

INDEX OF REFERENCES

OLD TESTAMENT AND APOCRYPHA

INDEX OF REFERENCES

INDEX OF REFERENCES

INDEX OF REFERENCES

INDEX OF REFERENCES

NEW TESTAMENT

INDEX OF REFERENCES

INDEX OF REFERENCES

ANCIENT NEAR EASTERN TEXTS

JEWISH LITERATURE

INDEX OF REFERENCES

INDEX OF REFERENCES

INDEX OF REFERENCES

INDEX OF REFERENCES

CHRISTIAN LITERATURE

INDEX OF NAMES

INDEX OF NAMES

Lincoln Christian College